Clinical Theology

Frank Lake

Clinical Theology

A Theological and Psychological Basis
to Clinical Pastoral Care

Abridged by
Martin H. Yeomans

Darton, Longman and Todd
London

First published unabridged in 1966 by
Darton, Longman and Todd Ltd
89 Lillie Road, London SW6 1UD

This abridged edition 1986

Reprinted 1986 and 1988

British Library Cataloguing in Publication Data

Lake, Frank
    Clinical theology : a theological and
    psychological basis to clinical pastoral
    care. — New ed.
    1. Pastoral psychology
    I. Title   II. Yeomans, Martin H.
    253.5   BV4012

ISBN 0–232–51676–6

Phototypeset by Input Typesetting Ltd, London SW19 8DR
Printed and bound by Anchor Brendon Ltd
Tiptree, Essex

Contents

Figures

Editor's Introduction

The publication of *Clinical Theology* in 1966 was a culmination of many years of pioneering work by Frank Lake. His early medical career began as a missionary doctor in India, with particular interest in parasitology. At the request of his missionary society he specialized in psychiatry and in 1958 began what might be considered his life's work. It was then he began to offer seminars in 'clinical theology' to ministers and clergy who were concerned to relate their theological understanding to psychotherapy and psychiatry. This work developed into a major pastoral training movement in Great Britain, pioneering in the 1960s a way that is now taken up by many others. Dr Lake became the Director of the Clinical Theology Association which was formed in 1962, and in over twenty years of the Association's life more than 1,500 seminars have been conducted by trained tutors and over 20,000 people have attended the seminars. This work continues.

Despite Frank Lake's wide-ranging eclectic mind which seemed readily to embrace so many hypotheses, he was powerfully influenced by two main sources. Psychodynamically he is in the British School of Object Relations Theory, and his indebtedness to Fairbairn, Guntrip and Winnicott is evident. Theologically he grew up in the evangelicalism of the Church of England and understands the heart of the faith pre-eminently in the redemptive passion of Christ. He lived in a catholicity linking the spirituality of the early Church with the present Pope, by way of Free Churchmen such as P. T. Forsyth. His correlation of psychology and theology has stirred, encouraged and restored many in the practice of pastoral care. For this reason I am glad to present this abridgement.

It *is* an abridgement, not a revision. Interest in the original work has been continuous so that both the Clinical Theology Association and the publishers consider that a volume such as this will serve to introduce the writings of Frank Lake to a wider public.

The first edition ran to about half a million words and was accompanied with ten teaching charts, all of which material was produced against an active background of promoting training seminars in pastoral counselling for clergymen and others throughout Great Britain. This severe reduction of the text to less than a quarter of its original length has been undertaken with several criteria in mind.

In the first place, I am a Christian minister, not a psychiatrist, and ask myself, what in that massive tome is currently pertinent to the work of the pastor today and can give him or her understanding in helping those in deep emotional distress? I believe the essence is presented here, though much of the author's extensive illustrative matter and case-histories has been omitted.

Secondly, I believe that in this abridgement we should let Frank Lake speak for himself. I have not seen it as my task to correct or contend with him in print. Since the publication of the first edition many have entered into discussion, and that debate still continues, not least within the Clinical Theology Association itself. By attempting this abridgement I acknowledge my own subjectivity in the choice of material. I have sounded out my approach with a number of the more experienced tutors in the Association and have been grateful for their confirmation and correcting of my guidelines. Nevertheless it is I, and not they, who take responsibility for this text.

Thirdly, Frank Lake wrote extensively in the 1966 volume on the schizoid personality and culture and he drew many findings from clinical work with his patients using the abreactive agent lysergic acid (LSD-25). I have not reproduced this to the same extent for several reasons, including the fact that he ceased using the drug in 1969. By then he was beginning to explore ways of reaching similar results by way of Reichian and bio-energetic techniques. His research in the field of primal integration and perinatal influences was continued in the 1970s and some of the findings were published in his book *Tight Corners in Pastoral Counselling* (Darton Longman and Todd 1981).

Another governing factor is the ongoing life of the Clinical Theology Association. The Association exists for the training of people in Christian pastoral care and counselling and to work in the interdisciplinary field of integrating psychology and psychotherapy with the Christian faith. The programme of training seminars and literature will now be supplemented by this abridgement. The teaching charts of the first edition, which will be of interest to readers of this volume, are used in seminars and can be obtained by writing to the Clinical Theology Association, St Mary's House, Church Westcote, Oxford, OX7 6SF.

Martin H. Yeomans
Advent 1985

1

The Christian Service of Listening

I THE RELEVANCE AND VALUE OF LISTENING AND DIALOGUE

The very language of the Word of God in the Bible is the language of the human heart. Dr Paul Tournier writes of the change he notices in his patients when moments of deep personal contact are made. Their style of talk changes. He notes:

> Images spring spontaneously to the mind, we begin to talk in parables, and we understand one another better than when the tone of the conversation was intellectual and didactic. The conversation becomes anecdotal, as the Bible is anecdotal, as the *Iliad* and the *Odyssey* are anecdotal; but the anecdote is no longer then merely a story, it is an experience, a personal truth.[1]

The Lutheran minister who first used the words 'clinical theology' in my hearing told me of the resolute resistance offered by theological professors to the introduction of practical training in pastoral dialogue for the seminary students. Yet after three months' involvement with suffering individuals, these students returned to college eager to ask many questions concerning theology, which had for them become burning questions, not academic ones. The theology professors found this most unsettling because they had no ready answers in terms which those who needed them could understand. Treating their anxieties by projection, as we commonly do, they complained that this early exposure to direct confrontation with personal problems was unsettling to the students.

When we turn to the methods of the Master in the New Testament we see how his communications are recorded at three levels. The general communications, such as the Sermon on the Mount, are for all. The group communications are for homogeneous groups, such as the Pharisees, and thirdly, the dialogues are specifically

1 Paul Tournier, *The Meaning of Persons*, SCM Press 1957.

concerned with particular people. The words to Nicodemus or the Syro-Phoenician woman cannot be transposed. It is when the disciples are in difficulties that we find recorded the dialogues of the Master with them. Each in his own way is beset by problems of belief, Peter having also problems of his own personality to contend with. For each of these the writers of Scripture turn aside to record the Master's dialogue with them. It was as they talked to him that they came to know themselves. What made the apostolic band into witnesses was not their ability to comprehend and expound a system of religion, it was their personal knowledge and observation of Jesus Christ himself. What qualified them as witnesses to Christ was rather a simple power of observation, of listening, of faithfulness to the concrete and historical details of the life of the Master, the manner of man he was, the things he did, and the things they had heard him say. The Lord interested himself in each one of them. He taught them to be interested in people rather than ideas.

Need for an attentive listener

Many small children, despairing of the adults around them, often confide their deep secrets to their pets or dolls. Yet when a child discovers again that an adult can be trusted with the truth we can see this represents a step forward to adult personality and selfhood. We oscillate between a desire to grow by communicating and a desire to defend by silence and secret withdrawal, with the tacit assumption that to leap the boundaries of reserve and become inwardly known by another person would be too painful to bear. It is only when external insecurity or internal anxiety threaten this equilibrium that we feel a desperate need to communicate. It is when we begin to have serious doubts about our solvency as persons that we need reassurance from a human listener who understands more than we do. For the most part we prefer to remain behind our masks in the anonymity of the crowd or the cosiness of the clique. It is when the symptoms of the frightened spirit begin to show that our need to be honest becomes pressing. We need then an attentive listener who can hear what we cannot put into words, and see what we dare not see ourselves. To avoid commitment to dialogue is to remain in defensive isolation.

Martin Buber

Martin Buber, whose writings have pointed us back to biblical thinking in the Hebrew mould after centuries of submergence under Aristotelian and scholastic modes of abstract thought, dates his conversion to the life of directness and commitment to personal dialogue to an occasion when he failed to be such an attentive listener. He relates:

> One forenoon, after a morning of 'religious' enthusiasm, I had a visit from an unknown young man, without being there in spirit. I certainly did not fail to let the meeting be friendly, I did not treat him any more remissly than all his contemporaries who were in the habit of seeking me out about this time of day as an oracle that is ready to listen to reason. I conversed attentively and openly with him – only I omitted to guess the questions which he did not put. Later, not long after, I learned from one of his friends – he himself was no longer alive – the essential content of these questions; I learned that he had not come to me casually, but borne by destiny, not for a chat but for a decision. He had come to me, he had come in this hour. What do we expect when we are in despair and yet go to a man? Surely a presence by means of which we are told that nevertheless there is meaning.

One who listens

Taylor Caldwell in her novel *The Man Who Listens*[1] describes the transformation in human personalities that occurs in the presence of an attentive listener. Her characters in a wide variety of human difficulties each speak to a man behind a curtain and talk themselves round to the point where they rail against the universe. If at this point the curtain is drawn aside, they see the Author of the Universe not complacently indifferent, but as crucified on the cross. Their whole attitude to life and to themselves changed profoundly. Each incident in this book is an illustration of the clinical theological method at its best. In her foreword she expresses her conviction:

> Man's real need, his most terrible need, is for someone to listen to him, not as a 'patient' but as a human soul. He needs to tell some one of what he thinks, of the bewilderment he encounters when he tries to discover why he was born, how he must live, and where his destiny lies ... Our pastors would listen to us – if we gave them the time to listen to us. But we have burdened them with tasks which should be our own. We have demanded not only that they be our shepherds, but that they take our trivialities, our social aspirations, the 'fun' of our children upon their weary backs. We have demanded that they be expert busi-

1 Taylor Caldwell, *The Man Who Listens*, Collins 1961.

nessmen, politicians, accountants, playmates, community direc-
tors, 'good fellows', judges, lawyers and settlers of local quarrels.
We have given them little time for listening, and we do not listen
to them either.

Let us remember there is someone who listens. He is available
to all of us, all of the time, all our lives. The Man Who Listens.

Mental pain and genuine relationship

The mental pain of a breakdown is the echo of the pain of long-
lost relationships. The echo resonates through into consciousness
because a painful loneliness has descended again upon the person.
The sound of friendly voices is lost, or is felt to be lost, or is feared
will be shortly lost. If we can see no companionable looks as we
search around us in the present, and hear no friendly voices, to be
afraid of actual loneliness is quite a reasonable fear. Neurotic anxiety
is the addition to that reasonable fear of strange, unreasonable
terrors, that is, of the long-repressed separation-anxieties of infancy.
Patterns of loneliness in the present tend always to invoke their
prototypes lying dormant at the roots of being. Working this way,
the buried past turns a tolerably fearful present moment into an
intolerably anxious one.

But this resonance from the roots of being works both ways. If
present loneliness can induce neurotic anxiety, then its opposite,
namely genuine company, can combat neurotic anxiety. Just as
recent social isolation can arouse the reverberation of separation-
anxieties of infancy breaking into consciousness, so also can the
return of good relationships, in which the lonely person is cared for,
resonate good experiences of infancy on the reverberating circuits
of memory. The anxious person is thus 're-mind-ed' that his infant
loneliness was met at times by mother love coming down to meet
him, to look and listen with attention and welcoming eyes. In this
way, the mere provision of an attentive listener can put to flight an
army of irrational fears.

This basic psychodynamic understanding of anxiety is fundamental to our whole case for the importance of listening. Let us
state this fully.

The roots of all the psychoneuroses lie in infantile experiences of
mental pain of such an intolerable severity as to require splitting
off from consciousness at about the time they occurred. These have
remained buried by repression. The actual cause of the panic may
be a time of separation-anxiety endured during the early months of
life, when to be separated from the sight and sensory perception of
the source of 'being', in the mother or her substitute, is tantamount

to a slow strangling of the spirit and its impending death. The various patterns of the psychoneuroses comprise and indicate a variety of defences against this separation-anxiety. For one reason or another to do with the loss of contemporary relationships in later life, the patient feels that 'as it was in my beginning, is now'. It is all happening again. He feels that the shades of the prison house of shut-in loneliness are upon him again. Those upon whom he depends for understanding and companiate fellowship do not seem to understand his continuing need of warm, loving, available dependable human relationships.

Now if we understand anxiety in this way, as a painful diminution of the power of 'being', due to loss of relationship with the personal source of 'being', it is simply the most logical step that a therapist or pastor could take to provide just this quality of accepting and undemanding relationship. In providing an experience of relatedness we are making it possible for the sufferer to move back into security from his area of primitive anxiety, in which all resources were obscured from the mind, in which perceptions of reality were distorted, and in which even co-ordinated behaviour may have been disorganized by the intensity of mental pain. By offering to be attentive listeners in a secure relationship, we draw him back into a place of safety and personal bondedness. Here he learns that the resources of 'being', in human fellowship and in God, are not lost to him. He is enabled to accept both 'being' and 'well-being' through the grace and graciousness of human and divine persons. He is then able to address himself to the problems of life again with a sense of status and personal adequacy which produces sensible, rational, adult, adjustive, problem-solving thinking action.

Ontological and theological listening
We have emphasized the importance to the human spirit in its anxieties, of the therapeutic practice of listening. Non-directive listening on the part of the clergy would be a valid human act even though they never got round to the specifically theological task of communicating the Gospel. I believe that every Christian working in this field, not only the pastor or psychiatrist, must wait until he has the freedom to speak which the Holy Spirit gives, before he advances from the universally acceptable human task of listening to his specific task of witness, namely to saying that Christ is also the great listener to every human conversation. This freedom to speak is not always given.

This theological necessity for Christian listening is clearly expressed in Dietrich Bonhoeffer's basic book on Christian living,

Life Together. Speaking as a minister and theologian he exposes the seriousness before God of our responsibility as Christians to listen to one another:

> The first service that one owes to others in the fellowship consists in listening to them. Just as love of God begins with listening to His Word, so the beginning of love for the brethren is learning to listen to them.
>
> Many people are looking for an ear that will listen. They do not find it amongst Christians, because these Christians are talking where they should be listening, but he who can no longer listen to his brother will soon no longer be listening to God either; he will be doing nothing but prattle in the presence of God, too. This is the beginning of the death of the spiritual life, and in the end there is nothing left but spiritual chatter and clerical condescension arrayed in pious words. One who cannot listen long and patiently will presently be talking beside the point, and be never really speaking to others, albeit he be not conscious of it.
>
> Secular education today is aware that often a person can be helped merely by having someone who will listen to him seriously, and upon this insight it has constructed its own soul-therapy, which has attracted great numbers of people, including Christians. But Christians have forgotten that the ministry of listening has been committed to them by Him Who is Himself the great listener, and Whose work they should share. We should listen with the ears of God that we may speak the Word of God.[1]

Karl Stern, the Jewish psychiatrist, in the story of his conversion to the Christian faith writes of his anguish in seeking an answer to the issues raised by the innocent sufferings of his people through the ideology of Nazism. For him the way through is Jesus Christ:

> If we are concerned with the suffering of those innocent ones, we have first to look at Him. If we are concerned with the evil which has brought it about, we have first to look at ourselves . . .
>
> There is something extraordinary in the suffering of Christ. It seems to include all human suffering, and yet it can be 'completed' by the suffering of individual persons. The more you dwell on it, the more it becomes clear that in His agony He anticipated the hidden agonies of innumerable individuals. For centuries the Church has meditated on the Five Sorrowful Mysteries of the Rosary or the Fourteen Stations of the Cross.

1 Dietrich Bonhoeffer, *Life Together*, SCM Press 1954.

And the more people did so the more the Agony of Our Lord became revealed. It has innumerable facets. It anticipates, it contains your life and my life in a singular way.[1]

Burdened by this suffering and by his own spiritual quest, Stern describes how he sought out Jacques Maritain and describes the kind of listener he was:

He asked me the most personal questions about my spiritual life, but there was not for a moment the feeling of obtrusiveness or indiscretion. I had from the first moment the deep impression of a strange and pleasant form of personal directness which was the result of a great charity and humility.

When those who represent Christ can listen in this way to disclosures at this abysmal depth, the transformation of personality which results exists not only in the ontological but in the theological order. God has not only spoken through his Son; what is perhaps more important, he has listened through his Son. Christ's saving work cost him most in its speechless passivity of dereliction. It is this which gives him the right to be called the greatest listener to all suffering. This gives his listening its redemptive quality.

The purpose of God for man in the universe is that he should come into a life-giving relationship with his Son through the power of the Holy Spirit in the fellowship of the Divine Society. Where this begins, even though between two persons gathered together in his name, it has truly begun, and the purpose of God in his universe is being fulfilled. In pastoral dialogue, initiated by the pastor's willingness to listen to one of his fellow men and concluded when both of them are listening to Jesus Christ, we have an epitome of that for which the world exists. Preaching without listening may fail to create the communion of saints. The deep mutuality of pastoral dialogue costs more, involves the pastor in more suffering, but its endurance in the presence and power of Christ is an indelible event in the divine order.

II CLINICAL PASTORAL RESOURCES

Resources in medicine are of two kinds, the general and the specific. Unless the general attention is given to a patient so as to maintain his proper functioning (e.g. adequate diet) no amount of concen-

1 Karl Stern, *The Pillar of Fire*, Michael Joseph 1951.

tration on the specific pharmacological treatment will bring him back into good health. The pastoral situation is similar.

Later chapters will deal with particular personality disorders and specific resources relevant to such conditions. In this section we draw attention to the basic general resources of the Christian life, in fellowship, word and sacrament which ought to be brought into fuller use. Clinical pastoral care cannot take them for granted.

This whole discipline of clinical theology depends on the truth of the Christian claim that in fellowship with God, through Christ and his Church, there are available personal resources which transform relationships and personality. We claim that there is here an inflow of being and well-being. In short: The fruit of the Spirit is love, joy and peace. Psychoneurotic persons need these resources above all others. They cannot love maturely, they are prone to gloom, and are anxious. If love, joy and peace are anywhere available, this diet will cure them.

Gospel-power paradox: strength perfected in weakness

St Paul constantly reminded his readers that these resources are now available. The 'tremendous power available to those who believe in God' is 'the same Divine energy which was demonstrated in Christ when God raised Him from the dead'. These 'incalculable riches of Christ' are now open to the Gentiles. He is confident of this unconditional gift, for he recalls how the gospel came to them: 'not as mere words, but as a message with power behind it – the effectual power in fact, the Holy Spirit'. And with firmness he writes: 'Accept, as I do, all the hardship that faithfulness to the gospel entails in the strength that God gives you.'

Anxiety states and depression were not unknown to St Paul. In the second letter to the Corinthians he writes:

> At that time we were completely overwhelmed, the burden was more than we could bear, in fact we told ourselves that this was the end. Yet we believe now that we had the experience of coming to the end of our tether that we might learn to trust, not in ourselves, but in God who can raise the dead . . . In Macedonia we had a wretched time with trouble all around us, . . . but God, who cheers the depressed, gave us the comfort of the arrival of Titus . . .
>
> I was given a physical handicap – one of Satan's angels to harass me, and effectually stop any conceit. Three times I begged the Lord for it to leave me, but his reply has been, 'My grace is enough for you: for where there is weakness my power is shown

the more completely.' Therefore, I have cheerfully made up my mind to be proud of my weaknesses, because they mean a deeper experience of the power of Christ.[1]

He is able to suffer the loss of friends and social status, the kind of hard knocks which often precipitate nervous breakdown, without neurotic complaint.

> We are looked upon as fools, for Christ's sake . . . we have found little but contempt . . . Men curse us . . . they ruin our reputations . . . We are handicapped on all sides, but we are never frustrated; we are puzzled, but never in despair. We are persecuted, but we never have to stand it alone; we may be knocked down, but we are never knocked out! Every day we experience something of the death of the Lord Jesus, so that we may also know the power of the life of Jesus in these bodies of ours. We are always facing death, but this means that you know more and more of life.

By the unchanging vocation of her Lord, the Church ought to take up again his ministry to those who suffer from personality disorders and mental distress. Our danger is probably a too wordy analysis without the power of synthesis. We need interpretation, but more than that, we need integration. We have less need of advice than of the power to carry out what we already know to be true in human relationships.

Christ's passion as the ultimate resource
St Paul is proud of nothing except 'the Cross of our Lord Jesus Christ, which means that the world is a dead thing to me, and I am a dead man to the world. For in Christ, what counts . . . is the power of a new birth.' It is in this act of the Son of God that all the resources of evil are deployed again him. And it is here that all the resources of God go into action against our evil and the very power of Evil itself which grips the world. It is this event, and our proper relation to Christ who undertook it, that is the primary resource for the ultimate transformations of human personality.

In his crucifixion, Christ gave up all rights to himself. For love of God and man he bore the ultimate throes of mental pain and physical agony. This he did, we are told, for the joy that was set before him. Beyond the crucifixion, obediently borne, lay the resurrection, not only his own, but that of the whole human race in him. By identification with his crucifixion, Christ empowers his

---

1 These quotations are largely taken from the translation by J. B. Phillips, *The New Testament in Modern English*, Geoffrey Bles 1960.

followers to a similar crucifixion of all that they are in terms of their old nature.

> Those who belong to Christ have crucified their old nature with all that it loved and lusted for . . . Live your whole life in the Spirit and you will not satisfy the desires of your lower nature. For the whole energy of the lower nature is set against the Spirit, while the whole power of the Spirit is contrary to the lower nature. Here is the conflict, and that is why you are not free to do what you want to do. But if you follow the leading of the Spirit, you stand clear of the law. The activities of the lower nature are obvious. Here is a list: sexual immorality, impurity of mind, sensuality, worship of false gods, witchcraft, hatred, quarrelling, jealousy, bad temper, rivalry, factions, party-spirit, envy, drunkenness, orgies and things like that.

This is a list of all those destructive emotions and insensate libidinal and aggressive drives which psychotherapy sets out to remedy. Our success in this is rarely commensurate with the effort involved.

> The spirit, however, produces in human life fruits such as these: love, joy, peace, patience, kindness, generosity, fidelity, adaptability and self-control . . .

It is an astonishing fact that the events of the crucifixion of Jesus Christ portray every variety of human suffering and evil, especially those crucial and decisive forms which suffering takes during the first year of life, where mental pain weakens the foundations of character and determines its distortions. Whether we speak about it or not, it is to this centre of the universe, where its Creator identifies himself with the evils of his creation, that all our dialogue in the end returns.

Clinical pastoral counselling has, as its introduction, the task of listening to a story of human conflict and need. This listening may be indistinguishable from that practised by non-directive counsellors. This is, in itself, a therapeutic resource. To the extent that our listening uncovers a human situation which borders the abyss or lies broken within it, we are nearer to the place where the cross of Christ is the only adequate interpretative concept. And this concept is historical fact, not ideology.

Just as it is the total work of God in Christ which is the ultimate source of man's redemption, so we have learned to look to specific aspects of his death and passion for the specific medicines of the spirit in its particular evils, both those which it has actively done as sin, and those which have been passively endured as affliction. These we take up in subsequent chapters.

Knowledge of complex human nature

We each perceive our human environment in a somewhat different way. When a troubled person is on the edge of a breakdown, such as could well lead to a clinical pastoral interview, his own particular 'prison house' of infancy closes in. He cannot 'see' people as they are. He misreads their intentions. He misinterprets what they say in terms of his own rigid emotional expectation of them, particularly their gestures and facial expressions. The troubled person cannot be reached except by someone who can see and feel with him the strange, limited universe into which his spirit, crabbed and confined, has shrunk. This is a stringent requirement. To communicate empathy with one whose basic experiences of the universe are utterly different from our own is not a natural gift. It requires deliberate study and costly identification.

Training for general pastoral care is correct in emphasizing the needs and resources which are common to all men. The basic requirement of a dynamic cycle of loving relatedness, in dependence on attentive and sustaining source-persons, and in opportunity for outgoing activity in significant service for others, is common to all men. If we forget that, all else goes awry. However, when we consider the training of clergy and medical laity alike for clinical pastoral care, we can be true to the realities of the subject only when we emphasize the ways in which individuals differ from each other. We must pay careful attention to each man's particular universe.

But are there no categories of pastoral understanding between the general and the specifically individual? When I go to my doctor with my array of symptoms I am not comforted by being told that I am so unique an individual that the pattern of my disease has never before been recorded. I am comforted by a diagnosis which classifies my illness as something physicians have met before, have understood and have treated with some measure of success. The same applies to clinical pastoral care.

Perhaps this accounts for the ironical situation that it is often those who insist most firmly that 'everyone is different' and that 'classifying people into types is an insult to their individuality', who are least patient in interviewing sick souls and more prone to limit themselves to generalized pastoral care. They need the halfway house of diagnosis, of that which sees through the multiplicity of symptoms to a particular kind of distorted perspective in the depths of the human spirit.

We do not all suffer from the same besetting sins. Yet the number of possible sins is not limitless. The Bible and the Church have always listed the sins – to some of which we are in bondage. We do not choose these chronic sins. They choose us. Here we meet the solidarity of the race, the nation, the community, and the family in sin and bondage to evil. The clinical pastoral task is to deal with the evils we have suffered rather than with the evils we have generated. It is for this special clinical care that the pastor ought to be given sound knowledge and personal training in the interpersonal relationships of parents and their effects on infancy and childhood, of psychodynamics, and of the mechanisms which the mind employs in denying or defending against these primary injuries to the identity of the ego, the being, and the well-being of the human person.

Pastoral care is defective unless it can deal thoroughly with these evils we have suffered as well as with the sins we have committed. At some point in our lives we may need someone who can preside over the healing of our memories of evil, especially the repressed 'memories' of personal injury, however early in our life history they came upon us and were imprinted. This is a pastoral task within the gathered congregation, not a medical one, except perhaps in the severest cases. In the established Church with its parochial system, this standard of care is possible only for the gathered congregation and a few fringers. There is no suggestion in Great Britain that the medical profession has any serious intention of occupying this field or providing these services. We are speaking here of the Church's responsibility to her own members and to those who appeal for help.

The life of Christ provides a norm

We cannot discover by averaging large numbers of specimens of humanity what is 'normal' or 'proper' human spiritual functioning. To place Christ at the centre of all we may properly know about man is admittedly an act of faith, not of unaided reason or logic. The model we use here is based on a study of the adult life of Christ as God's 'demonstration Man'. The hypothetical model for the origins of human personality in infancy which we have derived from this, follows the same law of spiritual life. It is a dynamic inflow and outflow based on dependent and interdependent relationships. The movement is biphasic, an inward movement in response to personal acceptance and sustenance, and an outgoing movement towards the service of others, characterized by the same acceptance and sustenance of them.

Our primary definition of anxiety is therefore derived from this Christocentric model. Ontological anxiety exists when the normal dynamic cycle of loving relationships is broken. Those who spend their days amongst anxious people can describe many forms of it. But the ontology of anxiety, what it actually is in relation to man's basic being, is more difficult to define. It could be said that only one who had undergone anxiety in all its forms could comprehend it existentially. Christ, as a man in the days of his ministry, shows a complete mastery of anxiety, and this distinguishes him from us more than any other facet of his character. Yet Christ, as Redeemer in the week of his passion bore upon his own person and in his own spirit every form of anxiety known to man or borne by him.

Paul Tillich in *The Courage to Be*[1] speaks of the three forms of existential anxiety; of death and ultimate non-being, of emptiness and ultimate meaninglessness, of guilt and ultimate condemnation. It is my experience working at depth analysis of the first year of life, that precisely these three forms of anxiety lie at the roots of the three main intolerable positions into which the infant spirit can be driven, the hystero-schizoid, the paranoid and the depressive, respectively. Certainly, before the age of one year, infants can suffer from all these three anxieties, the dread of death, the persecutory anxiety of emptiness and the depressive conflict of guilt and condemnation.

Beginning with this theologically derived dynamic cycle of normal relationships we show how deprivations of any part of this cycle lead to anxiety in one or other of its forms. Nothing in the model or its dynamic outworkings is contrary to a biblical doctrine of man. Indeed, the Christian doctrine of man and his redemption is at every point illuminated by 'depth psychology' stated in these terms. The model has provided a language of communication between theology and psychiatry which does not baulk even the most acutely paradoxical psychological issues or the deepest antagonisms of faith. We find this theologically based ontology and psychodynamic model a useful resource in clinical pastoral training.

Prayer and the people of God
As soon as the task of therapy is considered under the heading of resources of the power of being, of ontological factors and spiritual qualities rather than of learned techniques, it becomes clear that

1 Paul Tillich, *The Courage to Be*, Nisbet, 1953.

Christian pastors and laity alike ought to be engaged in the care and cure of the disorders of personality and human relationships.

So it is often within his own congregation that the pastor will find, as he uses a discerning eye, the habitually concealed needs which his Lord wills to satisfy. As life brings its unbearable frictions and the spirit winces, many a person who would have preferred to remain self-sufficient and silent, becomes ready, and if the pain is bad enough, eager to talk. The man of God who knows more about his people than they know about themselves is waiting for this moment. A few such people, faithfully and effectively helped, create within the congregation a sense of expectancy and open-endedness. There are second thoughts about people and about God. If he actually becomes 'a very present help in trouble' through the friendship of the pastor and a few members of the congregation, the level of interpersonal guarding and existential distrust diminishes a little. People begin to become real with each other, willing to bear one another's burdens.

It is in such a Christian community that the resources of Christ are meant to work. It would be a departure from the New Testament pattern to set up separate clergymen working like therapists or general practitioners in isolation from the therapeutic community of the Body of Christ. The resources of God are mediated in the whole life of the Christian fellowship, gathered to hear and study the word of God, gathered round the Lord's table where his Body sustains them, gathered in fellowship for mutual help and counsel. All the groups in which therapeutic change regularly occur are characterized by (1) a shared and avowed confession of need, usually of brokenness, (2) by the bond of a common experience of grace, of an unexpected, undeserved, almost miraculous breakthrough into acceptance, kindness, union, love and joy, and (3) by the ability to carry on this experience, propagate the message, without controversy over leadership. The gifts of the Spirit are for the building up of the whole body and of each member of it. Thus when a neurotic sufferer realizes that under God he has become a significant channel of help to someone else, and continues both to receive and to give on deeply interpersonal levels, he is well on the way to recovery. Gratitude to the healing community will impel him to a positive identification with its worship and service.

One of the reasons why pastoral dialogue is necessary with men and women suffering from the common symptoms of psychoneurosis is that prayer, their life-giving communication with God, may be re-established. When Christian people fall into despair, into bitter isolation, into depression, into separation-anxiety, or into dread of non-being, they have, to this extent, lost any clear sense of God as loving or personal, fatherly or friendly. There is no expectation that any relationship with him will of itself change the whole atmosphere of the spirit. The patient usually clamours for a change in external circumstances. What most needs changing is his own concept of God. This has become rigid, fixed and retributive. So he needs the god who is revealed in Christ definitively. He binds up the broken-hearted, befriends the solitary. He attends to true grief and brokenness. At every moment Christ is in full empathy with all the agony of our lives. Yet to this neurotic sufferer, despite mental assent, it has ceased to be palpably true.

So prayer as communication with God cannot be re-established unless he can bring his complaints, objections, demands, accusations, resentments, doubts and disbeliefs out of hiding and into conversation with the pastor and with God. But a man cannot say such critical things to a neurotically conceived god, any more than he can to a neurotically idealized parent. Idealized authorities must be buttered up, as they only want to hear nice things about themselves. While the patient maintains this façade, doublemindedness, hypocrisy and loss of energy over the internal conflict and its repression are inevitable. The task of clinical pastoral care is to evoke the truth in the inward parts, so as to bring the total actual content of the personality and its roots into the conversation with God – which is prayer.

Christ's own being on the cross contained all the clashing contrarities and scandalous fates of human existence. Life himself was identified with death; the Light of the World was enveloped in darkness. The feet of the Man who said 'I am the Way' feared to tread upon it and prayed, 'if it be possible, not that way'. The Water of Life was thirsty. The Bread of Life was hungry. The Holy One was identified with the unholy. He was deprived of all his rights, to be with us in our privation. He bore the ultimate deprivation of dereliction. A reconciliation is effected here between otherwise irreconcilable, offensive opposites. He carries the burden of all the miseries that disintegrate us. They are united in him, and we, united to Him, can be united also to these same aspects of ourselves which we have hitherto repudiated.

Whenever a man brings his total reactions to life as he has experienced it, before God as he is revealed in Christ, demanding that the badness of the situation be reconciled with his goodness, he has begun to pray. He may not feel like a praying man. He may not feel like a religious man at all. He is not. He is a Christian and that can be a very different thing. Prayer in this sense is entering into a forceful dialogue with God about the totality of our human experience, forgetting neither the wretchedness of our own predicaments nor the redemptive wretchedness of the cross of Christ.

Holy Communion, preaching the Word of God, the Bible

We affirm and endorse from our understanding of our psychodynamic model that the Holy Communion is a sacrament which literally carries ontological and spiritual strength and sustenance into the life of those who participate in it. Luther expressed it in forceful existential language that is a surprise and delight to contemporary Protestant and Catholic alike. J. S. Whale reports him thus:

> If I would have forgiveness of my sins I must not run to the Cross, for there I do not find it yet dispensed to me. Nor must I strive to know the Passion of Christ by an intense commemoration of it. But I must go to the sacrament or gospel where I find the Word which conveys, pours out, proffers and gives to me the forgiveness won on the Cross ... Although the work of salvation was accomplished on the Cross and the forgiveness of sins won there, it cannot come to us otherwise than through the Word. The whole gospel is incorporated in the Sacrament by the Word ... For though Christ had been given and crucified for us a thousand times all were profitless if the Word of God came not to administer it and to bestow it upon me and to say, This is for thee ...[1]

Nowhere is God's Word and act to man, and man's response by word and act to God, so clearly demonstrated. Thus the return of the psychoneurotic or psychotic sufferer to the responsive participation in the Holy Communion is a vital resource in the care and cure of his soul in its totality.

There is a genre of preaching which can reach down to the heart of psychoneurotic and psychotic problems and open them up to the resources of God. When the preacher speaks direct to those needs, present behind the façade of personality defences, he disturbs as only the Word of Truth can disturb. If he points on the way to further truth, that all these ugly facts can be accepted in the all-embracing truth of God's acceptance of unacceptable men in Christ, the result is a new and deeper integration of personality.

In caring for very intense Christians in health and sickness it is sometimes difficult to distinguish between their conviction that God

1   J. S. Whale, *Victor and Victim*, Cambridge University Press 1960.

has spoken personally through the Bible, which we should regard as valid and true, and a more extreme application of the text applied to themselves which can only be taken as a symptom of incipient mental disorder. Emotionally disturbed Christians supply their own diagnosis when they declare the texts which apply to them in the Bible. So the rigid obsessional person, for example, will see the key text for them as 'Come ye out from among them and be ye separate'.

The dominant factor in the neurotic mind is the regressed mood of infancy, pre-verbal now, as it was then. While faith is dominant the Scriptures will continue to be used however much the mind is overturned by uncovered repressed affliction. And it is in precisely such turmoil as the spirit is thrown into dark nights of flesh and spirit (actively or passively endured) that the Word of God is an effective counsellor to the Christian. It measures up to all the extremities to which the soul is driven.

However, to quote or not quote Scripture to a distressed person is a matter of delicate balance. Sometimes the appropriately addressed word of searching authority is most apt. In another case it is better to withold the direct quotation. God is healing the whole personality of the sufferer, the worst affected parts being those still sore from the earliest years, before words had any meaning. God may wish to express his loving parental care through us by what we are and do, rather than by what we say. To insist on quoting Scripture may be a neurotic compulsion in the helper, with hints of superstition, almost magic, with an unwillingness to let patient befriending precede verbal witnessing, as parents must do.

Whether then or later, the aim of clinical pastoral care must be to understand and overcome the intrinsic factors which have set the Scriptures in apparent opposition to the sick man, or turned them into a dead letter. Effective care will greatly deepen and enhance his awareness of the relevance to his condition of the whole record of God's redemptive commitment to man.

III DIFFICULTIES OF PASTORAL LISTENING

Not everyone can talk wisely or reason profoundly, but surely everyone can listen? In fact, the contrary is true. Listening to an anxious person is liable to be most provocative of anxiety in the listener. In order to listen to someone else who is anxious, we have to be able to sit still and stop talking. Attentive listening to the anxieties of another, which we intended should be a demonstration of empathy, may arouse our own anxieties in resonance and sympathy. The parishioner's separation-anxiety, his panic because of the one who never seems to come, may reactivate in the professional listener, terrors of the same sort. Whether the mechanism is a conscious one or remains throughout, wholly in the unconscious, whether the withdrawal is covered by face-saving rationalizations or honestly avowed anxiety, the reaction is the same in the end. The listener recoils from the whole threatening experience of listening.

It is not only anxiety that is liable to be aroused by the pastoral dialogue. As Karl Menninger wrote in an article for psychiatrists:

> The patient's symptoms and behaviour often awaken impulses and associations and reactions within us which we are having trouble enough of our own to manage. This tends to upset us, to disturb our objectivity. It may arouse pity, rather than sympathy, anger rather than regret, contempt rather than curiosity, erotic feelings rather than friendliness, anxiety about oneself, rather than concern about the patient. The patient's illness forces, or let us say permits him to do things which we do not permit ourselves to do, and sometimes this has the tendency to create envy and resentment. The patient may be provocative; he may be seductive. And the psychiatrist must control himself.[1]

There is a more subtle way of dodging the column of one's own anxieties. An infection may be avoided by shunning all contact with those who suffer from it. It may also be countered, paradoxically, by small repeated inoculations of attenuated strains of the infective agent one wishes to avoid. Thus, psychiatrists, case-workers and parsons can be drawn into personal involvement with those who suffer from the symptoms of anxiety, without at first recognizing that their unconscious motive and interest is of this kind. It is a self-protective inoculation. Hobart Mowrer[2] quotes De Wire, a theologian, as saying, 'Regardless of whether Freud was right or wrong in his theory, he at least tried to minister to a class of sufferers on whom the Church, Protestant and Catholic alike, had turned its back. This is to our inescapable and enduring shame.' This is true. It is also true that Freud's work with patients almost certainly provided a measure of defence against his own deep phobic, hysterical and schizoid tendencies. It is to his credit that he was always attempting to recognize and often succeeded in identifying these elements of neurotic motive in his own personality.

1 Karl Menninger, *A Psychiatrist's World*, New York, Viking Press 1959.
2 O. Hobart Mowrer, *The Crisis in Psychiatry and Religion*, Princeton and London, D. van Nostrand 1961.

Let us accept the fact that the deep compulsive motivations of our concern for case-work may often be the need to attend to a buried aspect of our own personality which is still suffering mental pain. This is not the same as repressing or warding it off. It is, in fact, utilizing it as a beneficent motive directed towards the help of other sufferers. Sooner or later we will discover the limitations of this kind of identification with our own grief, recognized and consoled in others. At some point our sympathy will get the better of our empathy and the question will arise whether our deep concern is not, in fact, directed towards the alleviation of our own suffering rather than that of the person we are ostensibly helping. Such sufferers may try for a while to please us by showing how much we can help them. If, however, their inability to improve seems to show that our help is no good, that our therapeutic potency is bogus or our motives contaminated, this can produce the most severe anxiety in ourselves and an angry rejection of the person we were, so recently, eager to help. Psychiatrists have discovered themselves reacting against patients who would not respond to their help by ordering electrick shock 'therapy', with ill-concealed annoyance and aggression. The parson's retributive armament is more limited.

It is at this point that as Christian therapists, medical or pastoral, we ought to be driven to accept ourselves as basically no different from our 'patient'. We have to step out of our role of professional superiority and stand with him, before the cross, at the place of help. If we retreat from this, both we and our brother face spiritual disaster. We cannot help an anxious person to the peace of God if that peace has not been given us by the Holy Spirit, making real Christ's justifying grace. We shall not help the depressive to handle his rage in consciousness to drag it forth in all its red-handed murder before the cross of Christ, if we have not so learned to handle our own. We shall not help the schizoid person to face his own complete inability to believe that there is any beneficent Being behind the universe if we ourselves are rigidly defending against the emergence of just that quality of utter unbelief in ourselves. We shall not help the hysterical person to come to terms with intolerable loneliness if we are using that need and our profession, in a dual collusion of attention-seeking, to engage in flight from separation anxieties common to both.

The sufferer wishes to sense that his physician is deeply concerned to help him; it will only add to his trouble if he senses also that the physician is anxious about the whole encounter. That is why, for the physician, whether his focus of attention be to body or soul or spirit, the primary task which will fit him for the life of therapeutic dialogue is to have faced and dealt with his own anxieties.

Compulsive personal detachment and intellectualization

Clergymen are always tempted to hide their anxieties behind the cloak of priestly office or ministerial authority. General Practitioners have a similar way of cloaking their anxieties by issuing authoritarian prescriptions and demanding obedience. These can have their virtue, but there comes a point when the patient realizes, whether the physician does or not, that they are merely childish evasions of his own inability to understand the disease or to cure it.

As a product of a scientific humanist age, Freud shared its assumption that reason was competent to solve all problems. It is now evident that this conviction and the method of therapy based upon it represent in themselves a compulsive reaction pattern to ontological anxiety in Freud himself. Pascal's phrase that 'the heart has reasons which reason knows nothing of' operates not only in those who believe that loving relationships solve more personal problems than rigorous rationality, but in those also, who, having lost the capacity for committed relationships, try to grasp and control them by the techniques of the observer and the objectivity of the scientific method.

Both the confessional and psychoanalysis share a faith in human reason which is, in fact, so overthrown in some distorted personalities as to render continued faith in its capacity simply pathetic. It is at this point that analysts and confessors begin to be annoyed with their unresponsive clients who ought, by rights, to get better. Depending, like the lawyers and casuists, on their books of case-wisdom, they search about for any ways in which they, or the client, have departed from the technique or infringed the rules. It would be wiser to recognize limitations and say that these methods were never commensurate with the problem presented by the severer disorders of being and spirit.

Analysts have tended to presuppose that there exists within the patient a basic power of personal being or ego-strength which lies intact below the complex which has to be analysed away. Likewise the priest tends to presuppose that there exists in the penitent a basic power of personal being which lies intact below the sins which have to be confessed. The competence of the conscious mind and the capacity of the will to decide and follow a course of action must be assumed by the confessor to be present. Those whose task is, in mental hospitals, to care for those whom neither psychoanalysis nor the confessional have materially helped, are forced to look closely and attentively at the specific problems presented by this category of suffering personalities. We find that the only kind of organization which shows any signs of being able to change these defeated personalities into new creatures is a lay organization, without professional status, without a priesthood, and without benefit of medical advice, such as Alcoholics Anonymous and similar self-help groups. We need to examine why they are so effective.

When we look for common factors in the deeply disturbed or emotionally inadequate personalities we usually find they can be described technically as being in the schizoid or the paranoid positions. Later chapters will take this up in more detail. Suffice it to say here that the schizoid position is one into which the infant has been driven in the earliest months of life by a serious failure of human persons to provide the necessary sustained personal relationships upon which the infant's selfhood could be based. Moreover, the failure gave rise to such unbearable mental pain that, once the margin of tolerance was passed, a paradoxical state had been entered, in which all desire for life through personal relationships had been extinguished. The selfhood became shattered at the very roots of being. This schizoid position is one in which the ego, still suffering in the depths of the unconscious mind in a vortex of mental pain, simply does not want to live by investment in outgoing relationships. Its deepest wish is to die. The ordinary bonds with human society may be, for such persons, intolerably difficult to accept. The ego in the schizoid position of dread opposes, in depth and intensity proportionate to its pain, any attempt to rejoin humanity in commitment. Even though it may concede commitment in caring for others, it will not do so for itself.

Hysterical patients and those in severe agitated depressions usually appear to cling fiercely to human help. But there is almost always, at the root of their being, a distrust which cancels out all their clamant faith. The roots of this distrustful anxiety are in, or very near to, the schizoid position. The root experience of life for hysterical persons is an imminent death of the spirit. One fundamental fact of their experience is an unrelatedness that is near to dereliction. At a moment of the most supreme need for the sight of a human face and the love that shines from human eyes they were bereft of consolation. They remained alone, without, as in the case of the schizoid, despairing of any return. They were almost identified with nothingness and non-being when they desired infinitely to be identified with a loving human person. Life for them is one long security operation. 'Am I really loved?'

Understanding these categories of sufferers in this way, we can expect therapy to be effective only if the helper can recapitulate acceptably the conditions under which personality is formed, ego strength assured and selfhood made intact. He must aim to reproduce as nearly as possible what should have been given to the nascent personality in its roots. But this time he must not fail the person by disappearing from view. He must remain faithfully and fully present, as a person, in order to evoke, on this occasion, a better and more durable response. If the conclusions of analytical studies are tenable, this would be possible only through a personal relationship, mediated by direct confrontation of the needy person by the one who cares, and whose genuineness of caring is manifest in the light of his countenance, which primarily is in the eyes. All the other sensory modalities by which the spirit of a person is made manifest to another needy person are important. Tone of voice is as important as the words spoken. The whole attitude of the spirit is expressed in the posture of the body and the movements of the face. Yet the 'umbilical cord' of interpersonal relationships does seem in some way to be mediated by the eyes rather than in some other way. It is not without significance that the Bible, though it affirms that no man has seen God at any time, is driven to use the language of the eyes to express the facts of faith in God. The pure in heart see God. The vision of God is given to man as the end of his spiritual journey. The blessing with which every service concludes sends us out with God's face shining upon us and the light of his countenance lifted up so that our eyes can reflect his in mutual recognition and joy.

We would expect, therefore, that those who can conceive of therapy as the re-establishment of genuine interpersonal relationships, mediated by face-to-face and heart-to-heart discourse, will be more successful in penetrating to the core of the therapeutic problem in these cases of extreme ego-weakness or paradoxical self-destructiveness than the analyst behind the couch or the priest behind the grille or the vicar who can never look anyone in the eyes.

As psychotherapists or as clergy we have reason to be grateful to those who attend on our ministrations, for obvious reasons. It is when our unsolved and unconscious personal deficits are compulsively seeking for satisfactions through the practice of our profession that an unhealthy collusion of neuroses is certain to occur, with harm to the patient or parishioner which is neither obvious nor easily definable. It is remedied only when the would-be helper himself declares his emotional bankruptcy and goes for help. When he, too, becomes realistically dependent on help outside himself, whether from man or from God, then he begins to be able, from a firm dynamic base of personal openness, honesty, and eventual well-being, to pass on to others the kind of help which leaves them free and ties no apron strings to him as helper. To accept this sort of close dependence on someone else, or to accept the close dependence of a needy person on himself, arouses intense 'commitment anxiety' in the schizoid personality. To enter into clinical pastoral training in order, in obedience to God's call, to be fitted for both these commitments, is indeed to take up his cross. He has a baptism before him, of water and of fire.

Compulsive over-attachment, perfectionism and moralism

Hysterical over-attachment, motivated by separation anxiety and schizoid over-detachment, in reaction to commitment anxiety, are two sides of the same watershed. They coexist in the same person, alternating in dominance. In place of the schizoid difficulty of detachment from human commitment being the obstacle to thera-peutic listening, the converse may become operative, namely an hysterical over-attachment to the patient or parishioner. This is just another way of manifesting the underlying experience of a panic-provoking uncertainty about human relationships in depth. These over-attachments can often be recognized by their specificicity. Some take to pretty women, others to pretty boys. Some make a bee-line for motherly women, others for strong men. Outside the category which betrays his fixation and therefore his 'weakness' as a balanced helper, the localized effects of excessive 'investment' do not operate; unless, in times of severe disturbance, he rejects every-body else.

Difficulties in ourselves as listeners may block communication just as effectively if our personality, not being so stressed so severely as in schizoid persons, has none the less been sufficiently threatened to make us adopt compulsive, rigid moralistic attitudes. There are many fine clergymen whose religion is based on compulsion rather than freedom. They take great pride in their work and become depressed if not appreciated. Being perfectionist, they tend to be sensitive, touchy, resentful of criticism. They cannot accept their own brokenness, nor admit failure, nor the need for any other than a very general confession. Outward expressions of anger with those in authority upon whom they are dependent have long been suppressed, rage has been repressed even from their own conscious-ness. To a variable extent their acquaintance with the sexuality of their own minds is also repressed. If so, their attitude to sexual misdemeanour becomes as harsh and rejecting when it occurs in others as when it occurs in their own deep mind.

Intolerant of weakness in themselves they have no welcoming word for those in whom weakness has broken out in undesirable ways. Since they have never overcome the difficulty of accepting their own bad side, whether of rage or truant sexuality, they have an insuperable difficulty in accepting the persons of those who manifest such morally undesirable drives overtly.

When a Christian minister becomes primarily a moralist he is creating insuperable difficulties in the way of pastoral dialogue. He remains a religious man, but he has ceased to be a Christian. In the biblical view, righteousness does not consist in the possession of a credible ethical record, but is, precisely, right-relatedness to God, and the behaviour that results from that relationship. Ethical behaviour by itself can too easily entrench a man in self-righteousness. He has joined the Pharisee, praying with himself to a god who is not the Father of our Lord Jesus Christ: 'I thank thee that I am not as other men are.' On the contrary, says the Bible, enshrining what we can now see is the first principle of interpersonal dynamics, this is righteousness: It is to be accounted as one rightly related to God. It is to trust in the One to whom you need to be rightly related for being and well-being. No mortal man can win by self-effort what in the nature of things must always be a gift.

In Christ, the representative Man, the proper Man, God does for us what we cannot do; he combines righteousness as moral perfection and righteousness as perfect relatedness to himself within the economy of the Blessed Trinity. In our place, substituted for us, Christ undergoes the hell of disrelatedness to God which our evil intentions and wicked deeds deserve. In Christ, his Son, the Holy God receives sinners. Not reformed sinners; it is broken sinners in their sin with whom Christ is united in his redemptive work. All Christian ethical motive arises in gratitude for these events in those who derive their very being from them. We are no longer related to God by obedience to the law's requirements. The law of holiness seems to serve only to break our pride in the attempt to fulfil it. We are now related to God by the obedience of faith.

It is fundamental to all pastoral ministry that those who undertake it should be living by this gospel. This is the greatest resource of the Christian physician of souls. To be a stranger to the dynamics of justification by faith in the gracious reception of God to sinners through the mediation of his Son, is a difficulty quite fatal to the pastoral task. If the pastor cannot, because of obstruction in his own personality see his way to receiving sinners and eating with them, listening to them and talking to them, he could properly consider retiring from his ministry until the grace of God, coming to him in his penitence, showed him that grace which is given to him as a sinner, in spite of his sin of religiosity. Experiencing this grace he would soon delight to give it to all others, in spite of their particular sins, in the name of Jesus.

Out of depth in the 'abyss'

Whether as psychiatrist, general practitioner or parson, we shall have to confront the difficulty created by our defensive desire to remain within the role of professional detachment. Yet we can only heal relationships by entering into them as deeply as the need requires. If we believe that God's love is effective we shall have to listen to one who has no experience of love but who deeply desires to love and be loved. If we believe in truth, we shall need to listen at one and the same time right down to the truth of this desperate person's history, and right down to the Truth himself, hanging in the darkness, crucified upon his cross.

Martin Buber wrote of this difficulty in his introduction to the posthumous work on psychotherapy by Dr Hans Trub. Though it concerns psychotherapists it is my conviction that in no sense are the clergy free to opt out of the encounter. Buber writes:

> ... the psychotherapist, whose task is to be the watcher and healer of sick souls, again and again confronts the naked abyss of man, man's abysmal lability.
>
> (He) practises with skill ... until, in certain cases a therapist is terrified by what he is doing because he begins to suspect that, at least in such cases, that finally, perhaps in all, something entirely other is demanded of him. Something incompatible with the economics of his profession, dangerously threatening indeed to his regulated practice of it. What is demanded of him is that he draw the particular case out of the correct methodological objectification and himself step forth out of the role of professional superiority, achieved and guaranteed by long training and practice, into the elementary situation between one who calls and one who is called. The abyss does not call to his confidently functioning security of action, but to the abyss, that is to the self of the doctor, that selfhood that is hidden under the structures erected through training and practice, that is itself encompassed by chaos, itself familiar with demons, but is graced with the humble power of wrestling and overcoming, and is ready to wrestle and overcome ever anew. Through his hearing of this call

there erupts in the most exposed of the intellectual professions the crisis of its paradox. The psychotherapist, just when and because he is a doctor will return from the crisis to his habitual method, but as a changed person in a changed situation. He returns to it as one to whom the necessity of genuine personal meetings in the abyss of human existence between the one in need of help and the helper has been revealed.[1]

It should be axiomatic of the man who takes his commission from the foot of the cross that such immunity as professional status and accomplishment confer upon him in Holy Orders should not protect him from the strain of walking with a fellow being into the abyss. 'This way of frightened pause, of unfrightened reflection, of personal involvement, of rejection of security, of unreserved stepping into relationship, of the bursting of psychologism, this way of vision and of risk is that which Hans Trüb trod.' This is a description of the Good Shepherd. The true pastor will recognize it as his own authentic road and wish he could be sure that he was walking on it.

Disinclination for radical change

Some difficulties are inherent in the human situation in which we operate. Sinful humanity would much rather have the effects of sin tinkered with and its deep wounds palliated than have them faithfully and radically dealt with. The pressure of the congregation on the parson is always in the direction of persuading him to accept outward compliance and reasonable acquiescence to church duties in place of that inner transformation of which the New Testament is in every part speaking. There are members of the helping professions, such as social workers, whose proper concept of their role is to help sufferers in mental hospitals and in society mainly by modifying their environment. Particularly with psychotic patients, who cannot themselves effect a responsible change in themselves, such work with their families is essential. It is essential, too, for the pastor. However, where responsible adults are concerned, the parson's central aim must be the transformation of the troubled person's attitude to life. He is suffering, less because of his actual environment than by what that environment has come to mean to him, by his own interpretation of it in the light of the earliest experiences of his spirit.

Resistance to change is primarily a fear of relinquishing well-tried defences against deeply repressed mental pain. The hysterical sufferer's separation-anxiety is matched by strong resistances when-

1   Martin Buber, *Pointing the Way*, Routledge & Kegan Paul 1957.

ever the compulsive pattern of attention-seeking is thwarted. Whether the means used to attract are beauty, glamour, power, or even ethical effort and religious behaviour the phenomenon of resistance to change is observed. The schizoid personality clings stubbornly to his detachment and to reflective centredness on his own ego. If commitment is impending, resistances rise to evade it. The depressive goes doggedly on complying with the approved line, keeping a law which he does not love, resisting what much of him cries out for, the release from the burden of the law's crushing weight which the gospel offers. Obsessional persons, above all, resist any attempt to modify by mitigation their rigorous control of environmental objects. They must wash and rewash by numbers. No one must interfere with their ritual arrangements. The paranoid personality resists imagined infringements of his rights with inflexible persistance and watchful suspicion. The psychopathic person resists all attempts to curb his compulsion to gratify impulses without a thought as to the consequences. The phobic person resists any attempt to override his limitations. The homosexual person resists all endeavours to push him or her in the direction of the opposite sex or separate them from their own sex.

These compulsive resistances operate, in varying degrees, in all of us. We are threatened by anxiety if we propose to act contrary to the dictates of our defensive systems. We are wise to keep our defences intact, unless, by constricting our lives too much, a greater pain results than the pain they guard. When Christ calls us to obey him, not only does his word run contrary to our defensive systems, he enables us to bear the pain of dispensing with them. Jesus said that whoever sets out to save his psyche with its built-in defensive systems will lose it. The person who obeys Christ is at first more conscious of the pain of disrupted defences than of the joyous integration which follows. Obedience is a watery baptism of mental pain from the waves and storms within or a fiery baptism of persecution without. Truth here is paradoxical. Painful dying to the old life precedes entry into the new. The initial step is in the opposite direction to the desired goal. No cross, no crown. Our Lord himself spoke with groans of the resistances within himself to the bitter cup of absolute degrees of suffering which obedience to God involved.

It is possible to reduce specific individual difficulties by pastoral interpretation of the particular resistance-pattern and of what lies behind it. But still the leap of faith must be taken. The overcoming of resistances to faith in Christ is not ultimately a work of interpretation but of intercession; not ours alone but Christ's and the Holy Spirit's prayer effects it.

The triad of openness

We who work together in this field, whether as parsons or laity, find that three facts invariably accompany one another for good. First, openness towards God in a life of closer obedience, with that alert readiness which arises out of a persistent prayer life, so that common talk slips naturally into conversation about the ultimates of existence. Second, openness towards fellow being about one's own unresolved fears and lusts, rages and depressions, sins and unsuccessful struggles, an openness that may have been hellish hard to reach, over the conventional high walls of religious pride, breached only through prayer and obedience. Third, an openness towards others, which they can usually recognize before we can. Our own inner openness to God and to a fellow being to gain help for ourselves brings a new coin into circulation.

Words cannot express the change this openness brings. At best they serve to identify an experience, but only to those who have 'existentially' been through it. Conversion, confession, fellowship, communion, all these are known only to those who have been opened to the experiences to which these words point.

When we have spoken of all these difficulties we recognize that in and behind them 'our fight is not against any physical enemy; it is against organizations and powers that are spiritual'. It is because of this that St Paul concludes his letter to the Ephesians, affirming 'be strong – not in yourselves, but in the Lord, in the power of his boundless resource'.

2

The Dynamic Cycle as a Model in Theology and Psychodynamics

The purpose of models is to enable us to come to a reliable under-standing of the phenomena of the universe and to be reliably articu-late about them. Our need in a clinical theology is for a model which correlates the biblical material concerning Christ and of the Church's witness to Christ and obedience to him on the one hand, with the sum of our knowledge of human personality growth and development and the disorders that affect them on the other. Most of the models developed by pastoral and ascetical theology tend to be as sin-dominated as the classical psychiatric models are sickness-dominated. We need a model which will correlate the dynamics of relatively well-functioning personality and of spiritual health, in its formation and maintenance, before it turns to the clinical conditions in which this integral wholeness is lost and replaced by deprivation, anxiety, conflict, distress, defences and various forms of disorder. By inference, the model must point the way back to health and wholeness, showing why the various therapeutic forces are effective and at what point.

The dynamic cycle of being. A basic model
The normal pattern of interpersonal relationships can be described as consisting of four factors, in dynamic relation to one another, and in sequence. This is set out diagrammatically in Figure 1 and is expanded into the model of 'The Womb of the Spirit' at Figure 2. This is an ontological analysis of the normal mother–child relationship concerned with the growth and development of the infant spirit specifically within the first twelve months of life.

The basic quadrilateral has an input phase consisting of the (1) acceptance and (2) sustenance followed by the output phase of (3) status and (4) achievement. There is something soundly biological about such a model based on the quadrilateral where two sides can be modified by divergent or convergent lines to indicate increase and diminishment of the 'powers of being', while the other two sides are free to indicate movement to and from the places where these resources are to be had and to be passed on. We expand upon this below.

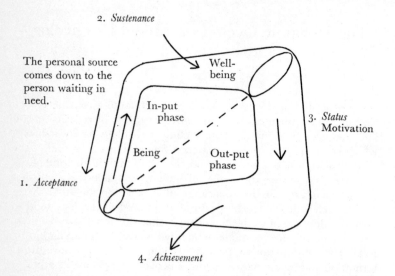

FIG. 1   The development of a model of the dynamic cycle of 'BEING' and 'WELL-BEING' arising out of and expressing presumptively normal personal relationships, in infancy and in later years

A. The dynamic input phase

1 *Acceptance* of the potentially isolated and, as such, anxious individual, by at least one other person, primarily by the mother, subsequently by the father, the rest of the family and society, is the primary ontological requirement. This access to human relationships ensures, on the personal level, his very 'being'. Without this he 'dies' as a person or as a member of society. Personal life is possible only when the seeking 'I' finds a 'Thou'. This alone makes possible the emergence of selfhood, of a steadily functioning 'I-myself'.

2 *Sustenance* of personality. Whoever enjoys relationships of a generous and gracious kind is enhanced by them in his power of 'being'. The quality of 'well-being', good spirits, courage and personal vitality is a reflection of what has been communicated

from others in this phase. 'Existence', in the form of good personal relationships, produces in the person who responds to this donative experience, a worthwhile spiritual 'essence'. These two phases constitute the dynamic input of personality. Ontologically speaking, 'being' and 'well-being' are achieved by an adequate response to an adequate personal source in this phase of absolute dependence.

The model as a basis for ontological analysis of mother–baby relationships through which selfhood, or human BEING and WELL-BEING are formed.

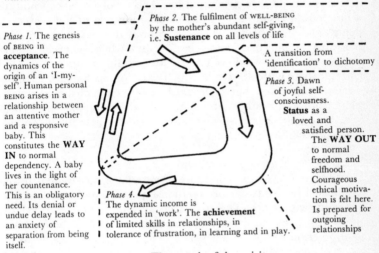

Phase 1. The genesis of BEING in **acceptance**. The dynamics of the origin of an 'I-myself'. Human personal BEING arises in a relationship between an attentive mother and a responsive baby. This constitutes the **WAY IN** to normal dependency. A baby lives in the light of her countenance. This is an obligatory need. Its denial or undue delay leads to an anxiety of separation from being itself.

Phase 2. The fulfilment of WELL-BEING by the mother's abundant self-giving, i.e. **Sustenance** on all levels of life

A transition from 'identification' to dichotomy

Phase 3. Dawn of joyful self-consciousness. **Status** as a loved and satisfied person. The **WAY OUT** to normal freedom and selfhood. Courageous ethical motivation is felt here. Is prepared for outgoing relationships

Phase 4. The dynamic income is expended in 'work'. The **achievement** of limited skills in relationships, in learning and in play.

FIG. 2   The womb of the spirit

B. *The dynamic output phase*

3 *Status.* The two ingoing dependency phases are normally followed by an outgoing movement, back to involvement in self-giving relationships in the place where tasks are taken up. At this point, the essential quality or status of the personal spirit that has resulted from (1) and (2) can be observed by introspection and inferred from the analysis of behaviour. If the input phases have gone well, motivation is strong, surgency is characteristic, the flow of energy is free, the mood joyful, the powers of concentration and decision adequate, with a readiness to invest interest in persons and concerns outside oneself. The natural desire in such persons is to care for others as they have been cared for, to love as they have been loved. Under these circumstances, mental processes function at their optimum. The quality of spirit that has been induced by the experiences of the first two phases is passed on to others. This

person is in good heart, and is able to enjoy, as a gift which has not been earned, the status of a courageous person. Standing in this large room, with ample psychological space, the fourth phase of work and service to others can readily be faced. This phase implies that status includes freedom from the dependency of phases (1) and (2) to go out, on one's own, without 'smothering'.

4 The *achievement* of the task appropriate to the person. Purposeful activity is required of every human being in society, whether it be the acquisition of skills in childhood or the performance of work and service in adult life. This involves the expenditure of ontological resources, that is, of the resources of the powers of 'being' and 'well-being' which have been derived from previous phases of the interpersonal cycle. 'Ideally', when the cycle is functioning normally, work is done with sustained application and concentration, with fair tolerance of frustration, with realistic adjustment to difficulties, but with steady persistence of aim. Personal relationships with others are characterized by outgoingness, openness, generosity, kindness, tact, warmth, and reliability of commitment, peacefulness, hopefulness and patience.

Blocks in the functioning of the dynamic cycle

This dynamic cycle is liable to be blocked, or so attenuated and diminished by unsatisfactory relationships as to nullify its value as a creative experience. This may occur at any point of the cycle. It may arrest personal development at any age. It is to be expected, at any period of life, that a person will react unfavourably to the loss of (1) acceptance, and (2) sustenance, in personal relationships; if the loss goes deep enough, by (3) some loss of the sense of personal status and worth and by (4) a lowering of the quantity and quality of personal achievement.

An emotionally healthy person, who has a personal record of existing from the beginning in reasonably intact dynamic cycles of loving relationships, will not make heavy weather of this contemporary loss of part of the cycle. Such a person will be sustained by the spirit and courage which derive from his beneficent past. The experiences of sustained and reliable relationships, in infancy and childhood, remain available on the reverberating circuits of the deep mind, to be used as resources of the power of 'being'.

Christ as the 'norm' for study of the 'normal' man

This model of a normal dynamic cycle of personal relationships, which permits of ontological analysis, derives from a study of the spiritual dynamics of our Lord Jesus Christ. When I met the Swiss theologian, Dr Emil Brunner, in India in 1950 I pressed him to show me where psychiatry could find a model of man's understanding of himself which could be acceptable to a Christian theology. He directed me to a long and repeated study of the dynamics of our blessed Lord as they occur in St John's Gospel. It was in studying the life of our Lord, in its interpersonal and dynamic aspects, towards God and towards men, that this ontological analysis arose (Fig. 3).

1   For Christ, his spiritual 'being', as Son of God, arises in a relationship between the Father who attends with love, mediated by the Holy Spirit, given to him without measure, and the Son who responds to the Father by the same Spirit. *Acceptance*, for this Holy Son, is always assured. The Son responds by withdrawing alone for prayer, with instant access.

2   His 'well-being' is reached as Christ abides in the Father who gives *sustenance* to him on all levels of his being. The Father, with whom he is united, in prayer, worship and communion, conveys to him the plenitude of love, glory, joy, grace and truth.

3   The dynamic outflow of personal 'being' and 'well-being' occurs when the Son of God proceeds forth from the presence of the Father, full of grace and truth, deeply conscious of his *status* as the Son of God, to work among men. His motivation is to love as he has been loved.

4   His achievement has all the characteristics of the Holy Spirit's indwelling. It is the fulfilment of his redemptive destiny in history.

These fourfold phases of the dynamic cycle are unmistakably present in the life of Christ. Moreover, he shows distinct signs of being aware of this dynamic fluctuation. Nothing is more characteristic of the achievement of our Lord Jesus Christ than his limitation of the demands which he would allow men and women to make upon him. When he healed, virtue went out of him. He returned to the presence of the Father in order that virtue should again flow into him.

How serviceable is such a model in guiding psychodynamic formulations?

When I began, in 1955, to spend many hours alongside patients re-experiencing the first year of life, whether normal or abnormal, under the psycholytic drug LSD-25, I found that none of the classical psychological or psychiatric models seemed adequate to organize the facts which were emerging. The work of John Bowlby and the neo-Freudians was obviously tending to conceive of the first

The references are to Chap: Verse, of St. John's Gospel, unless otherwise noted.

Acceptance of Christ the Son by his Father; the voice from heaven, 'This is my beloved Son' (Matthew 3:17; 17:5). Christ's response to dependence as a Son and as man, is to pray (Luke 6:12; 9:28). He went up into a mountain to pray. He is found alone, praying (Luke 9:18). He faces crucifixion in the Garden, praying. He knows he has constant access. 'I know that Thou hearest me always' (11:42). He is the only-begotten Son of God the Father. This is his being.

Sustenance and well-being as Christ abides in the Father. 'The only-begotten Son which is in the bosom of the Father (1:18). 'As my Father has loved me, so I have loved you' (15:9). Wisdom. The Father shows the Son 'everything that he is himself doing' (5:20). Christ is given the Holy Spirit and his gifts, love, joy, peace, patience all without measure (3:34). 'I am in the Father and the Father in me' (14:11). We are One (10:30).

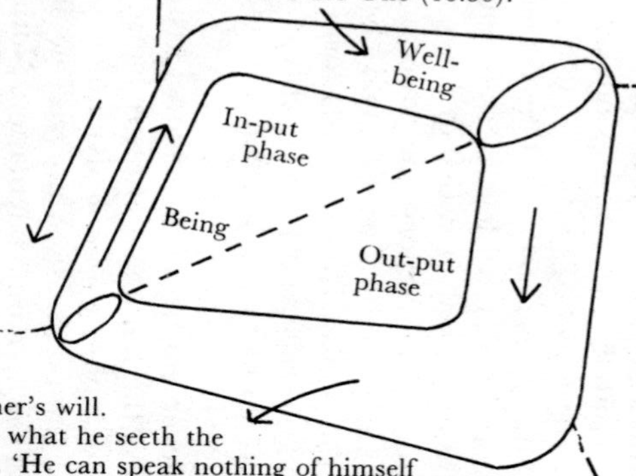

Status. 'I am from above' (8:23). 'I am the Son of God' (10:36). 'Not alone' (8:16–18, 29). He is sent by God, on God's work (7:18, 28, 29; 33; 6:38. 'I am the light of the world' (8:12; 3:19). 'I am the living bread come down from heaven' (6:51). 'I am the water of life' (7:37). 'Full of grace and truth' (1:14). Everything is entrusted to him by God (Matt. 11:27).

Being

In-put phase

Well-being

Out-put phase

Achievement is strictly limited to the Father's will. 'The Son can do nothing of himself but what he seeth the Father do' (5:19, 30, 36; 8:29; 10:36–7). 'He can speak nothing of himself but what he hears from the Father' (8:26, 28, 38). 'The words that I speak they are spirit, they are life' (6:63; 8:51); 'are everlasting life to believers' (5:24, 40; 14:6). He is the bread of life, eternal life, for all who believe on, and eating, partake of him (6:48–58; 6:33–5). To be the light of the world so that those who follow do not walk in darkness (8:12; 9:5). To finish the work of redemption God gave him to do (4:34; 16:5; 17:4; 19:30).

FIG. 3   Christ as the 'norm' for dynamic studies of 'normal' man

year in terms of interpersonal relationships. This was more cogent than Freud's own model. Adler and Jung were explained rather than explaining. Ronald Fairbairn and Harry Guntrip were stating this first-year material more specifically and perceptively. For Harry Stack Sullivan the first year signified much more than mere orality and the expression of pre-genital instincts. This view was supported by our findings. Under the pressure of the need for a satisfactory hypothetical model, I turned to see whether the ontological cycle of our Lord's relationship in the Divine Spirit to God the Father could provide a serviceable model for the growth and development of the human spirit in its foundation year.

One fact about our Lord's incarnation encouraged me to take this step of working from an 'analogia fidei' to an 'analogia entis', from a man believed in by faith to be normal, to the problems of being in men as we find them now. This was the surprising fact, that although the 'kenosis', or 'humbling' involved our Lord in the laying-aside of kingship and much else besides, this did not include the ultimate kenosis of being born in a brothel from a sluttish woman who would bring him up to know the seamy side of infancy. Tradition affirms the special holiness and godliness of the blessed Virgin Mary. From this it is not unreasonable to infer that God the Father was making provision for his Son's human spirit to come to 'being' and 'well-being' by response to a woman whose character was like his own, in loving-kindness, holiness and graciousness. Can we then regard the Godlike mothering of Jesus Christ as a normal pattern and expect to find that divergences from it in the direction of unloving or unGodlike behaviour towards the child will cause disturbances and distortions of the nascent spirit within the foundation years? Indeed, this is so. As my psychiatric colleagues and I have spent many hours with patients reliving the first year, this dynamic cycle of interpersonal relationships provided a better model of a normal ontological matrix than any other hypothesis we had encountered.

Alternative models

There are only two alternatives open to model-makers in the field of human personality. Either one proceeds from an examination of human beings as they are, to infer, and later affirm, that such and such a pattern is normal, or one must, as an act of faith, set up a certain pattern as normal, and proceed to examine existing human specimens in the light of it. It is evident that Freud, Adler and Jung studied human specimens as they found them, relying deeply on their own self-analyses to provide them with 'norms'. From that knowledge they then, by extrapolation, inferred, *as an act of faith*, a model of the normal man. That is to say, they proceeded from an '*analogia entis*' to an '*analogia fidei*'. Three quite different norms resulted. Aristotle says somewhere that if we want to examine what is normal we must be careful that we are studying unspoiled specimens of the species. The questionable assumption of the scientific method seems to be that you can escape from error here by examining a sufficiently large number of specimens. Psychiatrists, if they know a little more of what is in man than those who take him at face value, should be the last to subscribe to this assumption. Obviously we must look towards the few 'good' specimens rather than towards the many 'bad' ones if we are to have any light in this matter. What the scientist chooses to call 'good' and 'bad' is a value judgement whose criteria can never be other than an act of faith. It is only one further stage along this road to the conclusion that it might be that only one member of the species retained his true humanity and that even he might have to be introduced to the human scene uniquely in order to perform his task of demonstrating normality.

To quote Martin Niemöller, 'Jesus Christ is human, we are not'. His name for himself was 'the Son of Man'. Christ must be, at any rate for Christian theologians and for all professional men who would guide their thinking in Christian terms, the 'Logos', God's interpretative word to man about his own essential nature. If this is true, and it is the basic affirmation of the Christian faith, then we cannot know either what we are, or what we are meant to be, or how this is to be achieved through interpersonal relationships, unless we look first at him. This is to proceed from an '*analogia fidei*', a model based on Christ in the dynamics of his divinity and of his humanity, to an '*analogia entis*' which provides us with a pattern of the norm for our humanity and also, since we are invited to share his eternal nature, of our 'divinity'.

Everyone working in the human sciences chooses a model to work from, whether it is done explicitly by a deliberate act of faith, or implicitly by unnoticed, unexamined, unestablished acts of assumption. A model we must have, either an abstract hypothetical construction or an actual person or persons who can be observed, or a combination of these. If the model-maker does not think that his model is more adequate than existing ones to correlate the observed facts, in such a way as to make inferences and predictions possible, he should scrap it. The model to assist us in thinking about human phenomena, even though based on Christ, must always be servant, ready to be displaced.

The diagram entitled 'The womb of the spirit' (Fig. 2) is an ontological analysis of the normal mother–child relationship based on this model. It is admittedly structured by a primary act of faith in Christ, as Son of God, and Son of Man. It makes good sense of all that we know, with any certainty, of the origin and growth of personal 'being' and 'well-being' in the foundation year. It gives a valid hypothesis, which not only enables us to show the dynamic sequence of interpersonal events within which a human spirit may develop into healthy normality, but enables us to predict some of the effects of interference with the normal cycle.

3

The Understanding of Depressed Persons

The origins of psychoneurotic reactions
For reasons which are not apparent, certain people react to the loss, or even to the anticipated loss of acceptance and sustenance in personal relationships (which is the ontological input phase) in an excessive way. They react to minor losses of personal security, which do not really threaten their personal or social status at all, in a disproportionate manner. What is the origin of this excess, and of all the other compulsive, exaggerated, repetitive, non-adjustive responses which people make to apparently minor insecurities? Why do people react to moderate losses as if they were final and devastating? Why, in other words, do people behave neurotically?

Psychoneurosis occurs only when there has been an *antecedent conflict and defeat* in the same phase of experience in early infancy. The conditions under which a break in relationships produces the greatest effect and consequent liability to permanent deviation of character are:

(a) when it occurs within the first two-and-a-half years of a child's life,
(b) more especially when it occurs before a critical stage is reached, probably about the ninth month, which is the moment or period of transition from unitary life within the 'womb' of the spirit, to life in a growing consciousness of separate existence, apart from the mother,
(c) when the emotional trauma affects the phases of dependency and input, i.e. of acceptance and sustenance, and
(d) most traumatically of all if it occurs in phase 1, within the early months, when a break in the dynamic cycle results in a loss of 'being' itself. If the cycle is broken here by the mother's absence, life itself, as a person, is in jeopardy, and, if the obstacle is not removed by her return, this life, i.e. the spirit of relatedness in love, faith and hope, will ultimately be lost.

The severing of the essential relationship with the mother, seen and known to be present, which alone can give to the infant a sense of personal 'being' and selfhood 'in' the mother (i.e. an interruption of phase 1), cannot fail, if it occurs within this critical period, to result in:

(a) a progressive diminution of the power of personal being to the point of total loss, 'that is, towards the experience of '*dread*' or 'identification with non-being'. The infant can live as a person only by identification with a personal 'being'. If no person appears, it is still identified, but with 'non-being'. This is experienced as a dangerous waning of hope and expectancy, a certainty that one will not be able to last out long enough, a feeling that time passed in solitariness is equivalent to an imminent death of the spirit.

(b) a mounting anxiety which, if the block is in the first phase, is in the nature of '*separation-anxiety*'. Aloneness is intolerable where the nature of the infantile organism at this phase is to find it as impossible to survive the loss of the living face as it would be within the actual womb to survive without supplies of oxygenated blood. Instead of continuing to feel like a proper human person, by identification with a loving and coming person, through access to the desired maternal source of personal being, the infant experiences a painful state of non-acceptance and rejection; of being shut out from life as a person, cut off from 'being' itself.

This represents an essentially passive response to the loss of 'being-by-relatedness' or of selfhood and is diagrammatically set out in Figure 4. This passive response is not the only reaction to the loss of the maternal source of personal being.

Reaction into rage
In certain infants there is superimposed on these basically passive responses an active reaction summed up in the word 'rage'. In this phase of oneness (or obligated symbiosis), rage has no separable objects, but is a response to a painful 'identification-with-objectlessness'. The rage is felt against, literally, one's universe, which includes what are later distinguished as the other person, the 'I', and the spiritual bond between them. In this energy-arousing reaction the organism prepares for fight against the frustrating situation, and if there are fantasies, they are of combat and destructiveness towards this 'bad' ontological situation. Such reactions of insensate rage were noted by St Augustine when he observed it in the infant removed from the breast and another babe put there to suck. This

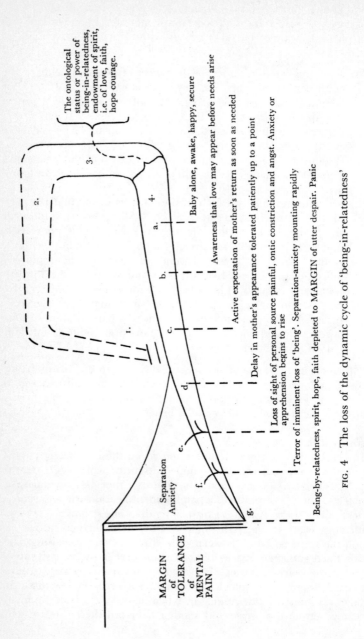

The ontological status or power of being-in-relatedness, endowment of spirit, i.e. of love, faith, hope courage.

Baby alone, awake, happy, secure

Awareness that love may appear before needs arise

Active expectation of mother's return tolerated patiently up to a point

Delay in mother's appearance painful, ontic constriction and angst. Anxiety or apprehension begins to rise

Loss of sight of personal source of 'being'. Separation-anxiety mounting rapidly

Terror of imminent loss of 'being'. Separation-anxiety depleted to MARGIN of utter despair. Panic

Being-by-relatedness, spirit, hope, faith depleted to MARGIN of utter despair. Panic

Separation Anxiety

MARGIN of TOLERANCE of MENTAL PAIN

FIG. 4 The loss of the dynamic cycle of 'being-in-relatedness'

reaction to loss of the first phase of access and acceptance by rage is expressed visually in Figure 5a.

Reaction into lust

An alternative defensive reaction to rage is to substitute for the real mother and her breast a mere fantasy of them as if they were back in possession. This substitution of a real loved object by an imaginary one is termed 'libidinal fantasy'. In the Anglo-Saxon sense of the word, this is 'lust', an absolute desire for that without which one cannot exist. In the first days of infancy the mind instinctively has a picture of the desired object, the nipple or breast, and a vaguely conceived picture of a desired person's face. In the painful absence of the real person or an acceptable substitute, fantasy 're-creates' the longed-for person, or a part of them, or an item of their clothing as a memento, in a mental image. Libidinal fantasy occurs independently of the reaction towards rage. (See Figure 5b.)

Defence against the 'bad universe'

The return of the mother or of an acceptable person as mother-surrogate at once removes the occasion of mental pain. Separation-anxiety is over. Whatever had been the reaction to it, whether diminution in trust, anxiety, rage or lust, all these suddenly become inappropriate. Yet they are very really present in the mind of the child, and memory cannot fail to retain a sense of the mental pain they have caused, for at least the time it takes to 'get over' the experience. What is to be done with these painful memories of recent deprivation to which the loss of a personal source gave rise? The return of the mother as the source of 'being' leaves these intolerable traumatic experiences in mid-air in the mind and memory. Unless some defence is possible against them, so that they are removed from the conscious mind, the restoration of the dynamic cycle would be quite spoilt and continue to be disturbed by painful memories of that terrible universe, that other world of desolation, to which the mother, by her unaccountable absence had, no doubt unwittingly, exposed the infant.

Splitting

The primary mode of defence against this evil universe of mental pain is that of 'splitting-off' from consciousness. This is an active process of forcible dissociation of the experience into an area of memory not immediately available to consciousness. The deprivation experience and its consequences are dealt with as if it were the 'not-me'. What cannot be borne is denied. What this process

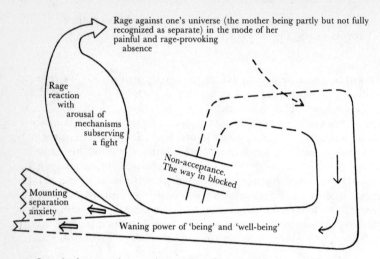

FIG. 5a Active reactions to impending loss of the source-person. Rage to avert anxiety

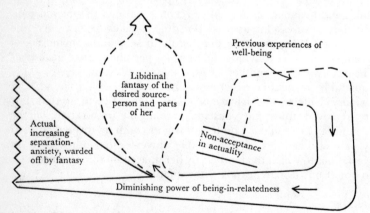

FIG. 5b Reaction to impending loss of the source-person by a fantasy of possession of the desired objects

represents in neurological terms is not known, but it is certain that it requires a constant expenditure of mental energy to maintain the dissociation. A person will tolerate the return to consciousness of split-off mental pain only when there is a relationship of trust with the therapist who is in charge of the treatment. The ability to allow the more severe forms of separation-anxiety to return from their split-off state into consciousness demands the continual presence of the doctor, therapist, friend or pastor, who must at this point be a deeply trusted person. The most severe forms of transmarginal separation-anxiety, which have actually turned into a dread of being united again to one who could hurt so terribly, can only be allowed to return to consciousness under even more stringent conditions. These require a certain quality of spiritual fortitude which is quite beyond most people. The deepest resources of faith in the nature of the universe, namely that the Son of God endured a like desolation and dereliction with us, alone suffices, in my experience, to allow this experience of identification with non-being to be expressed voluntarily in consciousness. If it has burst through, like a symptom, involuntarily, this is too shattering and of no therapeutic value.

Repression

Repression is an active mental process whereby a part or the totality of the painful experience which has been split off is forcibly not remembered. This defensive mechanism constantly makes demands upon the available mental energy. In depressive patients rage undergoes the deepest repression, while the libidinal fantasies are not usually under deep repression, though not readily admitted to other people. They tend to become the material content of confession to a priest. In contrast, it is the libidinal fantasies that are most deeply repressed for the hysterical personality. We take up this matter in a later chapter, but make mention of it briefly here. Rather than allow these threatening experiences to return into consciousness all kinds of mental defences are adopted to convert the mental pain into a less unacceptable symptom. This may be psychological, as in the case of phobias or irrational fears, or physical as when the mental pain is transformed into a physical symptom which substitutes for it. In the primary splitting-off of passively endured loss which occurred in the purely hysterical personality, the rage element was not present. It was all impending dread. Rage, in hysterical personalities of the kind who punish others when they suffer, is often not repressed at all and may be quite overt. However, the so-called 'hysterical' reactions, in which there is a conversion of mental pain into bodily or mental symptoms, frequently occur in those who are also depressed, who dare not rage against others, but turn all their rage and pain on to themselves. They are not, to use this confusing term, 'hysterical' personalities, but compulsively compliant or pre-depressive personalities.

Reaction pattern formation

The agent of this repression was named by Freud the super-ego. Partly it is a defensive system set up by the ego against the re-emergence into consciousness of painful experiences. Mainly it is synonymous with the neurotic conscience, which has been given the task of incorporating within the mind the anticipated reactions and attitudes of the parents, as the infantile ego perceived them – as often as not, mistakenly. It warns the ego of painful rejection if these standards are not kept. It sets a rigid unbending standard of prohibitions and negative ideals which must be observed to merit acceptance and right-standing with anachronistic parental figures. It is the 'Mother Superior' of those fast-bound in miserable morality and justification of themselves by works.

Part of the function of the super-ego thus constitutes the third mode of defence against unacceptable and intolerable emotions emerging into consciousness.

This super-ego, or neurotic conscience, acts to keep the split-off rage and lust under cover and, to complete the deception, covers up the lustful and destructive impulses by leaning over backwards to produce a character-type or neurotic ego-ideal which is precisely all that is opposite to that which is hidden away. The inside of the sepulchre is filled with the dead mother's bones and the inner walls are painted with lusts. Consequently the reaction pattern dictates that the outer wall of the sepulchre must be kept particularly well white-washed by a person who purports to be, and actually is, compulsively compliant and submissive, in whose mouth butter would not melt and who is virtuously prudish. We list the repressed emotions below in the lefthand column. On the right are the compulsive reaction patterns presented to the parent whose acceptance is an inescapable necessity to the infant.

Repressed activity and passivity	*Reaction pattern of behaviour*
1 *Lust*. Libidinal fantasies. The infant wants to touch and possess the apparently prohibited body of the mother	*A denial of sexual interest* constitutes the reaction pattern when, in any particular case of depression,

or the desirable parts of her. A picture of actually doing this has been exhibited and enjoyed in the picture gallery of the mind.

this libidinal element has undergone splitting-off and repression. Prudery is characteristic. Some denial of sexual elements in his own mind. Maintains interest in them by vigorous protest against them in others. God's gift of sexuality tends to be regarded as 'disgusting', not a 'nice' subject.

2 *Attention-seeking* fantasies are a defence when mental pain is caused by the failure of the source-person to pay attention. This behaviour is compulsively overt in hysterical personalities but in the depressive often undergoes repression and is reprobated.

Excessive self-effacement. This gives the impression that one does not wish to attract attention. Shyness and blushing express this conflict. The deep desire to attract attention, if it leads to any natural display of attractiveness and desire to be noticed, is immediately condemned by the super-ego as immodest, with a sense of guilt producing a reaction in the skin. The blush expresses ambivalence about being noticed.

3 *Rage* and *destructiveness.* Fantasies of compelling the mother and father to fall in with the will of the infant, which in fantasy is omnipotent. The super-ego has compelled the raging ego to turn the rage back on itself. This demands a reaction pattern which denies all these wishes, some of which may be for the death of the parents; of the mother for withholding herself, or of the father for his prior claim to the mother's

The compulsive compliant personality is the answer in consciousness. The ego-ideal becomes that of the inordinately meek person, the emasculated 'Yes-man'. There is an inability to express anger even to the point of loss of normal and moral self-affirmation in the face of injustice. As over against the inner rage towards the mother's ordering of life, the child becomes an intense supporter of every point of

attention, or of siblings in competition for her.

view the mother espouses. He will avoid a row at any price. Contradicting the inner desire to dominate and compel the parental figures, the reaction pattern is of submission and willingness to be controlled. The 'death-wishes' are covered up by an excessive solicitude for the health and longevity of those upon whom he depends.

4 *Separation-anxiety* has been split off and repressed as the 'not me'. Much of this anxiety may be conscious and put to the service of the ego-ideal striving to cover up and placate. There remains always a residue of split-off buried anxiety which is denied.

A brittle overconfidence and fussy desire to preserve the external appearances of equanimity, peacefulness and well-earned security. Is touchy about anyone who detracts from the perfection of performance, because this again forces the anxiety into consciousness. A compulsive need to rationalize and find good reasons for avoiding anxiety-arousing situations. The true explanation, 'I avoid this because it makes me anxious', is repressed.

5 *Fear of imminent death of the spirit.* If the separation-anxiety has approached, or exceeded, the margin of tolerance, this experience has to be severely split off and repressed.

A compulsive need to prove that one is not afraid. Dissociative mechanisms prevent the mind from coming into contact with unnerving experiences. A compulsive denial of the possibility of illness. Death is a morbid subject.

6 *Distrust of the 'bad universe'*, of the mother and possibly of the father. To be identified with a bad relationship is to

A compulsive idealization of the mother's perfect trustability takes place in consciousness. The fervour of one who cannot be 'bad'. One of God's little ones was offended and came to the end of its tether. This must be split off, repressed and denied. That which experienced the source-person as untrustable becomes the 'not-me'.

accept the actualities of his inner distrust of the mother compels him to excesses of identification with and idealization of her, and later of the group to which he looks for security. Trusting is replaced by its dynamic opposite, 'trying to trust'. This way of dealing with distrust of a bad universe is projected on to God. Oaths and vows are taken to prove loyalty. He proves the greatness of his trust by punctilious adherence to the tradition of the group he depends on.

7   *Despair* of the mother ever responding to the infant's need still reverberates in the memory. Hope is almost extinguished. Expectation of help has almost faded. All this must be denied.

Compulsive optimism and persistence. He shows an inability to accept the hopelessness of the situation of those who must gain acceptance by their own works. He refuses to admit defeat. Though despondent, he persists in flogging himself, in the vain hope that he will make the grade by his own efforts. He cannot 'affirm his despair' which, Kierkegaard says, is the first act of faith. He must deny despair to the bitter end.

8   *Desolation* actually occurred. The power of being-in-relatedness was attenuated to the point of extinction. Faith and hope in the promise 'I am with you alway' was realistically shattered. This must be denied.

The company of family and friends is clung to compulsively. This provides a further motive for compulsive compliance to the standards of the family group. Later it tends to make a mother cling to her children and friends possessively, for fear of desolation. The reaction pattern may dictate a need to be in an 'inner circle' of some sort. 'Who is right?' takes precedence over 'What is right?'

9   *A weakness of the will to go on living under such conditions.* The courage to be 'as oneself alone', with the courage 'to be as a dependent part of others', have both been almost destroyed. This must be denied.

Compulsive protestations of strength and courage. He strikes the attitudes of the dependable man, the strong man. A compulsive reaction dictates his trying to keep up a constant effort. Confession of tiredness or of failure of courage is intolerable. To rest, to give up hope in oneself, to give up trying, all arouse a neurotic sense of guilt.

10   *Apathy.* If stressing by the absence of the source exceeded the tolerable margins of mental pain; or if less than marginal stressing occurred too frequently; or if, when giving, the mother gave too little, apathy may be the true description of the split-off and repressed spirit. This must be denied.

A compulsive show of keenness and doggedness. Inwardly he has no desire to go on; this he cannot admit. He does not want to work at all, so he works all the time. He couldn't care less, so he pays the penalty in meticulous attention to every task. He cannot believe that God can raise his spirit 'from the dead'. He cannot see beyond the 'full stop' which would result from relaxation of his apparent zeal.

11   *A weakness of the will to be 'good'.* A positive ethical desire to keep and fulfil the spirit of the moral law arises as a result of intact relationships, not broken ones. If parents do not care to respond to him in need, he does not feel responsible to care about being good to please

Strong moral earnestness is a compulsive reaction pattern in his personality. He strives continually and without joy to keep the letter of the law. He does not delight in a moral law, he merely tries hard to keep it. Since such compulsive efforts and acceptance of prohibitions are complied

them. He has no positive love of their law.

with in order to gain acceptance, the factor of appreciation and approval is vital to the 'do-gooder'.

12   *Worthlessness.* If nobody bothers to answer the intense longing of the infant for life, by coming to it, this devalues the self to the point of annihilation. It would be intolerable to accept this as true of oneself. The reaction pattern must ensure its denial.

Compulsive striving to achieve worth and value. He has a compulsive need to be needed. Tends to take on too many key jobs. Constructive criticism of a performance is misinterpreted as destructive devaluation of the person.

13   *The need to live by denial, splitting-off and repression.* The mental defences of splitting-off and repression are themselves unconscious processes. They must undergo repression along with the split-off mental pain and the reactions which exist to obliterate it from consciousness. It does not do to *know* that we need to defend against unacceptable inner experiences and emotions. That is to say, the very fact of having to defend against intolerable emotions and impulses by splitting off with repression, demands a special reaction pattern formation as a permanent feature of character. This is known as the obsessional personality.

The obsessional personality is characterized by an apparent monolithic absence of splitting, in fact, by a very powerful cohesion and integration. But this is only an appearance. Similarly there is an appearance of absolute honesty and openness. Obsessional persons feel they have nothing to hide and are entirely open and uncomplicated. This too is a delusion.

The inversion of the dynamic cycle of relationships

Where the above reaction patterns of personality are found to be present, especially the compulsively compliant personality and the obsessional personality we are justified in adding a third term and describing such a person as a pre-depressive personality.

The essence of such personalities who are prone to depression is a total change in the grounds of acceptance into relationships. In the days before this splitting, repression and reaction formation occurred, the infant knew only one mode of relatedness to the mother, that of simple unconditional acceptance and trust. That open-heartedness is now replaced by double-mindedness. Acceptance no longer resides in the graciousness of the mother coming with love and, if necessary, forgiveness. The new grounds of acceptance are conditional on a prior ability to maintain the splitting-off and repression of the unbearable mental pain of despair and anxiety and to conceal the rage, envy and lust to which they gave rise. This new dynamic ground of acceptance is to gain approval by presenting a pattern of compulsive and fear-dominated morality of a largely negative kind. Theologically, this is to replace justification by faith in the gracious character of the mother by the onerous method of justification by works, so as to earn what had previously been a gift.

Consequently the whole fourth phase of the cycle, achievement, becomes the very workshop of his acceptance rather than the normally gracious outgoing fulfilment in interpersonal relationships of the, emotionally, well-nourished infant. It may be that the parents are essentially moralists, viewing parenthood as granting acceptance and access to loving relationships only to the 'good' child. Then the child has no opportunity within the family to learn that the good parent shows sorrow if, unwittingly, the child has been hurt, and gives comfort until the child is reassured. Nor can it learn the truth about God which Christ's life and death reveal, that even though we rage against the Source of Life, or lust after paltry substitutes, in the moment we return to him we are accepted by him in Christ; as every child should be by its parents, by the very fact of parenthood.

Once the splitting, repression and reaction pattern are established, the vital phase 1 of the dynamic cycle ceases to be a matter of grace and faith, or trust in the loving acceptance by a parent. It becomes a matter of self-justifying effort. The mentality of the servant has displaced the direct spirituality of the son. We can express this visually in the contrasting diagrams of Figures 6a and 6b. The contrasts between the normal and the inverted modes of the dynamic cycle are indicated in the columns set out below.

1 *Acceptance* as a gift. Unconditional access into full relationship with the person who is the source of 'being' and 'well-being' is free. The infant

1 *Acceptance* as a reward. Only conditional access is granted. The 'bad' side is felt to be rejected and one's 'bad' self with it. No genuine sense

feels accepted *in toto*, i.e. with whatever doubts or destructiveness he may own up to. Because forgiveness is assured, the personality remains open.

2 *Sustenance*. Close relationships with source-persons do not exhaust because there is nothing to hide. By abiding in the spirit of the greater 'Thou', well-being is assured and refreshed. Night brings sleep in which the spirit returns to its root experiences in the foundation year. Anxieties emerge but are resolved in the 'dream work'. We wake refreshed, new every morning. The anticipation of work brings pleasurable thoughts.

3 *Status*. He starts the day as a son, having rested in the given relationship and the powers of 'being' and 'well-being'. His obligations as a son, and his inclinations as a son, both born of gratitude for

of acceptance is possible. One's 'being' is no longer 'in' the person who was the source of 'being', but in oneself and one's own efforts.

2 *Sustenance*. Close relationship with personally important people is felt as a threat to security. The closer one admits them to intimacy the more likely they are to stumble on the wretched secrets. As this is construed as leading to inevitable rejection, close relationships are exhausting.

Night and its dreams is also exhausting. Dungeons of primitive experience are revisited. The enraged tigers and savage dogs which represent the primal rages and the imagined parental retribution, attack again. The censor stands guard keeping the would-be sleeper awake lest the destructive rages become too plain in the dream. Waking, the spirit is exhausted. The day ahead is viewed with distaste, as is the work that has to be done. There is no energy to get up and face it. 'Spirit' is at a low ebb, and so are courage, joy, caring, love and peace.

3 *Status*. He starts the day as a slave, having apparently nowhere to rest, no 'given' relationships, only those which can be earned. There is no 'being' or 'well-being' except his dogged willpower to battle

the experiences of care, are harmoniously united. He loves the 'law' of his family, which is the law of love. Personal and ontological status is high.

on joylessly in hope of picking up some reward. Obligation to get up and move is in conflict with inclination to stay in bed or commit suicide. Early in the day status is practically nil. By the end of the day, if work goes well and is approved he may feel better.

4   *Achievement* is an expression of ontological resources. Work is donative. He gives himself and his skills as the outflow of relationships in which he has a kind of 'freehold'. Having received so much, it is now better to give than to receive. Success or failure do not affect his essential 'being'. Justification is by faith in another person and their achievement.

4   *Achievement* is an expression of ontological needs. Work is extractive. He does it to feel better, not because he likes doing it. He performs in order to achieve relationships. His eyes are not wholly on the task itself, but on the effect his doing of it is calculated to produce. He likes to be seen doing it. His 'being' as a person is bound up with the acceptance or rejection of his work. Justification is by works, one's own achievement.

Blocks and displacements in the dynamic cycle

Factors such as these operate cumulatively, with the passivity factors in the constitution, to produce an ego which will feel itself compelled, by the poverty of its ontological status, to accept the mental pain of a broken dynamic cycle of personal relatedness, without visible or audible protest. It suffers acutely in silence, giving the mother the impression of an undemanding and unnaturally contented baby.

This is illustrated by the experience of some of my patients in hospital who under treatment were reliving their earliest memories of infancy. Knowing that a certain patient was not far from entering again into the experience of dread by identification with non-being, I was unavoidably called away to another ward. I assured him that I would be gone for only half an hour and that if he needed anyone he could ring the bell at his bedside and the nurse next door would immediately come. Returning after the half-hour absence I have come upon an acutely distressed person, trembling violently, but

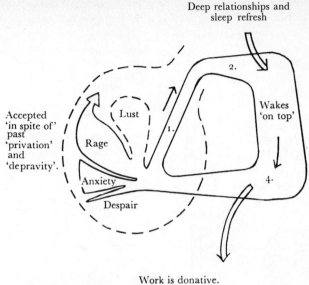

Deep relationships and
sleep refresh

2.

Accepted
'in spite of'
past
'privation'
and
'depravity'.

Lust

Rage

1.

Wakes
'on top'

Anxiety

Despair

4.

Work is donative.
Gives out freely.
Loves unconditionally, as *he*
was loved.

FIG. 6a The 'normal' dynamic cycle

seemingly unable to move for help, palpitating and sweating, with
a dry mouth and terrified eyes darting everywhere until they came
to rest reproachfully on me. My apology and reminder about the
bell are thrust aside with the confident assertion, 'But you knew.
You've known all the time what I was going through. You've stayed
away to test me to the limit. Don't you realize you've nearly driven
me mad?' When I protest that I did not know, for I would never
deliberately have caused such pain of absence, my protest is received
with incredulity. Then as we work over the experience of dereliction
the patient will say, 'Of course, that's exactly how it was with my
mother in those early months. I know I didn't cry out – as it seemed
to me, what is the point of crying out to someone who is part of
you, who must know everything you know about yourself, and must
intend everything that happens to you? You don't communicate
when you are part of the same system, and cannot conceive of the
possibility of separation.' Another patient commented later, 'I
would no more feel the need to ring that bell to tell you the state

I was in because you were not here, than I would, if short of oxygen in the womb, pull the umbilical cord to get a better supply.'

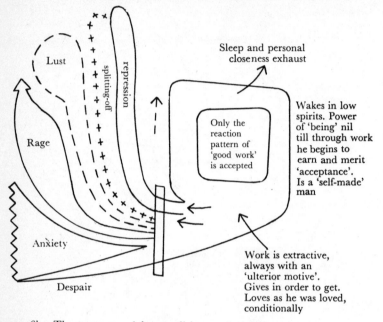

FIG. 6b   The commoner 'abnormal' inverted cycle

When we come to the hysterical and schizoid positions in later chapters we will take up the stages by which the gradual, quantitative diminution of the power of 'being-in-relatedness', by the progressive attenuation of what is left of the spiritual bond from previous good experiences of the mother's person, becomes, when a certain *margin of tolerance* of desolation is reached, a sudden qualitative change into dereliction and dread. As a result of mounting separation-anxiety, a state of panic at the impending loss of personal 'being' is reached. If separation-panic is further prolonged, mental pain reaches the margin of tolerance. What Pavlov called an ultra-maximal stress produces a sudden qualitative change, in which all the conditioned reflexes are flung over in the opposite direction. All that the infant sought and found pleasurable it now shrinks from as painful and dreadful.

Before the margin, though in *panic*, the appearance of the mother is longed for with most urgent expectancy. The baby longs to be touched, looked at, attended to, petted, kissed and fed. This brings secure relatedness to a human person. Every moment of waiting matters, each second's delay feels an eternity of dying. This is the hysterical position.

Beyond the margin of tolerance, in *dread*, all this is catastrophically reversed. The infinite desire to live on as a related person proved so intolerably painful, that now the infant experiences an equivalent desire *not* to live on as a related human being, but to die to all human bonds. To be thus bonded has become itself a bondage. No longer is it a joy, but a threat of imminent agony to be in love. The urgent desire in this schizoid position of dread is *not* to be touched, *not* to be looked at, attended to, petted, kissed or fed. And time has ceased to matter now, it is too late. 'Godot' can turn up when he cares to. His coming has ceased to matter.

Also in infancy, if there is a severe deprivation of supplies, particularly of milk from the breast, a sharp waning sense of well-being results. The beloved and generous source of sustenance, on which the baby had come to depend with such regularity as to count the gift as one of its rights, seems, when it runs dry, to have turned persecutor. The infant's covetous need for the breast can grow to be so threatening and produce such mental pain that, again, a *margin of tolerance* is passed. Beyond this, the desired object has changed into one from which the infant recoils in great fear. To exist in the presence of what could give 'well-being', satisfaction and fullness, but now will not, is to experience 'identification with emptiness'. 'To me, to be, is deprivation of rights and the endurance of injustice.' The whole meaning of personal relationships, of 'being' itself, is that through the generous care of the person who has called one into being, one should attain also 'well-being'. This is the whole purpose of life. To be bereft of this is to be 'identified with meaninglessness'. This is what lies behind the paranoid position in which the person lives with a constant sense of being persecuted. This also is taken up in a later chapter.

The relevance of psychodynamic studies to clinical theology
We find it is possible to make useful inferences from psychodynamic studies, based on symptoms and syndromes, as to the condition of the spirit, the basic position of the ego, the form mental pain took, and therefore the view of the universe in the foundation year. We can summarize these basic terms in human experience.

1   To have been caught in the trap of the anxiety-depressive position is to go through life with a painful sense of the unreasonableness and injustice of 'God'. He does not seem to provide the

conditions necessary for 'being'; yet to be angry with him, or protest against the injustice of his world seems to be asking for damnation. At times he seems to be warmly accepting, at others hard and rigorous in his rejection. One thing is certain, he asks the impossible. One cannot trust him, only propitiate him. One can try to make a good show in the hope he will overlook all that one has swept under the carpet of lust and rage.

2   To have suffered the passive loss of being-in-relatedness to the source person, into the hysterical position, is to be identified with a 'God' who absconds. Leave him to himself and he would never come in time to save you. Depending on him is an anxious business. You cannot trust him, you can only try to trust him, against painful inner evidence to the contrary. You must attract and hold his attention by some means or other. To have gone beyond the margin of tolerable mental pain into the schizoid position is to be dependent on a 'God' who is a devil, cruel beyond telling, utterly unfaithful to any word of promise made to his own. Pain and fiendish punishment characterize his world, not love or kindness. The schizoid person lives with a dominant death wish. This world of 'God' is so full of affliction, for which he must be responsible, that the only sane desire is to die.

3   To have been consumed in infancy by feelings of hate, envy and jealousy, is to incur throughout life a constant sense of guilt and meanness, because these emotions will keep projecting themselves, in unappreciativeness and detraction from the good qualities of others, in the family and in society. If these are repressed and reversed, a strained character results, leaning over backwards to be compulsively generous.

'God', to this person, is one who gives life reliably. There is no anxiety about being itself. He also gave well-being. But, fixated in the unconscious mind is an experience of 'God' who took away his support, who hatefully withdrew, who gave himself to others, provoking jealousy. Moreover, one is powerless to assert one's will over his. This increases the bitterness against him, but one must turn it all against oneself. Even so he is in us as an accusing voice, breathing guilt and condemnation. He is himself envious, jealous, touchy, retributive. This view of 'God' is implicit in the depressive position when anxiety about 'being itself' is absent.

4   To have endured the painful emptiness of the paranoid position is to live in a universe in which one's dependent spirit is surrounded by persecutors. God keeps us alive for the purpose of persecuting us. The god of the paranoid is a sadistic god. To get on with him one has to be a masochist (using those paired words without their

sexual connotation). He makes the whole experience of life empty of any good, devoid of meaning. But since he is absolute and powerful we must praise him for being what he is, or worse will befall.

These are the basic positions of the human ego when it has fallen away from simple human relatedness to its personal source. A moral theologian would say that they look like the first experience of 'privation' and 'depravity'. The primal anxieties and the besetting sins are laid bare for inspection at the roots.

In adult character, far from being laid bare, these roots are all covered up by layers of defensive manoeuvre. There is no resemblance but only a dissemblance between the root and the branches. The hidden face of rage wears a mild mask. The face full of hate contorts itself into a winning smile. The screams of hysterical panic are suppressed under gusts of hysterical laughter. Deepest of all, the wretchedness and hollowness of dread become the dungeons below the ivory tower of 'His Sureness, the Philosopher', or 'His Eminence, the Professor'. He builds as high as he does to be able to live away from – the truth – his personal nothingness. The scientist, in secret despair of becoming a person, posits his own being in terms of rationality, neatly omitting the existential question. He offers, as proof of himself, a few impressive but really unimportant certainties, proceeding by way of methodological doubt – to despair. As Kierkegaard remarked, 'Lying is a science, truth is a paradox'.[1] Certainly the truth about the heart and mind of man is that it is 'deceitful above all things'.[2] To reduce this complexity, by a superficial science of behaviour, to observable morality is to embrace a lie. It is also to reject Christ, the Word of Truth.

Nothing is more astonishing to those who have recovered some of these actual dreads and rages in therapy than these two facts: first, that such red and raw emotions could have lain so long undiscovered, and second, the strange certainty that part of the mind has known about the dungeons and their inhabitants all the time. At the end of a session in the period of psychosynthesis they say, 'Oh! of course, that's why I always did this, or avoided that, or never could stand the other'. It all seems so clear – when you can accept the painful truth.

The Psalmist and the face of God
The Psalmist sets the sights correctly for the troubled human spirit. Surrounded by seemingly unhelpful or hostile faces he looks beyond

1 Søren Kierkegaard, *The Diary*, Peter Owen (1961), p. 158.
2 Jeremiah 17:9.

them towards God's face with the expectation that God will reveal his countenance, welcoming and acceptable. In the depths of memory our spirits are surrounded by many strange and puzzling faces. The human spirit is formed, in so far as its proneness to neurotic disorder and depression is concerned, within the first three years or so of life. This is true as much for Christians nowadays as for the Jews before Christ, for Hindus or for Animists. There are two vital needs of every child in these foundation years, which could be summed up as the face of the mother and the voice of the father; the smile of loving recognition and the word of guidance. We do not expect the child of three to have acquired much knowledge of revelation truth about the face of God and the word of God from 'holy history'. Yet it has acquired many permanently imprinted attitudes of expectancy or non-expectancy towards vital relationships. It has learned to expect a welcoming face or a rejecting, scornful, angry face, with correspondingly powerful defensive manoeuvres to mitigate the encounter which promises to be too terrible. When the loving face of the mother, by which the baby lives and without which its spirit dies, is absent for too long, the mental pain may be too severe to be retained in consciousness. The loving face is obliterated from the mind by prolonged absence but the threatening faces which take its place cannot be tolerated in consciousness. They undergo splitting-off, repression and fixation and so remain for ever a threat to the security of the inner world. Unfortunately for God, though perhaps fortunately for the offending parent, this 'death mask' usually becomes one of the faces of God, if not his only face. Disbelief in his existence and hatred of his 'providence' arise here.

1   Where disappointment provokes infantile rage against the absent, and therefore supposedly merciless face of the mother, it seems for ever, to this split-off buried self, as if the source of life itself, by demanding the impossible waiting, distorts its face, the face of 'God', into hard, pitiless lines. The infant fantasy sees its own rage reflected in greater rage on the face of a presumptively angry 'God'. In depression this predominates.

2   The mind of the infant may, in lieu of the real, visible face, and impatient of delay, fix its inner eyes on substitute fantasies of the loved persons, or parts of them, of a lovely face and shapely breasts, distorting reality by the acceptance of mere fantasy, friendly and always accessible, but phoney, unreal and false. Moreover, there is often a sense of guilt at having done this lustful thing, so that the

face of 'God' takes on the punitive angry gaze of the accuser. It is
this face which threatens in hysteria.

3   The most terrible face of all is the faceless face of dread and
fear. Rather than face this, the infantile mind searches the racial
unconscious and brings forth birds with great beaks and claws,
spiders, crabs and scorpions, all of which are preferable to the
faceless face of the mother who absents herself beyond all bearing.
We meet patients for whom the 'face' of 'God', on the earliest levels
of being, pressing through into consciousness at a time of illness, is
hideous. And behind the hideousness is the paralysing facelessness
of an identification with non-being. Facelessness is schizoid.

4   If, when the mother's countenance is visible, it is so dead,
lifeless, and utterly ungracious towards the baby, this imparts to
the countenance of its own spirit or self-image a sense of worthlessness. That one who could give so much, gives so little, is felt to be
persecutory. The infant spirit looks out fearfully towards a 'God'
whose face is full of scorn at its own, evidently contemptible, face.
In paranoid disorders this sour face threatens.

These bitter memories of supposedly or actually unloving faces
seen in the foundation year, when the human spirit must come
to 'being' and 'well-being' through the 'umbilical cord' of visual
encounter, or die, are at the root of all compulsive unbelief, of all
our neurotic defences, and, ambiguously, of much of what becomes
our sin. Here are the beginnings of man's distortion of the truth
about the ultimate personal reality, God himself. This is where the
lie is first told about God, the lie which bedevils humanity, which
determines our solidarity with the race in ignorance, pride, fear,
anxiety, despair, idolatry and lust, unbelief and murderous hatred
of God himself.

With all these universal emotions the Psalmist is entirely familiar.
He, too, has odd feelings about God. He is puzzled by what goes
on in God's world, indignant, resentful, despairing, apprehensive,
persecuted and rebellious by turns. Paradoxically, this is precisely
the strength of the Psalmist's position from a psychological and
spiritual standpoint. He has no more of that certain knowledge of
God which came into the world by Jesus Christ than the infant has
in those primitive years when these dark and inexplicable things
happen, which are recorded in the spirit's indelible memory for
unbearable hurts and offences. In the history of God's progressive
revelation of his true face to man, the Psalmist is much nearer to
the situation of the human spirit in its formative years. He, too, is
dependent on the family, the race, the culture with its ups and

downs, its tragic crises and festivals. What course is possible to such a spirit, limited in the objects upon which spiritual vision can be focused, when beset by the cross-accidents of life which are the precipitants of depression? This same limitation of the objects of faith in the mind is characteristic of depression. When the onset of depressive illness has resulted in the inevitable regression to infantile perspectives and has constricted the spirit's vision, so that the adult knowledge of God in the face of Christ is entirely obscured, what keyhole is still available to the eye of faith?

Psalm 42. A way with depression

In a few condensed phrases in Psalm 42 the writer not only describes some of the universal symptoms of depression, but also lays down the attitude of mind and heart which will find a way through the experience of melancholy.

First, he is honest with himself about his feelings. He expresses the depressive emotions in full. 'I pour out my soul in me.' His stiff-upper-lip attitude melts. He grieves unashamedly for the past, remembering how once he would lead the throng into God's house. He admits the sluggishness of his spirit.

Secondly, he does all this in the presence of God. His statement of the problem of spiritual depression is not explained away in terms of ancient medical science, mythology or culture. He expresses it in terms of a soul athirst for God. 'I will say unto my God, why hast Thou forgotten me?' When God is manifestly present in the heart, the spirit rejoices. This he knows. Therefore he associates his depressive lack of joy with the absence of that relationship of which joy is characteristically the product.

Thirdly, he affirms that this is all in God's world, even the tragic elements in it. Though overwhelmed in spirit he does not allow his universe to disintegrate. By an act of faith, even these offensive elements are given due place in the universe which is still God's. 'All *thy* waves have gone over me.' He does not take refuge in a false dualism to save God's face by limiting his sovereignty.

Fourthly, he takes a standpoint outside his depressed self and enters into dialogue with it. He uses the painful splitting of the ego and its contrary experiences of the self, to turn the tables on his depressive feelings. 'Why art thou cast down, O my soul?' He demands that all the facts be taken into consideration; of God known and enjoyed in the past and who is alive beyond this present turmoil.

We go under neurotically, either when we refuse to listen to the complaining self at all, so that our symptoms do the complaining for us, or when we listen to nothing else. The mournful ruminations of a depressed person actually consist in attentive listening to the unhappy self at the moment dominant in consciousness. The Psalmist does not fail to listen to this desperate self. He allows it to state its full case against things as they are. But he does not allow this aspect to be the sole speaker. He does not let complaint drown the voice of the self that has known what it is to be loved by God and true companions. He insists that the contrary voice of God's word, still reverberating in the self and available in personal and national history should also be heard. The crucial point is that he identifies himself with the protestations which are calculated to increase depression and nevertheless affirms that the truth is not with the miserable majority but still with God and faith in him.

Fifthly, he counsels himself to wait on God. Tolerance of frustration, courage in the face of apparent isolation, the capacity to wait patiently, suffering in hope, is a primary manifestation of the power of 'being'. Hope is that dynamic bond by which we remain tethered to longed-for persons, even when apparently isolated from them. 'Hope still in God.' This is active passivity. It bridges the gap between the needy 'I' and the source in the 'Thou' with a trust based on previous experience of reliability. To know this means that trustful waiting strengthens faith.

Sixthly, the secret of his deliverance will be an encounter between two countenances, God's and his own. This is always how human language speaks about the triumphant vindication of faith, hope and love between God and man. It does so because there are clear analogies for this between the mother and the infant within the first year. The Psalmist encouraged his despairing self, 'Put thy trust in God . . . give him thanks for the help of his Countenance.' Though in one sense no man has seen God at any time, yet in the only important sense spiritually, our Lord affirms that the pure in heart see God. We see how God relates us to himself by the love in his eyes, as he looks at us in the face of his Son, Jesus Christ. It is the upturned eyes of the man of faith, who, in spite of sins and sufferings, looks expectantly for the appearance of the One he confidently calls 'my God' which enables him to retain the initiative and live actively through his depression, making creative use of its evil.

The difficulty is always in allowing the split-off experience to become conscious. The Psalmist says that 'God requires truth in the inward parts' (Psalm 51:6). If he really does, he must be prepared for the relevation of some shocking paradoxes. The Christian estimate of man is so paradoxical as to offend the natural man's judgement. The liberating truth is in the right holding together of apparently irreconcilable views of the self and of God. Even in depression it is possible to hold to these complementary facts:

1　To be honest and open about one's negative and unacceptable feelings, sins, doubts, rages, lusts, dreads, accusations of persecution and every kind of anxiety.

2　To do this in the presence of 'God', even if this is, at the time, little more than a protesting before the 'truth', however one perceives the truth.

3　To affirm that all that happens must be reconciled with a God of love and truth, without loss of integrity.

4　To look with the eye of faith and listen with the ear of faith beyond the present depressing sights and sounds, to take up the argument within oneself and give to the depressive feelings the best back-answers of which the spirit and the memory are capable.

5　To wait – on God – determined neither to despair of the depression lifting at all, nor, through impatience, to let mental fantasy seize upon substitute 'libidinal objects' or lusts.

6　To seek God's face, for a revelation of the way out, for the truth of the matter, for the life which transcends death, for the power of being that can embrace non-being, and to look for it in the form of personality and godliness.

7　To rest in the character of God as revealed in his historical acts of redemption and rescue.

Psalms for the depressed and afflicted

Among the Psalms there are forty-eight which are of particular value to those prepared to make the Psalmist their contemporary. The Holy Spirit will use these prayers for us as a revelation of the face of God and the word of God, the mothering and fathering of the eternal Source of Being. The list of these Psalms, which come from the deeps of human grief, despair and melancholy, follows below. Those of particular value are in italics:

6, 13, 18, *23*, 25, 27, *31*, 32, *34*, *37*, *38*, 39, 40, *42*, 43, 46, *51*, 55, 57, 62, 63, 69, *71*, 73, 77, *84*, 86, 90, 91, 94, 95, *103*, 104, 107, 110, *116*, *118*, 121, 123, 124, 130, 138, 139, 141, *142*, *143*, 146, 147.

Those persons who have had experience of helping depressed people will have learned to recognize severer injuries to the spirit which we refer to as schizoid stressing (to be taken up in a later chapter). This is a more extreme feeling of unworthiness and dereliction going to the point of an infinite desire to die. In this dreadful condition the fundamental spirit of the sufferer is in collusion with the forces of death and does not, at times, even desire deliverance. The Book of Job in its Psalmlike portions speaks to the condition of the schizoid person. However, there are some Psalms which go deeper into the expression of this chronic agony than any other ancient literature except Job. I suggest these Psalms be considered:

22, 44, 55, 71, 73, 79, 88, 102, 109, 118, 123, 124, 130, 139, 141, 146.

The evidence of psychoanalysts working on the origins of depressive illness is agreed that its roots are found within the first year of life of the mother–child relationship. The mother's face and eyes are the bearers and communicators of personal spirit and without them all is lost. It is certain that all the severer classical anxiety depressions take their origin here in conflict over mothering. However, personal identity – the 'I' in relation to one's own self – arising in the maternal relationship also requires social identity. This comes with the addition of the paternal relationship, summed up as the guiding voice.

Without the father's guardianship, his reassurance, his explanation of the way things are done, his introduction to the commandments of society, the child is lost. For the adolescent attempting to discover his social role it matters a great deal to have had a good antecedent personal relationship in which the guiding voice and supporting voice of the father have been heard. Not to have enjoyed this, either by default or by the father's surrender of role in a feeble 'ask your mother', or by his use of power to dominate the child, is to have incurred a considerable personal injury. If the indignation this arouses dare not be expressed, depressive symptoms can be expected, usually not so pathological or suicidal as those arising from the primary 'rejection' conflict with the mother.

The Psalmist deals with the fatherless situation in Psalm 119 which takes up the 'guiding voice' aspect of God.

In the cross of Christ God bears truth in the inward parts
The truth in the inward parts of the human race all came out in the crucifixion of the Son of God. Now we know, if we could not believe it before, that God is well aware what it is like to live in the world he has made.

1 *Rage.* We attended the crucifixion in our crowds, turned on the Healer, strengthening the hands of his persecutors, yelling full of rage and spite, 'Crucify him!' Our rage is focused on him as they

hammer the nails through his hands. The Roman soldiers are caught in a trap, an insoluble conflict of murder and mercy like that in the anxiety-depression position. They do not want to be the murderers of this innocent man. Their centurion saw him for what he was, the Son of God. It was thoughtful of Jesus to pray for the crucifying soldiers at that moment, just the prayer they needed: 'Father, forgive them, they know not what they are doing.' So even as the soldier hammered the nails into God, facing the naked truth of his anxiety, his rage and guilt, he could know from God himself that he was not cast out of his sight as a murderer, but forgiven and restored. While he kept this in mind, he would never need to turn away from the painful truth in the inward parts.

2 *Hate and envy*. The rulers of the people attended to the hate, mocking Christ, jeering and reviling even as he was dying. The gospel records: 'Jesus knew that for envy the Chief Priests had delivered Him to be crucified.' Having brought him low, as the envious do, they mocked his power. 'Let him come down from the cross. He saved others, let him save himself.' He did not come down, he willed to remain where he was, and in so doing saved the world and them. Saul, the persecutor of the Christians, consumed with deadly hate and proud of it, discovered the shocking truth about himself: that he hated the Truth, hated God, and loved only his own fanatical principles. This he no doubt repressed when he saw the stoning of Stephen. Saul accepted the truth about himself when confronted with Christ on the road to Damascus. The inward vision blinded him. His hateful and envious self-righteousness gave place to an entirely new way of being related to himself and to God, the acceptance of righteousness, right-relatedness to God, as a gift. Since this is always a gift, and a gift for all, envy, jealousy, greed and hatred of what others possess become redundant.

Christ knew all along that the hate and envy of the religious leaders whom it was his destiny to replace would be his destruction. From childhood he knew from the messianic Psalms, and from Isaiah's Suffering Servant, what was in store for Him. 'All they that hate me whisper together against me; they devise how they can hurt me' (Psalm 41:9). As the gospel takes it up, 'from that day forth they took counsel together to put him to death' (John 11:53). 'But he was wounded for our transgressions, he was bruised for our iniquities, the chastisement of our peace was upon him, and with his stripes we are healed' (Isaiah 53:3).

3 *Persecution*. The persecution that gives rise to feelings of inferiority, loss of rights, chronic weakness or fatigue, and paranoid feelings, was certainly part of Christ's passivity on the cross. The

'well-being' that was his right, either as Son of God or Son of Man, was extracted from him by stages and nothing at all was put back by way of relief. Betrayed by a friend, denied a proper trial, not allowed to make his defence, outlawed and condemned before the charge was heard, he protests in the name of justice and is struck across the face by a menial court servant. All his rights are taken from him, all his powers of command are superseded. His right to the companionship of friends is taken from him. Of his own disciples it has to be written, 'They all forsook him and fled' (Mark 14:50). In the terminal moments of the crucifixion Jesus cries, 'I thirst'. They gave him vinegar to drink mixed with a bitter drug. When he had tasted them, he would not drink (Matt. 27:34).

The loss of well-being, of rights of sustenance, and the persecution which makes mockery of natural justice has been endured passively by human spirits when such mental pain could least be understood. Human life is at times persecutory. Hungry people are forced to swallow what purports to be food, only to find that it is roughage without nourishment, or milk so watered down as to be useless. This is as true of washy mothering as it is of watery milk. Some investigators regard it as quite typical of the mothers of schizo-phrenic patients that they should be fulsome in their language of endearment, while remaining under the surface emotionally detached and incapable of real warmth. Such an infantile experience is in the literal sense 'disgusting'. In deep therapy paranoid patients may spend hours feeling identified with a most 'distasteful' experi-ence, as if the mouth were full of a substance so insipid, mawkish or tasteless, and so useless as the food they hoped it was to be, that they will spend hours in abreaction as if spitting out some cloying stuff. This 'disgusting' truth compels consciousness to tell a lie and deny that one could ever have been identified with such an insipid and offensive source. By projection, however, such people cannot fail to feel that life is treating them in a 'disgusting' fashion.

So Christ who is the Truth for every man must become even this unpalatable and disgusting truth. The fullest human life that ever existed submits himself willingly to be, in the end, the most attenu-ated of lives. No one suffers the mental pain of persecutory empti-ness without his participation. Since this is true, and God has, in Christ, reconciled the world of the persecuted to himself through his cross, it is of the utmost importance that we should learn how to make this fact meaningful to those who suffer like him. A fuller consideration of the paranoid personality is taken up in a later chapter. This reference here is to note that paranoid feelings can be an integral part of many depressive illnesses, especially in middle and old age. The depressive element is more amenable to psychiatric and spiritual treatment than the paranoid. The latter carries a combination of passivity and pride which makes the establishment of a therapeutic relationship very difficult.

4   *Non-being.* Some people who on first encounter seem to be depressed show, on deeper acquaintance, that their spiritual problem arises from a psychological fixation which is termed 'schizoid'. A later chapter deals with this. Here we wish to define this most malignant paradoxical dilemma of the human spirit. Whereas the uncomplicated depressive patient is on the side of the therapist in wanting to live and get well, the presence of schizoid components indicates a person who always, at a deep level, wants to die. The root of this condition lies in the infant experience of splitting off the mental pain of an experience of dereliction so unbearable as to destroy all confidence in dependent relationships. Infantile dereliction is the worst indignity we know of. Personal being-by-relatedness-to-a-source-person is irreparably destroyed. This is to have passed through the hysterical position of separation-anxiety into its exact opposite, non-separation anxiety or commitment anxiety. Where such reactions occur in an ostensibly depressed person we will find that the spiritual measures and resources of Christ which prove adequate in the willing and co-operative 'reactive depressive' person are not enough. We do not despair of them, for Christ in his dereliction reaches them.

The stressing across the margin of tolerable mental pain by privation of interpersonal contact into the schizoid position may occur only once, or rarely, in the infancy of someone who was in fact a deeply loved child, actively able to respond to generously given mother love. The schizoid experience represents, say, less than one per cent of the total input of experience; ninety-nine per cent had been a normal experience of dynamic cycles of loving relatedness.

Thus, so much heaven cannot be disbelieved in because of a moment of hell; but it makes us believe in 'hell'. It makes us compassionate with those who are 'in hell'. The presumption that 'no hell exists' is not truthfully possible. But neither is 'hell' so overwhelmingly present in the infantile universe that we have to dissociate ourselves from it, as hysterical extroverts or schizoid introverts do. Many of those engaged most fruitfully in pastoral and medical care seem to me to have the marks of this composite involvement in much heaven and a little 'hell' in infancy. I say 'seem to me' because in depressive illness (in spite of a few schizoid features of detachment) they respond much more readily to the simple, uncomplicated and less paradoxical invitations of Christ in the gospel than the genuinely schizoid person ever truthfully can. They need to know from the cross that God accepts them with their murderous rages, but always, when he calls out to them, 'Come unto me, all ye that are weary and heavy-laden, rest on me', they unmistakably want to come. They are not afraid of commitment. Involvement and personal bondedness is ninety-nine percent joy. But with the truly afflicted schizoid person the same loving invitation of Christ, reverberating on the circuits of association of the deep mind, brings back a response of ninety-nine per cent terror. Commitment spells disaster again, with dread, despair and mental agony to threaten them away from it. Thus, with an apparently depressed person where schizoid symptoms predominate, he should not be regarded as depressive at all, however 'depressed' he may be. Apathy or disgust will be more fundamental than rage in the content of the conscious.

5 *Dereliction.* Let us therefore complete the picture of Christ's redemptive work for those in whom anxiety depressions overlie an element of deeper, more paradoxical stressing into schizoid affliction. This component of the personality is in recoil from any invitation to life in commitment. To spare themselves from pain they must keep at a distance anyone who asks to enter them, as God does. An infinite distance would be safest, if it were not equivalent to a total loss of social contact and the annihilation of one's humanity. How can God get across to them? Only by himself accepting their lot, and inflicting upon himself their affliction. He must himself overcome the infinite distance they have had to place between themselves and any would-be rescuer. He must taste death for every man. He must make his own bed in hell. This, to his eternal glory by Christ Jesus, he has done. Nor was this an afterthought. The Lamb was slain before the foundation of the world. Before the depressive person with huge schizoid roots wedged into the rocks of his experience can say 'Amen' to that, and let go, he must examine the evidence. If he can be truthful enough to admit that his present standpoint is not that of a 'man' in methodological doubt, but of one 'who has no real existence' in existential despair, he will make faster progress towards the Truth.

With his disciples in the upper room, our Lord declares over the broken bread, 'This is my Body which is broken for you'. He speaks of the grain of wheat falling to the earth, dying to bring a good harvest. For this very purpose now he comes to the appointed time (John 12:24, 27). At Gethsemane in deep distress he prays that the cup might pass. The sleeping disciples add to his isolation. 'Could you not watch with me?' and so 'they all forsook him and fled' (Matt. 26 and Mark 14). At Golgotha, the place of crucifixion, he is mocked and jeered at and enters the darkness of dereliction. He cries out: 'My God, my God, why did you forsake me?'

From the Psalmist's cries of protest in those Psalms of dereliction (see Psalms 22, 69 and 88) and from Isaiah's picture of the Suffering Servant of the Lord (see Isaiah 53 and 54), our Lord would know what it was that he set his face towards in going to Jerusalem. These are not things he suffered for three hours at Golgotha, but for a lifetime. Must we not say that he knew them from the foundation of the world? That he knew that he was the Lamb of God, slain before the foundation of the world?

The task of the pastoral person

Here we see how Christ, the Good Shepherd, goes into the hell where his sheep are lost, paradoxically entangled, where every desperate struggle to get free has done nothing more than aggravate their entanglement in briars and thorns of mental pain. The first task of the Christian shepherd, the pastor, which means every Christian in relation to his neighbour, is to ensure that 'the Passion of Christ shall not go unrequited in the hearts of men' (to quote Temple Gairdner of Cairo). The man with the word of God from Christ's cross in his heart must learn to recognize, from every interpretable indication, when deep needs are stirring. Thus he should know the kinds of information that psychodynamic studies can offer, not to provide him with experience, but to help him to notice things and tie up the significance of things which he is, in direct encounter with people, experiencing. Sound textbooks put words to our ill-formed notions, enabling us to clarify and conceptualize them, thus making our own accumulating experience available to others, and most importantly, our next needy person. Clinical theology is not a diagnostic exercise. It is an interpersonal encounter of infinite complexity in which God the Holy Spirit is using one 'dead' man (glad that God has enabled him to die to any other desire than to be lived in and used by God) to communicate with another 'dead' man (who is just beginning to realize how dead he is – and worried about the past and the future). The task of the clinical theologian is to be a whole person, in Christ, open and defenceless, prepared by the Holy Spirit in dialogue, for dialogue. Discerning, by his ability to see into the depths behind the symptoms, the extent of pain that has to be revealed, he spends most of his time at first in attentive and structured listening. If, as preacher, he has already spoken of human needs in depth, and shown how the resources of Christ's cross are applied for their cure, he has made more possible the emergence of those painful truths into the consciousness of his hearer, which, but for evocative preaching, might remain for ever wordless aches, gloomy fears, unmentionable secrets. His first task, as preacher or pastor, is to reach the wounded self whatever defensive system is being used for concealment. He has something reassuring to say. 'You can come out now. Christ and we know you are there, and exactly how you feel. All your feelings are accepted, whether or not they were justified, as no doubt many of them were. You need hide no longer. See, if this is your dilemma, how Christ has acted to deliver you from it. No amount of rage or pain of persecution or dread is beyond the power of the crucified Christ to heal.'

The pastor may help the unhappy family of 'not-me's', shut away for so many years in backrooms, to come out into the open again, calling them by name. The clinical and diagnostic part of clinical theological studies will help the pastor to call the right name. But the message and the power by which the deeply afflicted man, dead and hampered by his grave-clothes of repression, can be brought to life and given strength to walk out of his tomb, is not ours, but Christ's. It is to him, not to us, that the afflicted are indebted for the harrowing of hell. That is why we take on, not like the wise analysts only those patients who are assuredly helpable, but all comers. This is simply a measure of our experience of the boundless resources of 'new being' and surgent 'well-being' which Christ brings with him down to the depths of depressive, paranoid and schizoid hells. This rescue work is twofold, seeking and saving, identification and redemption, the discovery of the lost entangled sheep and the climb back from the valley of the shadow of death to the fold, until it is back with the flock, feeding peacefully.

A new dynamic cycle
Whatever went wrong with the primitive dynamic cycle of relationships, where the human spirit should have been founded, but where, in fact it foundered, there is in Christ and His Church a new dynamic cycle of loving relatedness, a new creation of God, a new 'being', the new person in Christ, and a 'well-being', the fullness of the Holy Spirit.

There would be no point in Christ's rescue work on the cross if he had not retained on earth a fellowship, his Body, with its limbs or members, to offer a new dynamic cycle of relationships to those whose natural cycle had broken down, and who needed his divinity to replace their mortality. In this fellowship are shared the symbols

ACCEPTANCE offered to man by God.
We are 'accepted in His Beloved Son'.
'We have boldness of access by faith in Him.'
'Through Christ we have access to God.'
The Biblical term for acceptance with God is

JUSTIFICATION, through grace, by Faith. God, Being justified by faith we have peace with
As many as received Him . . . were born . . . of God.
You must be born again . . . of the Spirit.
If any man be in Christ, he is a new creature.

BAPTISM 'You are all the children of God, for as many of you as have been baptized into Christ have put on Christ.
Made ONE, you *are* all one in Christ Jesus.

Truly our *FELLOWSHIP* is with the Father.
They gave their right hands in fellowship.
Jesus said, 'I have called you FRIENDS'.
I am the WAY, the TRUTH and the LIFE.
To guide our feet *INTO THE WAY* of peace.
God so loved the world that He gave. . . . that we might have *ETERNAL LIFE*.
In Him, we live and move and have our *BEING*.
Given the *Spirit of ADOPTION* whereby we cry 'Abba', *FATHER*.

SUSTENANCE. Filled with the being of God. The God of Hope fill you with all joy and peace in believing . . . that your joy be full. Christ's coming brings life, more abundantly. A phase of *REST and ABIDING* in the life of God, that is

SANCTIFICATION, through grace, by Faith. Whom He justified, them He also glorified. Out of the glorious richness of His resources to know the *strength* of the Spirit's reinforcement that you may be FILLED with all the fullness of God.

HOLY COMMUNION Except ye eat of the flesh of the Son of Man and drink his blood ye have no life, in you. He that eateth me shall live by me. Jesus said, 'I am the BREAD of life'.
We are all ONE Bread, *ONE BODY*.

GIVE US, this day, our daily bread.
Evermore dwell in him and he in us.

GRACE has overflowed into our lives, full and generous.
Pray the Father, He will give.
. . . The Paraclete

ACHIEVEMENT. To love one another as I have loved you.
It is God who is at work within you, giving you the will and the power to achieve His purpose. We are His workmanship, created anew in Christ to do those good deeds God planned for us to do. He who abides in Me, brings forth much fruit. He comforts us so that we in turn may give the same strong sympathy to others.
The outward man suffers wear and tear but the inward man daily receives fresh strength.
Live your whole life in the Spirit and you will not satisfy the lusts of the flesh. The Spirit produces these fruits in human life, love, joy, peace, patience, kindness, generosity, fidelity, adaptability and self-control, without ambition, envy or jealousy. Limited by obedience. Live with a due sense of responsibility as men who know the meaning and purpose of life.

STATUS
The Spirit Himself endorses our inner conviction that we are *the children of God*. No more strangers, the *HOUSEHOLD of God*. Because ye are *SONS*, God hath sent forth the Spirit of His Son into your hearts, crying (as He did) Father! A member of the Church which is His Body. The fulness of Him who fills all things. Christ, 'a tremendous power inside you'. God has flooded our hearts with His light. The same Spirit brings to your whole being new *STRENGTH & VITALITY*.
The glorious *LIBERTY* of the children of God. The Son makes you *FREE*, you are free indeed. The law of the spirit of life in Christ Jesus has made me FREE from the law of sin and death. We reflect like mirrors the glory of the Lord.
Handicapped but not frustrated.
Puzzled but never in despair.
Persecuted but never standing alone in it.
Knocked down but never knocked out.
Experiencing in our bodies both the death of the Lord Jesus and the power of His risen life.
God's heredity within us will conquer the world outside us.

FIG. 7   The dynamic cycle or 'law' of the spirit of life in Christ Jesus, which sets a man free from the law of sin and death in fallen nature

of his continued self-giving. We are 'accepted through his blood'. His broken Body is also the food of the sacrament by which his eternal life in us is fed. It is this centrality of the cross which causes Paul to cry out at the end of his letter to the Galatians, 'God forbid that I glory about anything or anybody except the cross of our Lord Jesus Christ, by whom the world becomes crucified and is a dead thing to me, and I am dead to the world.'

So we can delineate the elements of the new dynamic cycle of the law of the spirit of life in Christ Jesus (see Fig. 7). The sacrament of baptism is the sign of God's *acceptance* of us. This declares the existence of a pact of love and assured acceptance which is always God's work, not ours. The act of birth or of adoption takes place only once. The son may wander into prodigality or, like the elder brother, into pettymindedness, but the same way back to the Father stands open for both. Christ's righteousness, not ours, is the ground of our acceptance and our access. So the central doctrine of phase 1 of the spiritual cycle is this: that we are justified by his gracious and costly act of road-building from man to God.

The *sustenance* of the life God gives to his adopted children is not something they have to work for or could merit. He provides the necessary food of the new life he has brought to birth. So we pray, 'Give us this day our daily bread'. We hold out our hands to his holy food in the sacrament. We must change our habits. We take our eyes off our libidinal picture gallery and fix them, wide open, on Christ. Our minds need prising open to new truth and a double insight – into our misery and Christ's majesty. It is a struggle to keep an open heart even for so generous and glorious at Guest. But these are short sharp struggles if we keep the cross in mind and plant it in our path as we run away from dread or persecution. When we see in our path someone whose dereliction and persecution are greater than our own, his cross set down in hell can turn us back from our headlong flight to destruction. It becomes possible to turn with him and return to life in him. We 'convert', turn around with him, and the struggle is over. Whether for justification or sanctification, for 'being' or 'well-being', the mode of our partici-pation in him is simply to listen, to come, to sit and to eat. We neither grow, nor earn, nor prepare the food of our eternal spirits. That is God's work. Our response is to abide and rest in him, to enjoy his gift of Himself as the Bread of Life in the joyful Feast. Since now there is no shortage of beloved persons and sustaining objects, our lusts and rages because of the lack of them, become pointless.

These are the two spiritual 'input' phases. Since it was in these ontological input phases of acceptance and sustenance that our human spirits were driven most seriously astray at the beginning, it is here that they need most correction. When these change in response to God's grace and graciousness, our *status* changes to the position of sons of God, whose obligation and inclination are no longer discordant, but unified. Furthermore, the whole concept of *achievement* changes from being the prelude to, and precondition of, neurotic acceptance, to a free outpouring of the 'well-being' we have so generously received and will receive again, whether, in work, we seem to succeed or fail. If, from the heart, we have been responding to this account of the gracious work of God in Christ with steady gratitude, we have the root of the matter in us which will enable us to bring Christ's joyful resources to the depressed. In the next chapter we consider the criteria of recognition of depression in the pastoral setting, and the stages by which dialogue may proceed.

4

Depression – Practical Considerations

In this section we deal with the treatment of spiritual depression without the help of diagrams or recourse to the model of the dynamic cycle. Many clergy have found the model helpful towards the understanding of what is going on in depression but, rightly, want to keep it out of sight when dealing with depressed persons. The 'I–Thou' of interpersonal meeting must never be displaced by a premature and depersonalizing attention to diagnostic labelling in an attempt to 'locate' the problem in relation to a model. However, in so far as the model of the dynamic quadrilateral with its extensions is demonstrably Christ-centred, I think it has more chance of survival than those which are just as demonstrably based on existing man. The behavioural dynamics of the average man do not innately supply any model for the delineation of mental health. Nothing arises ultimately out of man himself but variations on the theme of his despair. For the man whose main interest is in psychodynamics he will find what follows is in line with classical analytical formulations about depression. Whether the relevance to depressed persons of the death of Christ at the hands of raging men comes home to him with the 'Aha!' reaction of surprise and wonder, or does not, is another matter.

I am concerned about the clergymen who may feel suspicious of this mixture of oil and water, of spirituality and psychology. At least this psychodynamic arrangement should commend itself as one which acknowledges again the primacy and normative force of Christ as the Word of God, in his Person the Living Theology. This rapprochement was not possible while psychoanalysts wandered uncertainly from one hypothesis to another about the origins of anxiety on too-late, oedipal levels. Even the clarification of depressive dynamics within the second half of the first year could not fully effect the synthesis.

It was not until the definition of the schizoid position, within the first half-year of life, made it clear that the primal anxiety is onto-logical and that the basis of existential trauma is despair or dread, that an effective correlation could be made with Christian theology; centred in Christ, crucified and risen. For the word of the cross is addressed, not only to our mistaken activities of rage or hate, but also to our miserable passivities.

Existential or ontological analysis reaches down through those areas of psychodynamic conflict which Freud held to be open to analysis until it reaches the final predicaments of loss of being or well-being. These Freud affirmed were unanalysable. But the Word of God in the cross reaches down to identify himself with the desolation which is almost in despair of life's renewal (what we would call the hysterical position). He reaches down beyond that to dread of life itself, to the final despair that death is not possible (which we call the schizoid position). These are not 'questions' that can be 'answered' by knowledgeable explanations addressed to the intellect. Each of them constitutes a dilemma of being itself, or indeed of non-being. To state this dilemma, as the existentialists have done, and as psychoanalysts now can, is to invite all those whose thought is centred in the cross of Christ to come alongside and speak with poignant relevance to the human condition.

It remains, as ever, a free decision whether we accept or refuse the implications of God's work in Christ's strange victory over rage and dread, hate, envy and persecution. All that honest accounting of what goes on in the depths of being and non-being can do is to undermine the manifestly inadequate psychodynamic formulations which historically come first. In so far as they have become, for some, articles of belief (and inferentially of disbelief in the theological assertion, that man's basic requirement is redemption from his despair) they can no longer be held with any confidence. Doubtless, where compulsive group loyalties prevail, they will be. Further than this, intellectual demonstration cannot go. No Christian would wish it to. Faith in Christ is never to be a syllogism. It does not wait for a cleverer proof or irrefutable evidence. However, within the 'household of faith' this rapprochement, highlighting as it does so many aspects of the redemptive work of Christ, gives us further solid ground for joy and responsiveness to him.

It is my wish that those clergymen who regard the study of psychopathology as the strange occupation of a queer and unreliable profession should not turn away from this opportunity of discovering the Lordship of Christ in these peculiar hells which we and our patients inhabit. Even if this particular psychodynamic formulation of depression displeases, it must be admitted that not a single major item of this analytic account is not already clearly defined in the theologians' descriptions of accidie. Thus we turn now to the spiritual responsibility of leading depressed people from the law of sin and death in which they lie, to the Person of Christ and the law of the spirit of life in him.

A ladder to rest and joy in Christ

1   The depressed person is fatigued beyond all ordinary weariness. He is heavy laden beyond the weight of any external burden. His load is mental pain, impenetrable blackness in the mind, and a sense of guilt that defies absolution. To all such, Jesus Christ said: 'Come unto me, I will give you rest, I will refresh you' (Matt. 11:28). Here is his open invitation to acceptance and sustenance, to the gifts of being and well-being out of the Person of Christ, open to all comers. In so far as men will thus define themselves, Christ promises them rest and refreshment.

Unfortunately, the very habit of his mind is to imagine these are not for him, or if they are, they must be earned by him. He cannot rest. He cannot, in despair of himself, rest back into the bosom of the Father for that refreshment of spirit which was promised alike for him in word, sacrament and the fellowship. He is unfamiliar with the dynamics of grace. His ultimate concern lies, not in a reconciled relationship with the source person, but in an egocentric argument between himself and his neurotic conscience. The pastoral task is therefore a clinical theological task, to take up, one by one, those fixed and regressive attitudes of mind which are preventing the person from enjoying Christ's promised rest and refreshment.

2   Thus the pastor must take up the matter of hidden rage, directed (as all authors on accidie and depression agree) against 'God', and against significant persons in the family circle, and against himself. He cannot rest in a 'God' he is secretly enraged against. He must come clean about the rage, see it and feel it in himself and learn how Christ can invite even those who rage against him murderously to rest in him. This the cross of Christ itself teaches, with a little help by way of exegesis.

3   He cannot rest in God while his mind is ceaselessly resting in and gazing on a whole picture gallery of desirable libidinal objects. These will be at times readily available for inspection and appraisal. Some of the more mature objects might be worth resting in. Most of them, in depressed people, are regressed, infantile and unsatisfying when looked at in the light of day. But in depression the lack of desirable objects leads the mind's lust to rest itself in all kinds of impracticable imaginary situations. The pastor who himself rests upon the face of Christ will draw the restless depressed idolater

to stay his eyes on the divine countenance revealed in Christ and there be satisfied.

4   He cannot rest in God while he remains a religious moralist, resting for his being and well-being on his own activities. The slave must become a son. However alien it is to his inbuilt sense of what is reasonable, he must come to terms with God's foolishness, which offers all that the religious man strives for as a free gift. He needs to live again by the experience of Paul's letter to the Romans as to justification, or right-standing with God, solely by responsive faith to what God has done. As he has also lost well-being, he needs to live again within the experience of the letter to the Galatians, where all the abundance of the divine indwelling is a gift to those who abide in the Triune God for refreshment of spirit in the uncomplicated receptiveness of faith. What could never be achieved by effort is given freely to affiance.

There may be other obstacles to a joyful rest in Christ which may be encountered in pastoral dialogue with depressed persons. However, these four main obstacles to change and cure must always be borne in mind in the depressed. No claim is being made that the understanding of psychodynamics is any more than a handmaid to theology. It is the direct activity of God in the gospel of Christ which alone has power to transform a person trapped in depressive dynamics into one who is rooted and grounded in the life of the Son of God. That this spiritual transformation also solves completely the psychological dilemma of privation, anxiety, rage and lust, the impasse of compulsively compliant personality dynamics and the bankruptcy of moralistic religion, is an added bonus God delights to give. There are no rules as to the order in which these points should be taken up. Since it is agreed that rage, fixated and turned in upon itself, is an invariable component of depressive illness studied psychodynamically, we turn first to this factor of unacknowledged aggressive emotions.

Hidden rage and resentment

In the process of giving the history of his illness the depressed person has probably described various people in authority as behaving in ways which would provoke any ordinary person to anger. In spite of this admission, the depressed person feels justified in denying the anger because most, or all, of it is unconscious. A good part of the skill of dealing psychotherapeutically with depressed persons consists in talking delicately, lightly and uncensoriously, reflecting upon the person's life situation with him until he recognizes that it is perhaps not so terrible a thing to feel his rage, which appears to be turned in upon himself, is actually directed primarily against his frustrators. The task is made more difficult for the pastoral counsellor because of the universal expectation of religious people when depressed that they are judged, condemned and rejected by God and all other decent people. The whole truth of the gospel about God's acceptance of broken sinners is obscured in depression. Moreover, the admission of rage is guarded against by its very close association with the severe ontological weakness which is subjacent to it in the unconscious. We know that what originally provoked the rage was a most painful sense of falling out of relationship with the source, and the separation anxiety to which it gave rise. This whole area is shut off as being part of the unacceptable experiences of infancy, the 'not-me'. In front of the parson the religious depressive feels he must never admit to feelings of weakness, despair, apathy or weakness of the will to be good. He must put a brave face on, steadfastly refusing to give up.

In the depth analysis of depressed people, invariably there are found occasions in infancy when the child was shut in to utter unreasonableness on the part of the mother. Her ideas of infant rearing deprived the child of adequate love or attention at a time when it felt urgent need of them and felt they ought, in all justice, to have been given. Mothers of depressives, after early months of dutiful attention to the child, tend to take the tough line of discipline and demand too early, before the infant has arrived at the most primitive usages of speech whereby it might understand what the mother's insistent dissatisfaction is driving at. To the infant the whole of life seems monstrously unjust. Patients, recalling these experiences in later life, record the predominant emotion as resentment at injustice. They say, 'Why couldn't she see that it was an impossible demand to make of me?' or 'She left me alone all night, scared and crying'.

, We recognize that it is impossible for parents to bring up infants without incurring at some point frustration and rage. However, where there are severe clinical depressions it is found on analysis that there has been some actual prolonged deprivation of acceptance and support, and there is justice in the infant's pleas that he was at some point denied the necessities of being and well-being.

This is not to say that the parents were aware of this. Often they were perplexed at the onset of disturbed nights and the obvious unhappiness of the child. On recollection, a mother may say that had it not been for an older person, such as a grandparent who lays claim to authority in these matters, her own intuitions would have led her to err on the side of generosity in staying with the child for reassurance and allowing more generous sustenance. Frequently we are told by the parents that the baby was very troubled for a period of its infancy, that they themselves would have acted tenderly and mercifully to the child, offering it a loving presence in its inexplicable mental pain. But this was forbidden by the doctor or the nurse, who declared with utmost rigour, even with threats, that such attention would do damage to its character, that it must be left to cry. In what other period of human life is disconsolate sorrow supposed to be eased by solitary confinement?

Yet in depression the whole human person is thrown back into this primitive environment. What he feels bears no relationship to contemporary relationships. In all things that concern his life and well-being he is now exactly as he was then. He is no longer in the presence of the God of Christian theology, he is in the presence of the merciless 'God' of his first year. He is back in 'hell', crying out to someone who does not come, praying with utter longing for one who is evidently not there. All the smouldering rage and bitterness of the infantile situation is aroused in the depths of the unconscious mind, and Gŏd seems to be precisely as unjust as the 'bad' mother was. As there was no fairness about the initial situation, so the depressed person feels there is none now. Comparing the God of the promises with the 'God' of his unhappy experiences he aligns them emotionally in pairs alongside his primitive certainty that there are two sources of his being, the one who came lovingly as she was accustomed to and gave him 'being', and the one who played him false and gave him hell. The state of affairs is such that the depressed person would rather suffer the accusations of guilt from the super-ego than call off the inner aggressive accusation of injustice against the sources. He is not going to own up to his rage to anyone he feels will condemn him for it, since his inner conviction is stronger, that the rage was, in its origins, a righteous anger which he will not disown.

The clinical theologian sees all men only under the cross and recognizes that the rage of the depressed is no bar to Christ's acceptance of him. The whole enactment of the cross, whereby Christ becomes the willing victim of the rage and spite of men, while yet praying to God for them, 'Father, forgive them, for they know not what they do', is an object lesson to the depressed person, enabling him to recollect his rage without further need of repression. Jesus died for, and at the hands of his own people, but though his death is a judgement on their rage, it is also, since it did not end there but in His resurrection, a guarantee of the reinstatement. This reinstatement can only take place when we, or they, acknowledge our guilt: not guilt of having committed sins, or of coming short of a self-imposed ideal of moral perfection, but the guilt of having rejected, despised, raged against and crucified the Son of God in human form. The Christian is not interested in condemning persons for unrighteousness, whether it be law-breaking or raging at real or imaginary injustice, because the inference would be that he approved its opposite; that is, the ability to justify oneself by having performed the works of the law, or by having ceased to rage, either by repressing or displacing the anger. The essence of the Christian message is that 'righteousness' or right-relatedness to God is now no longer a matter of law-abiding behaviour. It does not depend on the ability, by introspection, to give oneself full credit marks for morality. It is a matter of looking away from ourselves towards Christ Jesus. We hear and respond to his invitation to become rightly related to God by what he has done. 'Christ is the end of the law-way for righteousness to everyone who trusts him.' There is no danger whatever that any man exposed to the clinical theological approach is going to go away with the feeling that, since his neurotic guilt has been lifted, he is thereby freed of guilt. His actual guilt, as over against the goodness of God, is established, in order that by the further goodness of God in Christ it too may be dissolved.

The cross discloses truth which offers freedom

All is changed when a man comes to view himself and all men as under the cross. He recognizes his kinship with those who took pleasure in seeing the nails driven through the hands and feet of Jesus. The only ones who enjoyed the spectacle were the punctilious religious, the indignantly self-righteous Pharisees. What distinguished the disciples of Jesus from the Pharisees was not that the disciples were morally admirable and the Pharisees were not. Rather, the secret sins of the Pharisees are hidden, whereas no attempt is made to minimize the faultiness of the disciples on every count. What differentiates the disciples from the Pharisees is that the disciples follow, are found with, and are related to Jesus, whereas the Pharisees are not. Though this may sound offensive to those who regard morality as the final criterion of human self-acceptance, and religion as only a means to that end, the Christian view is precisely to the contrary. It affirms that if this relationship is maintained and responded to, ethical behaviour, loving as one has been loved, is certain to follow. Because the relationship which Christ offers is one of entire sufficiency, in spite of all that the world can do to deprive us of good relationships, this is in itself an entire contradiction of the depressive delusion that one has lost all one's good object-relationships. Martin Luther summed up this paradox when he said, speaking of the Christian, that he stands, '*Simul justus et peccator*' – at one and the same time a sinner and a justified man.

While the dynamics of depression are on a man he is not pure-hearted, he is essentially double-minded. He is not humble. Though humiliated he is basically proud. No amount of spiritual direction, if it fails to diagnose and deal with this concealed fact of double-mindedness, will ever do any Christian spiritual good, much less any psychological good to depressive persons. The aim of psycho-therapy is thus to restore emotional truth and reality to all our relationships, however painful this revelation may be. It is the truth which frees. It is because the depressed person cannot tolerate the truth of his destructiveness that psychotherapy is prolonged. Anything which makes the truth more tolerable, more credible, such as a belief, shared both by the depressed person and his counsellor, that the cross of Christ catches the whole world raging against its Source of Being, cannot fail to assist insight into the hidden elements of rage. If the depression is in its early stages it may be quite possible for the person to recall festering occasions of resentment and discuss them in a manner both adult, sensible and therapeutic.

History-taking can be therapeutic

The opportunity to discover where the resentment is directed and why, occurs as we listen to the recounting of the personal history. Direct inquiry frightens it further into hiding. Patient listening reveals it indirectly. A concerned but morally relaxed opportunism, listening to everything simply as fact, creates the opportunity for self-disclosure. History-taking or pastoral conversation, is not just getting to know essential facts so as to fill in a hypothetical form of information about the patient. It is, with all distressed persons, an essential part of the therapy. The therapeutic process inheres in a combination of at least two factors, the relationship which grows up between the client and the counsellor, and the increased insight which arises within the relationship as a result of a joint search for facts and their meanings. The dialogue advances these two elements. It is not so much the compilation of a factual record as the increasing knowledge, inseparable from loving acceptance, of a person. It is the counsellor's opportunity to show that he is much more interested in the totality of the real person and every one of his genuine feelings and experiences, than he is about symptoms, omissions, commissions or beliefs and unbeliefs. He shows himself to be unconditionally at the disposal of the needy person, granting to his faith the same unquestioning certainty that it will be justified, and he himself accepted whatever disgrace is revealed, as the pastor himself received from Christ. Here he is putting the gospel in its ontological roots into action as maybe nowhere else in his ministry.

One important function of history-taking is to restore a proper distancing. Until this is done no problem-solving is possible. That is why, in the severer depressions, complete rest in hospital is such a profound relief. We must recognize that in listening to the unstructured tale of woe of the depressed person we are hearing a selective account of the past and certainly a distorted one. When this has spent itself, a more structured history must be attempted. This will be based on a more systematic inquiry into previous personal history. If such conversation is possible, the therapist will ask direct questions, looking not just at the events of the past few weeks or months, but at a long cross-section of the person's life from childhood, through schooldays and adult life in an attempt to appreciate something of his total life experience. This quietly encouraged recalling of all kinds of past experience, including the happier ones, tends to restore a better 'distancing'. At the end the person may say something like, 'It's done me good to talk. Remembering the better bits has helped me get a grip on reality again.'

In depression we know what the general pattern is. There has been a falling away from the dynamic cycle of relatedness into a painful disrelatedness to the sources of being. Diminishing powers of the spirit to maintain waiting are accompanied by increasing anxiety. Aggressive and libidinal fantasies spring out of this situation, but both are liable to be crushed down by the weight of anxiety. We go to the history-taking with this pattern of anxiety depression in mind. It structures our listening. We are less anxious as we attend to the jumbled story presented to us. But we begin to listen first as if we had no patterns at all in mind. The depressed person alone possesses the data of relevant information. We possess a variety of patterns. As he talks some patterns fall away as irrelevant, others are confirmed time and again until they are established. Consequently it is folly to come to any definite conclusion as to what the final important pattern will be until the end of the interview. Even when we are sure that the fixated pattern is such and such, it is a matter of fine judgement to decide when to offer the interpretation to the patient as a clue to understand himself.

Such interpretation should never be more than we feel the patient can bear.

Evaluation is therapeutic in the light of God's justice

More important than any evaluation by the pastor is the ability he has to help the depressed person to re-evaluate all aspects of his own previous evaluations of the event he relates. This is the crux of therapy in depression. His evaluation emotionally of certain recent losses has been excessive. Recent relative losses are treated as though they were the original total disasters. Because of the depression he evaluates similar patterns of experience as if they were identical. He requires help in evaluating the relative strengths of the forces inside himself and in his environment which are tearing him apart. Our task is to strengthen the elements of truth which are in danger of being suppressed by violence or intimidation. He is a man at civil war. A powerful majority, claiming absolute right on their side, has attempted to put the minority absolutely in the wrong and stifle their complaints. Since his freedom, self-affirmation and possibilities for maturation lie with the minority, it is important to him that we put a high value on them and help him to express their just demands. No one in such a situation is helped by a counsellor who echoes the opinions of the oppressor. Nor is he helped by one who, without appreciating the strength of the opposition, encourages him to rebellion, without counting the consequences. He needs someone who is without fear, who pursues the truth of the matter without deviating, who insists that open court be held to hear both sides in full. The aim is never to impose our evaluations on the person. Dependence on us will perpetuate the depressive immaturity. Our task is to set the court in motion for him to be the judge.

The statement above has to be qualified in certain cases. If he proposes a criminal act to get revenge on those who have oppressed him, we must evaluate this for what it is and dissuade him, for good reasons, from pursuing a felony. In Christian pastoral care the same applies to any proposal which, before the event, warns us of an intention to sin high-handedly. Our silence can rightly be construed as approval and we do the person an injustice by it. To take the matter up in discussion is by no means to invade the person's proper freedom. I would feel justified in saying to an infatuated man who proposed elopement with a married woman, 'It would be wrong to take this woman away from her husband and children. Your conscience would never approve of this to the day you die.' What comes to our notice after the event needs no condemnation from us or evaluation of any kind. Unless it is boasted of, we do well to regard the telling of it as a confession, and therefore to be accepted. In coming to lay his whole life before us, a man is showing a degree of penitence which many of us will never equal.

All evaluation based on clinical pastoral history-taking begins and ends within the fact that structures all our work with individuals, the over-arching fact of Christ's justifying, accepting love. This puts all of us, the weak, the bad, the indecisive, the scared, the outraged, and even the despairing, nevertheless in the right with God. The only ones it excludes from being in the right with God are the proud, the pompous, those who when praying thank the 'God' of their imaginations that they are not as other men are. They will not be submitting themselves to clinical pastoral care. They also, by an act of inner blindness to the cross of Christ, disqualify themselves from conducting a clinical pastoral interview. Their evaluation of men and events is always based on something other than the cross of Jesus Christ, and to say that it is based on 'moral theology' or 'ascetic counsels' or 'casuistry' is no excuse. My conviction is that it is fatal to the best kind of therapy to jettison the patient's expectation that there should be justice in the universe. Depressed people have a strong and central notion of justice and injustice. If the clinical theologian were to encourage a person to throw this overboard, he would certainly be casting his Christian faith away at the same time. No one can read the Scriptures without being impressed with this primary fact, that the God of Judeo–Christian revelation is infinitely concerned with justice. To have to forgo a confident belief in ultimate justice should make any sane man depressed to the point of utter despair.

Has there been any world religious teacher who spoke so sternly of the duty of adults always to accept children? Did any of them utter such terrifying words as those of Jesus when he said, 'Whoso shall offend one of these little ones which believe in me, it were better for him that a millstone were hanged about his neck, and that he were drowned in the depths of the sea' (Matt. 18:6). When his disciples told the parents of young children that he was too tired to welcome them, Jesus rebuked his followers and insisted that little children should always have access to him. Christ adds, to the natural instinct of a mother, the divine injunction always to be available for her infant when it has grave need of her. If, therefore, the history demonstrates that the depressive sense of injustice takes its roots in actually unjust infantile situations, we are not concerned to show the patient that the rage is futile. We ought to say that it has the whole weight of God's indignation and condemnation behind it.

Where there is manifest injustice the pastor must not be afraid of declaring that it is so, and that God is concerned to redress it. Pastoral care requires that degree of empathy which shows understanding of the variety of suffering which all the actors in the drama have undergone. He shows by empathy that he understands, while avoiding sympathy with any one party at the expense of the other. As long as the patient is struggling to express emotions that he has never dared express before, the pastor is entirely with him. This is creative activity. The pastor does not encourage reiterated complaints. He reverts to facts and history-taking. He may remind the complainer of the injustices which we all are continually inflicting upon others by the very nature of our own compulsive egocentricity. This is not a judgement on the person which excludes the pastor. It is a statement of fact. We recognize that he who has caused injustice has also usually suffered it. Christ's truth for him lies in the cross and resurrection, and in the giving of the Holy Spirit within the sacraments and fellowship of the Church. This is God's final answer to injustice, which he shares and redresses.

In all that has gone before, the clinical theologian has been a listener. When some pattern has emerged which seemed would be readily acceptable to the person, this is stated as one possible way of interpreting the events and symptoms which have baffled the parishioner. The significance of some of the physical symptoms may have been simply interpreted. Without being a doctor it is possible to explain that in a complex state of mind conflicting orders are sent from the brain to the internal organs. Some organs are ordered to prepare for a fight. The heart pumps full and fast as if fight were on. Digestion stops, muscles tense for struggle. Other organs are prepared for flight. Yet others are made ready for a luscious meal or an exciting sexual experience by the free play of the imagination. The internal organs are bombarded by irreconcilable and contradictory orders, so that nothing is ready for anything. This is the functional basis of hypochondriachal symptoms. A depressed person worries about the state of his stomach and his bodily workings. The reassurances of the doctor, examining him and in organic terms declaring that there is nothing wrong, often fall flat. The patient knows perfectly well that there is something wrong with him, and cannot accept this reassurance. The pastor may at times be the first one to make sense of this paradox. If the pastor hears that the doctor is satisfied, organically speaking, he is able to give great relief to the patient by simple explanation of elementary physiology. It would come better from the doctor, but a simple interpretative

word can link with the emotional conflicts and the person will find
the symptoms easing.

Sometimes all that clinical medicine needs to do for overstrained
organs and physical systems is to order rest, rest and more rest.
Everything that a clinical theology can do for the overstrained spirit,
whether the strain be due to sheer suffering (as in the hystero-
schizoid position) or to having attempted the impossible morally
(as in the depressive and obsessional reactions), is summed up in
Jesus Christ himself, and in rest, rest and more rest in him. The
revival of the Church will come about when we learn how to live
resting and abiding in Christ Jesus, pouring himself out by the
operation of the Holy Spirit in the corporate life of those who,
passing through the waters of baptism, gather round the holy table
for the bread and wine of eternity and feed on his word.

Steps in the pastoral task

In this chapter we have emphasized the clinical theological
approach to depression rather than that of simple supportive
therapy by befriending. Both are part of the 'total push' which the
Church's diaconate offers to the doctor and the patient. We
conclude by setting out a summary of the steps in the clinical
approach to the theological task of leading men and women out of
the multiple psychopathology of the depressive state to rest and joy
in Christ.

1   Establish a rapport with the sufferer by relaxed, attentive and
prolonged listening. Say no more than serves to lower the tension
and diminish the inevitable difficulties a patient has in talking
about things so long concealed. Your own contributions may be
summaries of what the person has said, in such a way as to let him
know you have accepted this so he can pass on to the next point.
Avoid all judgemental attitudes. They are out of place here. Leave
what advice you may have to give to the end. By that time you
may understand that it would have been pointless to give it.

2   Let him tell his story in his own way with just enough
prompting from you to keep him going.

3   If he becomes reiterative, lift him out of the groove by asking
direct questions about his life, now and in the past, at home, at
work and in recreation. Clergymen should avoid asking about the
sufferer's 'faithfulness in religious duties'. This puts the patient
immediately on the defensive. It sounds like the parson demanding
his dues. It is best to leave all about religion right to the end. The
emotions of the depressed person date from eras of his personality

which antedate knowledge of holy history. He is helped if his pastor puts into words what he already knows, that prayer, worship, assurance, joy and warmth have passed right out of this person's religious experience. It is the depressed parishioner who harps upon religious duty and bewails his failure to fulfil it. The Christian pastor talks about Jesus Christ as God's infinite grace and gift, in whom all men crushed and killed by the law are invited to rest.

4   Allow him to state his case against life. You know he has one, encourage him to state it vigorously. If he seems afraid to do this, help him to put it into words. Be in empathy. Show that you understand that such emotions arise naturally out of such experiences, interpreted as the parishioner has interpreted them. Do not say, 'I simply cannot understand anyone feeling like that'. Do not indulge in too much sympathy. Empathy is the ability to relate situations to the feelings that arise out of them, and accept them as matters of fact. The pastor may never have felt this way himself. Christian empathy, by which a person makes himself available to the Holy Spirit to feel for others far beyond his own experience or capacity, is as desirable as it is rare. Do not be afraid that the case against God, against Providence, against the Church, and against his neighbours and family is mounting up. Allow him to continue until he has no more to say on this account.

5   Begin to formulate in your own mind the patterns of his despairing, fearing, dreading, resenting, raging, hating, envying, lusting, coveting, and any other besetting emotional compulsions. Formulate also the positive and meaningful relationships and purposes round which his integrative forces have been gathered.

6   Do not leap to conclusions. Work steadily through the whole life history until you begin to sense where it is that the major conflict lies. Recognize that the area of conflict is most often defined clearly by the sense of resistance which you feel when the crucial relationship is under discussion. Notice at what point he changes the subject, breaks off to reiterate his complaints, switches to other issues or talks about you instead of himself, suggesting that he is taking up your time or that he has to get to a fictitious appointment.

7   If you think you can see what his half-concealed problem is, tentatively speak of this sort of conflict as a likely one for a person in this situation. Throw it out as a suggestion or something which might be so. Thus you indicate you are prepared to discuss such things without embarrassment or condemnation. The patient may say to you, and with gratitude, 'That's just the point', then proceed to tell you about it.

8   By tentative inquiry about infancy and childhood, look out

for presumptive evidence of the origin of these dynamic patterns in emotional stresses in the first and subsequent years of life. Do not by any means imply the person should accept the relevance of this. He may be loaded against psychodynamic interpretation. Offer your suggestion as to the ways in which his life situation and his present distressed emotions and symptoms can be linked up. State it as a matter of fact that these linkages do occur. If the interpretation is approximately correct it will produce an answering resonance in the parishioner. At this moment he may move on with eagerness and further insight. On the other hand it may produce an intensified volume of defensive protest, with idealization of parents and childhood. This would indicate that the interpretation is too painfully true for the patient to accept it at this stage. Never try to argue a person into acceptance of your understanding of him. You must wait, prepared to modify your formulation or collect further evidence from his history of its truth. It will be fully acceptable when the depressed person is sure of your acceptance, and indeed of God's acceptance of his shadow side.

9   Encourage the parishioner to accept, first intellectually, and later with as much genuine feeling as possible, the fact that he has more angry resentment at life's injustice buried within him than he is readily aware of or has dared to show openly to others, particularly to those in authority.

10   Explain how this inner raging, turned back upon oneself by anxiety, is depression. Show how all the various spiritual, psychological, emotional and physical symptoms he complains of arise from this internal civil war.

11   Assume that, as part of his depression, he will have had difficulty with his libidinal drives. In which direction has his fantasy life got out of hand? Do not indulge your eagerness to enjoy sexual exploits vicariously, nor, on the other hand, indulge your fastidiousness by denying him the opportunity to speak of his sexual vagaries in so far as they trouble or accuse him.

12   When the history as such is concluded the experienced pastor will make a few direct inquiries. The answers to these will enable him to assess the extent to which the depression has affected bodily functions. You wish to know to what extent sleep, appetite, concentration, decisiveness, incentive, normal interests, speed of thought and activity have been affected.

13   It is always wise to ask directly whether the person has felt like ending it all. If he replies affirmatively, inquire if he has at any time made an attempt, or has definite ideas as to how he would do it, whether he has acquired the necessary drugs or planned the

details, and whether he has tidied up his affairs or written farewell letters. If there is any serious thought of suicide, equally serious arrangements must be made, medically, to prevent it. The pastor may need the person's permission to get in touch with his doctor and to consult with members of the family. This should be the procedure if you have made no rapport during the interview and there has been no lifting of him out of the groove of his ruminations and you sense he is beyond your capacity for personal helping. Do not be dilatory. Pastoral care, even if not your own, continues in hospital.

14   If insight is developing, you will have come to some sort of understanding of the interpersonal dynamics of his depression and what it means to him. This good relationship is the primary thera-peutic factor. Having come to terms with various shadowy aspects of himself, in the presence of a person whose judgement he has come to respect, gives him a new and secure base from which to act upon his deeper life problems. If he expresses eagerness to see you again, propose a further hour within the next week, sooner if you sense that breakdown is not far away. He may be satisfied and stop at this point. You will have done a most useful piece of psychological first aid even if he accepts no further help. This is as proper a task for the Christian 'diaconate' as the work of medical missions or of social relief. The works of love express the Word of Life in you, but they do not always lead to an acceptance of the Word of Life in those who are healed. Only one may return to give glory to God.

5

The Understanding of Hysterical Personalities

The word 'hysteria' and the adjective 'hysterical' carry many meanings in psychiatric terminology and it is not easy to relate them to
each other. The word is neither exact nor a construct of modern
psychiatry. Used by Plato and the Greeks it means 'the wandering
womb'. From earliest times hysteria has been associated with frustrated sexual and marital functions, especially in women, manifesting itself in a variety of symptoms in all parts of the body and
the mind. Freud amplified the Greek idea by attributing the infantile
origins of hysteria to the 'oedipus' conflict in which the little boy
has genital-sexual wishes towards the mother and hostility to the
father; and to analagous sexual conflict in little girls. More recently
the neo-Freudians, Melanie Klein, Fairbairn, Guntrip and others,
have shown that the real root of hysteria is in a much earlier period
of infancy, well within the first year of life. It had to do primarily,
not with sexuality and the genital areas, but with interpersonal
deprivation during the primal phase of personality development.

The core of the hysterical position
The core of the hysterical position, from which all the protean
manifestations of the disorder are derived, is the mental pain of
separation of the infant from the presence and countenance of the
mother, or the substituted personal source of being. Unable to bear
aloneness, able to live only by identification with a personal source
who can be seen or felt or otherwise known to be present, the
baby reacts to dereliction by diminishing tolerance of isolation and
concomitant increase of 'separation anxiety'. It is probable that
hereditary or constitutional factors, or both, render some infants
less able to tolerate such frustration in maternal delays and
absences. The experience of separation-panic in these infants is not
terminated by the mother's return. It is split off from consciousness,
a process referred to by some analysts as hysterical splitting.
    The hysterical position of 'identification with terrifying separation
from a personal source' is near to the margin of pain tolerance.

There is an imminent threat of 'identification with non-being' if the pain of hanging on to life by relationship with one who never comes becomes literally intolerable. Hanging on to the cord of 'attachment-to-life-by-relatedness-to-human-persons-as-the-source-of-personal-being' is near to breaking point. In some hysterical patients who show signs also of powerful schizoid reactions it has certainly broken. The intense hysterical wish for life through someone's coming, to whom one can cling and be fed is replaced, if the margin is crossed and the schizoid position entered, by an equally powerful wish for death, not to be held, not to eat. But though this schizoid position must always be borne in mind in hysterical persons, the predominant reactive movement in hysterical behaviour is towards people in an attempt to gain and keep their attentive acceptance.

This intensely painful experience of separation-panic is suffered initially as sheer passivity. The baby is too young to 'think' of fighting or raging to attract attention. It has no consciousness of separateness from the mother, thus everything the baby experiences is inferred to be known by the mother and intended by her. The only defence at this stage is fantasy.

The infant in its first year is person-seeking. Its spirit must feed on the personal relationship given by the mother, mediated by the sight of her face and by every other mode of experiencing her love and care. If it cannot have these precious whole-person experiences of interpersonal relatedness, which it is painfully deprived of in the hysterical position, it has no alternative defence against absolute anxiety or schizoid dread but to take refuge in fantasies of desirable part-objects, and to comfort itself by rubbing the most painfully excited places, genital and oral. When repression follows the splitting-off of these experiences from consciousness, nothing changes in the deep mind. The panic-stricken baby is buried alive in the mind. It is as alive twenty, forty or sixty years later as at the moment of repression. Drug treatment may return it fully to consciousness. More commonly it manifests its presence in the whole variety of psychiatric conditions to which the adjective hysterical is attached.

The hysterical personality disorder
An hysterical personality disorder is the direct expression, in terms of dynamic patterning of the personality, of a lifelong reaction to the constant threat of the buried situation in which, because no one is spontaneously responding to the absolute, infantile need for an attentive source-person, the pain of final separation-panic and the dread of non-being are perpetually imminent. This can be kept at bay so long as attention-seeking behaviour is maintained. Every-

thing is sacrificed to the clamant emotional need for someone to cling to. Frustration is poorly tolerated, waiting time is like dying time. Impulsive, thoughtless, unreasonable bids for attention rise rapidly to temper tantrums. This can make for accident proneness, especially if there is a schizoid death-wish in the background. Before resorting to violence or blackmail the hysterical personality tries to please. To this end, as a woman, she is seductive, exhibitionist and histrionic. Her self-dramatization is supported by a high level of suggestibility, self-deception and emotional manipulation of prospective helpers. He, or she, is faithful to the one idea, to attract and hold attention. The gaze is extraverted, seeing what is wanted to be seen. To look within, even for a moment, gives her the creeps. Because there are many ways of attracting and holding favourable attention in different environments there are many modifications of this hysterical personality reaction pattern. In some families, religion, morality, compliance or prudery are necessary to acceptance and security. In others one has to fight for it with power as the key. For others it is sexual seductiveness even as between parents and children. Others are lawless and irresponsible. Thus we come to speak of compulsively compliant hysterical personalities, compulsively dominating hysterical personalities, hysterical liars and hysterical psychopaths.

Paradox constantly encountered
The paradoxical is constantly encountered in the study of hysteria. The disorder is characterized by fierce, clinging attachments and equally violent detachments and dissociations. The hysterical person is exquisitely sensitive, showing enhanced powers of observation where self-interest is concerned. Should the environment present stimuli which link with ideas and persons from whom, perhaps unconsciously, the sufferer wishes to be dissociated, then there is a marked insensitivity, and the field of vision is narrowed so as to exclude whatever would be disturbing. Some hold these dissociative mechanisms to be the fundamental characteristic. Hysteria parades itself as a great lover, seductive, imperious and powerful in the affairs of the heart. This is a function of the strength of its 'need-love'. It has little or no 'gift-love' for others. The hysterical woman may appear to be 'over-sexed', but in the marriage bed is all too likely to be frigid, withdrawn and resisting. To caresses of a superficial, tactile kind she will respond with exquisite sensitivity. But this is often a counterpart of a complete inability to tolerate a deeper caress of the penetrative kind. In the pursuit of attractive objects and flirtations she is faithfulness itself.

The fruition of a courtship in a marriage bond which expects the continuation of her faithfulness may be sorely disappointed.

To the hysterical patient her states of mind are 'desperately' serious. Despair is embodied in her seriousness. She is often able to compel unwilling professional men to take her states of mind as seriously as she takes them herself. Reality is for her so structured by the mood of the moment that she is able to draw others into her private universe with consummate skill. In retrospects it still seems to have been devilishly clever. Yet we must not attribute to the hysterical person herself any conscious fabrication. To her, at that moment, the universe did appear exactly as she expressed it. We shall never understand the problem of hysteria, or of any state of mind foreign to ourselves, unless we are prepared to concede that every individual person's perception of the universe around them is a highly specific view which is, for them, indisputably the true one. Pastoral care must take this fact seriously. Every possibility of obtaining empathy with the parishioner depends upon it.

It is difficult to decide whether the basic impulsion of the hysterical sufferer is the need to be loved or the need to be hated. Is she really aiming to create security in relationships, or to test them all to the point of their inevitable destruction? She is for ever conducting 'sincerity operations' on her friends, but does not the way she does this indicate an even deeper need to prove their insincerity? Every movement of the body, the supplicating hands, the beseeching eyes seem to say, 'I want to live by dependence on your love'. But before long your love is proved conclusively to be lacking in some essential quality. Your love is no good. Then every movement of the body expresses withdrawal; of the eyes, rejection; there is a desire to die. The fervent life-wish seems so often to be matched in depth by an almost equally pressing death-wish, that the primacy of either one or the other is debatable.

Technically speaking, we must ask is the separation-anxiety always matched by a commitment anxiety? Is there always beneath the hysterical position a schizoid position? Is the final truth this, that the hysterical person is in love with life, anxious about separation from persons, walking in dread of non-being in which the spirit would die? This is certainly the presenting truth of the hysterical condition. Or does this represent only a superficial orientation, overlying a deeper position of mental pain in which it is death which is longed for, and being as a human person in dependence on other persons which is feared? If it is the former, then the therapeutic task is to create the conditions of security in which the sufferer can gain complete and constant reassurance. But if it is also the latter, then the therapeutic task is complex and paradoxical. It must address itself, at first alternately, and ultimately simultaneously, to two diametrically opposed wishes, for life and for death. It must be familiar with the absurd: 'as dying and behold we live'. It must set off in an apparently opposite direction to that in which common sense says that it should.

Instead of enabling the patient to avoid pain, it prepared her to bear it. Instead of strengthening the fingers which feel to be slipping off the cliff edge, it strengthens her spirit to endure the drop into the feared abyss, to the point where it can ask permission, so to speak, to tread on her fingers. Since hysteria itself, as a disorder, has to be defined so resolutely in terms of paradox, it is not surprising that in determining a rationale for treatment, we are baffled by the complexity of things it seems we ought to do. This is a particularly thorny pastoral problem. The physician of the soul is placed on the horns of a dilemma. Ought his basic attitude to be kind or stern, approachable or distant? Which is the better pastoral act, to care deeply for the person and show that he cares, or not to show any special care, particularly not give much time to personal counselling? Is this so fraught with pitfalls that there is no safe and proper individual pastoral care by the man of God for such women? Should it only be done in groups with other women present, or when in cassock and surplice before the whole congregation, or only by secret prayer? To descend too heavily on either side is either to cease thinking in therapeutic terms of a cure of souls, or to misunderstand and underestimate the problem of therapy. This misunderstanding is usually motivated by intense emotional reactions within ourselves, either of complicity in the case-work relationship by which we are at present bound or of furious rejection because the memory of a previous 'gruesome twosome' still rankles. It is necessary to 'keep one's head' in the dizzy situation of cliffs and precipices which hysterical experience inhabits. This is not easy in the presence of one who seems dedicated to driving her helpers crazy.

The importance of pastoral recognition

The importance of pastoral recognition of the hysterical condition, despite its complexity, is simply this. There are resources from within the Christian faith, for those who will appropriate them, which radically alter the fundamental problem. The apprehension of the universe which constitutes the basic hysterical position is indeed full of apprehension. It is based on an infantile conviction that no one spontaneously pays any attention to you. Hysterical persons stretch out eager hands to the universe of persons, but they cannot accept the suggestion that this comes to them of its own accord. Their own fully determinative experience at the roots of life still states inflexibly that unless by one's own continual and sustained effort to attract attention and manipulate the source-persons into action, there is no love, no life, no acceptance, security, status, nor any achievement of human personality.

The whole revelation of God in Jesus Christ gives the lie to this fundamental misimpression of the universe in which humanity is set. It is true that the suffering, ignorance, sin, and folly of human parents continually create the conditions of identification with non-being in infants which lead to hysteria. But the gospel is as continually reaffirming the fact of God's free and gracious approach to persons in their need, accepting them neither because of, nor in spite of their deprivations and their depravities, but out of the essential lovingness and graciousness of his own nature. Moreover, the Christian faith affirms that through the Word of God, through the sacraments and through the fellowship, this continued presence of God in the human soul is effectively mediated and communicated. That is why the parson is to concern himself with hysteria and its derivative syndromes. That is why he must be able to see it, however disguised; hear its voice, however unfamiliar the accent; see the terror behind the eyes, however they may brazen it out. This means to say that the pastor is less interested in the variety of hysterical manifestations than he is in the central fact of the hysterical personality and ultimately in the ontological hinterland of all such persons. By convention we speak of the hysterical personality as a woman. This does not mean that hysteria, taking into account all its forms, is not almost as common among men. It is true, however, that the uneasy burden of medical or pastoral care of hysterical personalities is concerned mainly with women.

It is part of the necessary task of the parson, as well as the psychiatrist, to come to the point where he is able to deal just as objectively, warmly and rationally with the hysterical patient as with any other kind. For few patients arouse such violent emotions of love and hate in the analyst as this sort. He can do this so long as he bears in mind that at the roots of this attention-seeking personality there is an infant agenda that was never completed. Scrawled in red across one of the pages of babyhood is a sentence to the effect that, 'I was, after all, in passive dependence, trusting my mother, when all hell was let loose upon me, with panic and stark terror.' Two forces are therefore operating, the one which, thinking of her chronic unmet need says, 'The book must be opened again in spite of the pain', and the other, which, remembering her deep-set mental pain, says, 'The book must never be opened in spite of the need.'

The hysterical patient always denies that this infantile agenda of attention-seeking is governing her behaviour. Thus it is absolutely necessary to feed back to her what it is she is doing, when, for example, she wastes fifty-five minutes of an hour's interview, and then with a rush in the last five minutes presents a host of problems to be solved. There is perhaps no more important dictum in the treatment of hysteria than this: that one must learn early to say 'No', while it can still be said reasonably, or else the time will come later, if not too late, when one will have to say 'No' unreasonably.

There is a paradoxical sense in which the hysterical person attempts to force a man into the mothering role. Some psychiatrists and clergy have powerful identification here, and that is no bad thing; shepherding and mothering have much in common. If, however, such men have a compulsive need to act in a mothering way, we have two active neuroses in collusion. By projection, the professional helper may be dealing with his own basic anxieties in a substitutive fashion, proving his capacity to sustain the frightened child within himself by concerning himself with a similarly frightened child in someone else. The hysterical personality intuitively recognizes that this man is one who needs to be attentive to the motherless child within, and cannot say 'No' to distress. If this helper has not recognized the extent of his own neurosis, he is unaware of the extent to which he is open to manipulation.

Proper pastoral control
How can we do justice pastorally to the fact that the hysterical parishioner is emotionally sick, and yet maintain proper control of the therapeutic situation so that it does not become an uncontrollable and non-therapeutic regression? The first point is that the helper should remain at all times in firm yet kindly control and understanding of the situation. He must not allow himself to be manipulated beyond what he believes to be reasonable caring. Put bluntly, I would say that a man needs to love such a person with the love which Christ gives him, and not on the basis of any human love he may have, either of a libidinal, an erotic, or even companionly basis. The hysterical parishioner will be quick to recognize any of these and will begin to work on them. Even if she learns that he collects postage stamps she will begin to make herself indispensable as a sub-collector of them on his behalf. In the desperate scramble to save herself she will become all things to all

men. It is therefore essential that we ourselves should need nothing
from the hysterical woman. We must come to her replete in the
armour of God, with the sword of the spirit, and the breastplate of
right-relatedness to God. I cannot trust myself to put myself across
to an hysterical woman. She always makes either more or less of it
than I intended her to. What we 'put on' that day must not be our
self-supportive, self-inflationary role of professional helper, much
less that of the nice friendly male, but the role of Christ's
compassion, trusting him to get his quality of loving and caring
across to her. If Christ has dealt with us at his cross, we will be in
no mood to give credence to the blandishments of this poor woman
who tells us that 'nobody has ever understood me before, as you
do'. We will remember that she has probably told this to at least
half a dozen people in the past.

I would also make this point quite strongly. That if an hysterical
person is to be seen at all, it ought to be by interview arranged by
deliberate appointment. We tend to dodge her altogether until she
manages to get a foot inside the study door and compels us to give
her more time than we intended. Our own mounting annoyance
prevents any good pastoral work then being done. To offer her
deliberately arranged time breaks right across the basic hysterical
assumption that 'I am only attended to when I scream for help'. It
means, perhaps, that there is a God who cares and knows all the
time the state she is in.

The pastoral goal is 'Christ-realization'

The skilled therapist has one clear goal if he works within the
framework of the Christian Church. It is that this hysterical and
anxious person may come as soon as possible to live within the
whole full life of the Church of God. No part of it can be neglected.
There must be a response to the word of God, spoken to the
individual, calling her to accept the new birth and gift of the Holy
Spirit in baptism and confirmation. With an ever-growing inward-
ness she will come to feed upon God and the life of Christ through
the bread of the word and the bread of the Sacrament. She needs
also to be embodied in the fellowship of the Church, not only as
one of the many in the congregation, but as a member of a small
group fellowship, prayer circle or caring therapeutic group. It is
here in the provision of discipleship groups in which people with
problems can discover the divine meanings and resources, that our
churches are weakest. If they are ever to be therapeutic, it is here
they must be strongest. In such a group, more than anywhere else,
the hysterical sufferer will ultimately find her capacity to accept

herself and become mature. She must be able to take her part also, along with others, in the outgoing works of the Church in service to other people. This means giving up the dependent role; here her resistance will be great. Yet when she is healed, it is at this point that her service often becomes most fruitful. She knows how great a salvation has been needed to deliver her from the abyss of personal nothingness and bankrupt defences, to the enjoyment of reliable relationships based in Christ's new being. This is an enormous goal of therapy. I do not think we dare contract it one iota without running the risk of failing her entirely. We must not accept, either consciously or unconsciously, the neurotic patient's goal that 'I am always someone who will have to be carried by the Church fellowship.' We can only accept this goal if we despise, not only the patient's own personality and possibilities, but Jesus Christ her Saviour and his capacity to work within her.

The aim of Christian therapy is 'Christ-realization'. It clearly sets Christ in the centre of the field of vision and points to his offer of a new being through relationships with God in him, of sustenance and status within the divine family, and a daily achievement of such good works as God has for us to do, all bound up with an eternal destiny. This allocentric orientation aims radically to replace the basic egocentric neurotic orientation. It has no aims for self-improvement, nor regrets that I had not a better start or a more integrated selfhood. The neurotic's 'if only' is swept away in a strong affirmative 'Thou only'. The Christian view of maturity is one in which there is and continues to be absolute dependence of the self upon its true Self, Christ. Dependence is not a mere developmental necessity such as having to pass through childhood to achieve manhood. Daily dependence upon God was a necessity for Jesus Christ and it characterizes every mature Christian person.

The implicit goal of humanistically orientated therapy is that, at the end of treatment, the patient will have ceased to be dependent upon another human being and will have all his life situations within his own independent control. For the Christian pastor this is at best an intermediate goal. He may be properly grateful when psychotherapists undertake it and succeed in substituting a knowledge of right relationships for distorted infantile ones. At this moment, should the healed person hear the gospel, he will recognize that dependence has to begin all over again. Human life suffers continual diminishments, even through the natural processes, of ageing, decay and ultimate death. It is delusion to pretend it is not so. If there is any destiny of eternal relationships open to us, we are utterly dependent upon God for any knowledge of it, dependent for the gift of the One by whom we could be related to the Divine Life, and dependent on his Holy Spirit of relationships to effect it. Our critics may say what they like about this being a prolongation of infantile dependence translated into a theological sphere. We have in mind a Master who said, 'Without me, ye can do nothing.' One who was closest to him wrote, 'He that hath the Son hath life, he that hath not the Son hath not life.' We are not ashamed to be reminded of our weakness, for with Paul we find that 'his strength is made perfect in weakness'. This being so, it is obviously advantageous to the hysterical person to recognize that there is nothing ultimately to be changed in the psychological fact that she feels utterly dependent upon life outside herself. Within Christian therapy she can begin to enter upon that life of dependence on Christ, knowing that, however long she lives, or mature she becomes, this will always be the nature of her personal dynamics. Christian therapy does not interpose any intermediate goal of humanistic 'self-realization'. It would have to be unlearned as soon as it was learned. It is not about this great ontological fact of utter, absolute, and continuous dependence of the human spirit on its sources that the Christian psychotherapist is in conflict with his hysterical patient. The conflict is only as to the manner in which she wishes to manifest this dependence. She is unlikely to have noticed what is going on. The faithful pastor must assist by offering feedback, however unacceptable it is, until she comes to an insightful admission about her fixated agenda. It is not her dependence which is at fault, but the infantile, clinging, all or nothing, neurotic nature of it. Only when she recognizes this and accepts it can she begin to control its inner and outer manifestations.

Courage to face aloneness

The demands for sympathy and care which the hysterical woman makes are her misunderstanding of her problem. She thinks she needs company; what she actually needs is courage to face aloneness. That can only come when experience of attentive caring has enabled her to possess for herself the reverberating circuits of information within the cortex which enable the normal person to feel, 'I am never alone'. She thinks she needs just a little attention here and a little there. The basic therapeutic task is being evaded so long as she declines to face the depths of her inner solitariness, the infant in utter panic and near dereliction. If these could be repressed again, we might be content, but that is not a very adequate ideal of therapy, for it leaves the personality always on the defensive. Our experience and our confidence is this, that when the infantile separation-anxiety is openly declared, then, in the power of the Holy Spirit's abiding presence, there is an entirely new ability to come to terms with separation-anxiety.

Clinical theology, stemming from both theological resources and psychodynamic understandings, finds it valuable to use each line of approach. We are concerned that the fellowship of the human Church should become so pervasive in the mind and spirit of the sufferer as to be a reliable factor for her, even in moments of physical isolation. Also, that she should increasingly enjoy the fellowship of the Holy Spirit, calling Jesus as Lord constantly to her mind. In addition it is valuable to interpret these anxieties and direct the patient's attention to the necessity of facing them at some time, pressing a way through them, rather than by appealing to present helpers always to go through the motions of avoiding them.

I had a patient whose hysterical need for company forced him to plan carefully never to be alone. He would either be with men friends in the pub, or with a woman with whom he would spend the night. He came to see that until he was prepared to challenge this anxiety by deliberately staying at home in his flat one evening he would for ever be in the position of running away from this infantile experience of dread and panic. One evening he decided to do this. The inner demands to seek refuge in the pub or with his ladyfriend became tremendously insistent, but he resisted them firmly. The panic within him rose, and he said, 'I just threw myself flat at the edge of the bed, and in trembling and terror, said ·'My God, if you are there at all, you've got to help me now." ' He described the panic rising to great heights, palpitations, cold sweat and fear of death and madness. However, he was determined to stay there alone and work it through. 'After about half an hour,' he said, 'there came over me a tremendous sense of warmth and of another presence. I knew I would never be afraid in that way again. For the first time in my life I had gone deliberately right through and into that place of terror and come out the other side.'

I do not say that this is the only way, or the best possible way. I would affirm it is radically sounder than the treatment target which, as psychiatrists, we often have to accept as the only feasible one, that is the establishment and reinforcement of neurotic defences with sedatives and tranquillisers. However, the clinical theologian, though he may consider an encounter with the mental pain in the depths is not possible at any given moment, remains expectant that when the parishioner's sense of being and well-being is strong enough, she will have courage to enter into the threat of non-being in such a way as to vanquish it.

Maturation dispels hysteria

To the extent that any personality is recognizably hysterical it is also recognizably immature. Maturation dispels hysteria. 'Be your age', we say. In hysterical personalities the whole psycho-physical development remains childish, at best juvenile. The body retains the youthfulness which belies its middle age. The mode of experiencing life which is normal in, and common to, infancy and youth, persists beyond its proper time in the stages of human development. What is acceptable and admirable in its right time and place becomes grotesque when it is inordinate. Men and women of adult years cannot devote themselves to the fantasies and pursuits of adolescence without becoming increasingly unacceptable as age advances. Yet a large part of our entertainment and advertising world is devoted to evoking adolescent fantasies and a juvenile dream-world for the 'benefit' of adults. Adult reality is eluded in a mental game of make-believe. The experience of growing older and its necessarily changed objectives is not accepted. Within Hindu culture, for example, a normal pattern of development is expressed by speaking of stages whereby a man leaves his adolescence to become a householder and eventually leaves his house and business behind to prepare himself for eternity. An hysterical culture, highlighted by its overtly hysterical personalities, does not even accept contentedly the loss of adolescent possibilities in the solid actualities of domesticity. Hysteria is the sworn enemy of domesticity.

Mary of Magdala

If Mary Magdalene in her unconverted days had been brought before a modern magistrate to face the charge of her sexual promiscuity, those presenting her social report would almost certainly have labelled her an hysterical personality. If she is to be identified with the sister of Martha, then the account of her needing to sit and gaze into the eyes of Jesus fits the picture also. Our blessed Lord was perhaps the first religious leader to invite popular derision by welcoming such a woman into the travelling apostolic band. He was never afraid of explosive situations. Characteristically, in his death and resurrection he is surrounded by persons who represent every type of extreme human brokenness. The condemned criminal alongside him is the first man to hear the promise of paradise. Blustering Peter, denying him at the trial, is the first to be forgiven after his resurrection. Mary Magdalene is present among the broken company representing a type of extreme human weakness characteristically found in women. She follows him from the cross to the tomb until the stone is rolled across the doorway.

Why did she need him so deeply? Surely because on the human level she had had so little to give life or strength to her spirit. Many of us were fortunate enough to be given the security of our mother's and then our father's continual presence to support our being until it became so much a part of us that we could say I-my-self in such a way that we could carry our mother's spirit and our father's strength about in us. We can always enjoy this tripartite 'I-my-self' nature. Much has been given to us, and there is nothing lacking to our essential humanity that we have not received.

This is not so with hysterical personalities. Faith in one's basic spiritual relationship, in the 'self' which should have been mother, has been shattered. It can be represented only by 'I-my-?' or indeed by 'I-nothing-nothing'. This is what we mean by depersonalization, a sense of the complete unreality of the self when it cannot rely by faith on the other necessary elements of its spiritual totality.

In despair Mary Magdalene had learnt to replace her 'I-nothing-nothing' by a neurotic defence of 'I-my-?' where the question mark represents the man on whom she happens to be positing herself at the moment to gain semblance of a personal relationship. When she met the Lord Jesus her personal equation changed from 'I-nothing-nothing' to 'I-my-Rabboni'. He had looked at her and this look had created life. She had only to respond by looking steadily upon him and there was no part of her being which she could not affirm joyously. When her basic ontological annihilation of spirit into panic and dread threatened, she had only to look again into the eyes of Jesus to be affirmed as a person, and a person of value. If memory of her awful past threatened her moral self-affirmation, her invited presence in his company gave sufficient answer to her inner accusers. If he accepts me, the unacceptable, he closes the mouths of the moral dogs of conscience.

For no one, therefore, was the death of Jesus on the cross a more appalling cataclysm than it was for Mary Magdalene. Others might lose their leader but keep their selfhood, with their disappointments. Peter had lost his leader and his self-respect. His moral self-affirmation was shattered. Deeply depressed, he was still very much Peter. But for Mary Magdalene, with Christ's death she had lost her very personality. There was absolutely nothing left of her. Every hope of life for her died when the Body of Jesus died, and near that dead body she stayed.

'The first day of the week cometh Mary Magdalene early, when it was yet dark, unto the sepulchre.' Twice during his lifetime she had anointed her Saviour's feet. Again she leads the other women in bringing spices to anoint the body, the last act that her love can do. Arriving first in her haste she sees that the stone has been removed. At once she imagines the worst, not as St John later, who believes the best about the empty tomb. She rushes to Peter and John with the bitter news. 'They have taken away the Lord, and we do not know where they have put him.' Her message was not what she had seen, but the inference she had drawn. Sober facts are not hers to relate. Her purpose is to rouse them to action, and this her despairing interpretation does.

Mary returned to the tomb on the heels of the men. They, seeing the empty tomb, had 'therefore' gone away, John in full belief, Peter just not knowing what had happened. Mary cannot leave. A stronger affection riveted to the spot one of a weaker nature.

'But Mary stood without at the sepulchre, weeping; and as she wept she stooped down and peeped into the sepulchre.' What catches her eye is not the linen clothes, but 'two angels in white sitting one by the head and one by the feet where had lain the body of Jesus'. The place of his death was between two thieves; 'he was numbered with the transgressors'. The place of his burial was between two angels; for God hath set him forth in his blood to be a mercy-seat, a place where God's forgiveness meets human sin. Mary the sinner, Mary the one who most needs mercy, is the first to see this, even though in her need of Jesus, not even angels are any comfort to her.

Two fundamental questions

'Woman, why weepest thou? Whom seekest thou?' are the questions the unrecognized Jesus, mistaken for the gardener, addresses to Mary. These are the two fundamental questions for every hysterical person. She is always seeking the attention of someone who will give her a reason to stop crying inwardly. Jesus speaks her name, 'Mary'. Recognizing her own name spoken in her own country tongue she hastens to clasp those feet she once had bathed with tears. But she is not now permitted to cling to him, in the sense of holding on to the bodily form. He declares to Mary that the time has come for him to ascend to the Father, and therefore for the inauguration of the new order. Within this order believers will in very truth be sons of God. What Jesus is by nature, his disciples are by grace.

The first appearance of the risen Christ, after the experience of dereliction, is made with a woman whose personality represents humanity at its most shattered and clinging wretchedness. He knows that she, the most derelict among all the disciples, needs him first. The spiritually strong, like St John, can draw their own conclusions. Jesus, the Word of God, comes first to the defeated, Mary Magdalene and then to Peter. In that order. The agonizing need of hysteria is always more urgent than that of depressive guilt.

Mary is to give up clinging to the humanity of Jesus because she is shortly to become a member of that new humanity in which he dwells in person through the operation of the Holy Spirit. She will then be willing to let the eyes of faith and the touch of faith relate her to him, rather than the sight of the eyes and the sense of touch. The wise Physician does not leave her without fellowship. He gives her an important task in relation to the fellowship. 'Go, tell the brethren.' So 'she cometh, telling', not 'having come, telleth'. How like her, to be talking while still on the move. How like the disciples hearing the announcement of their Master's resurrection and ascension at the mouth of an hysterical woman, to refuse, as Mark tells us, to believe her.

So for forty days Mary Magdalene lived in a strange half-world, richly alive because Christ was alive, yet not fully able to grasp his continuing presence within her until at Pentecost the Holy Spirit was given. Then she came to have within her Christ, indwelling by his Holy Spirit, abiding within her for ever. She can now define herself for all eternity as 'I-my-self' where the self is Christ, and the relational element the Holy Spirit, now given to relate us to God our Father in the Person of his Son. As St Paul writes, 'To me, to live is Christ. I live, yet not I, but Christ liveth in me.'

That these are the stages of our Lord's redemption of the broken personality of Mary Magdalene there can be no serious doubt. I find that those who have had most experience of wrestling with the devils in hysterical persons until Christ is born in them, are those who most readily recognize this identification. If you dislike the identification, I would say from experience that if such persons are to be helped at all by the clinical theologian, they will go through stages very similar to these we have seen in the Lord's dealing with the woman out of whom he cast seven devils.

Recapitulation of the stages of clinical theological therapy

Phase 1   First (still using the feminine for both sexes), the hysteric must be able to posit her insecure selfhood in some Christian person, or better still, a family or group of accepting Christians. Here she can recapitulate with another set of parents and brothers and sisters something of what was lost in the vicissitudes of her own unfortunate babyhood. We must interpret this transference activity as a necessary kind of bridge-making bringing her from distrustful isolation (however concealed) back to the reality of the social family.

This way she replaces her own neurotic bridge, with the force of forbidden impulse and retributive punishment surging back and forth over it, and substitutes a new and as yet untried bridge of actual trust of a real person outside herself. Only when she has tested the bridge to see if it can carry her weight can she begin to respond in mutual trust again. She has to ensure the new relationship can stand the weight both of the ingratiating attractive side of her personality as well as the unattractive fears and rages and paroxysms of envy and hate that are inalienably part of her tortuous self.

The clinical theologian will expect this to be part of the programme of recovery and will not be too perturbed by it. His task in interpreting this behaviour both to patient and the helpers is part of the process of testing the therapeutic bridge. In making this interpretation he enables the other members of the church community, both men and women, who may at first be put off by these antics, to come to accept them maturely as just one of those things that happen when the cure of really sick souls is taken seriously by the Christian community.

Phase 2 'It is expedient for you that I go away.' As Jesus spoke to the Magdalene and his other disciples about his impending death and departure, so the clinical theologian must 'admonish' the hysterical person towards the end of a lengthy counselling relationship within the fellowship of the Church that it is expedient that he go away, 'because if I go not away, the Holy Spirit will not come unto you'. Like Simon Peter, but with even more fervour, the hysteric will cry, 'Far be it from Thee, Lord'. At the mention of this separation all her symptoms are likely to return in apparently more distressing magnitude. This final kick of the symptoms almost always precedes the resolution of the transference in orthodox analysis of such persons. Until we reach this point we do not know how much solid work has been achieved during therapy. Under this threat of loss, the hysteric may feel that all the recent times of fellowship, friendship and growing security are as if they had never been. It is certain we cannot be faithful to the hysterical sufferer's true need at this point unless we are prepared, like our Lord, to hurt this still somewhat infantile Mary Magdalene by insisting on disappearance for a while from the human scene.

Timing is vital. The analyst's experience and intuition are his only guide. The patient herself is not a reliable guide in ordinary psychotherapy. Her natural pull is always to prolong the dependence. How is the clinical theologian to know when the time is reached? Sometimes forced absence, apart from deliberate planning, may compel her to face the next necessary step in the transition to separate selfhood and to discover the courage to stand alone in the power of the Spirit within, which now assures her she is 'never alone'. At other times the praying helper becomes aware, by an inner impulse of Christ's healing Spirit, that a transition to a maturer mode of dependence needs to be urged upon this parishioner. If we are working with colleagues it may be their wisdom, as they see in a proper perspective what is happening, which gives the clue for the loosening of the dependent phase. Whether engineered by life itself, or by deliberate action of the pastor, the break has to come. Now the hysterical person realizes that she is, in a sense, on her own again. We are alongside her only with the prayer of our Lord, 'We have prayed for you, that your faith fail not.' She knows now that Christ has overcome the infinite distance between herself and the sources of being by traversing that distance himself, and that this redemptive act of his has been duplicated in the caring of one of the Church's own shepherds.

Phase 3   The dark night and the dawn. She will now know that she must learn to trust in the reality of the Christian family and its relationships, without the confirmation of sight, touch and sense, except those which come in the ordinary ministrations of the redemptive word, sacrament and fellowship. She may no longer be special, she is to be one among sisters and brothers. All her old anxieties will be aroused, but she is in an infinitely better place to face them. In the dark night of her fears she will find herself in the presence of Christ Himself. If she is forced to cry out again with utter realism, 'My God, my God, why hast Thou forsaken me?' she knows this also, that he who as her Saviour uttered the same cry is now risen and ascended and operative within her. She now has power to wait in the darkness of her infantile solitariness until it is worked through. As she looks confidently for his appearing, in and beyond the darkness and the emptiness, Christ will come to his own. The Holy Spirit exists to make his constant presence real to us, this he will do for Mary Magdalene, now, as then. If she endures the bleak period after the destruction of the blossoms of inordinate hopes, the fruit of true hope will set and grow. There is much undergoing and overcoming.

The pastors of the Church of Jesus Christ have to decide whether the hysterical persons who come to them in despair, having received little help from physicians of the mind or of the body, must go away from them, too, without any lift of their despair. Must we confirm their despair? It all depends on our practical experience of the cross, the resurrection, the ascension, and the filling of the Holy Spirit.

6

The Understanding of Schizoid Personalities

The term 'schizoid personality' finds a place in *The Standard Psychiatric Nomenclature*, adopted in 1950 by The American Psychiatric Association for the classification of mental disorders. It is there characterized by (1) an enduring and maladjustive pattern of behaviour manifesting avoidance of close relations with others; (2) inability to express hostility and aggressive feelings directly; (3) autistic thinking (i.e. thinking unduly directed towards oneself and the inner personal view of the situation, at the expense of the information actually available from the external world); (4) a shut-in, seclusive, withdrawn, introverted personality.

Other terms could have been used, as the condition has a long ancestry. Following the tradition of naming a disease after the one who gave it the first classical description, the name 'Job's disease' could be applied to it. Job speaks of it as 'affliction'. Simone Weil[1] suffered such affliction and describes the condition of spirit minutely in her writings. Søren Kierkegaard[2] calls it 'the sickness unto death'. He associates it with dread and the abnormal, paradoxical, wish to die and to be annhilated, so as to escape the perpetual pain of it.

Colin Wilson[3] gathered together a group of sufferers from the schizoid problem in *The Outsider*. Other terms abound such as the Rebel, the Nomad, the Introvert, the Disinherited Mind, the Ivory-tower Intellectual, the Word-monger. All these in their proper context refer to people whose behaviour patterns illustrate several or many aspects of the schizoid personality defence.

Following the *Standard Psychiatric Nomenclature* we have become accustomed to using the term 'schizoid personality'. The root 'schizo' derives from the Greek verb 'to split'. In this condition there has been a radical split in the ego, in fact in the total person. This took place earlier, and goes deeper than it does in hysterical splitting or depressive splitting. As a result of this overwhelming

1 Simone Weil, *Waiting on God*, Collins, Fontana 1959.
2 Søren Kierkegaard, *The Sickness unto Death*, Princeton University Press 1941.
3 Colin Wilson, *The Outsider*, Gollancz 1959.

infantile trauma, the ego, which was beginning to develop a relationship of trust in persons in its environment, is split from top to bottom. Only a semblance of trust remains. A part of the ego splits off and becomes regressive, seeking the intra-uterine security from which it has been ejected. Another part of the ego, forced into continued contact with the 'terrible mother', is split off and is identified with a longing for death and annihilation. This ego-splitting experience may be due to 'biological pain', such as crushing or distress in the birth passages during a difficult delivery, or to 'ontological pain', such as the post-natal suffering of the too-prolonged absence of the mother who is the necessary personal source of being. Whatever constitutes the ego-splitting experience, it is like the splitting of a tree-trunk. It may be that the split opens out so that the main part of the trunk remains on the 'hysterical' side, still clinging to life mediated through relationships with the outside world. A small part, soon deeply repressed, defends by schizoid withdrawal. On the other hand, the split may leave only a sliver still attempting to keep contact with objects outside the self. The main trunk then veers away into the schizoid defence by detachment, away from people and from extraverted investment. It turns upon itself in introverted investment, centring upon aspects of the self accessible by reflection, especially those based on mental activity. Since the schizoid position involves the most fundamental splitting which can occur in a neurotic illness or personality disorder, the term 'schizoid' is appropriate. We do not observe here the 'molecular splitting' or fragmentation of mind which is characteristic of schizophrenia. The picture is not one of a stone shattered to pieces by a hammer, but rather that of a tree-trunk cleft from top to bottom, or almost to the bottom.

Factors calling for pastoral attention

Many factors contribute to the reason why the schizoid personality disorder is relevant to the clinical theologian and the attention and understanding of pastoral carers. We list some of them below:

1 Clergy are often asked to help in 'end of the road' cases, which have proved stubbornly resistant to all psychiatric treatment. The 'hard core' of this resistance, as Fairbairn, Guntrip and others have pointed out, is the schizoid position.

2 The schizoid position typically leads to anxiety, not about separation or loneliness, but about commitment, especially to marriage, to steady employment, and to social and religious decisions. These matters concern clergy rather than general practitioners.

3   Schizoid breakdowns in adolescence often take on a religious or philosophic flavour, commonly leading these young people to consult, or be referred to, clergymen.

4   One pattern of defence by detachment and introversion, characteristic of schizoid personalities, seeks to emphasize separateness from common and material things to find exclusiveness in hidden and mysterious powers. This may find expression in the occult, the metapsychological or ritual.

5   The schizoid personality disorder has some of its roots in innocent infantile affliction of great severity. As this emerges in the conscious mind the goodness and the existence of God are brought into question. The problem of innocent affliction raises fundamental questions for theodicy, as Job's protest shows. Christian faith claims that the innocent affliction of the Son of God effects a reconciliation between the Creator and the oppressed sufferer. It offers a possible meaning to existence at its worst, and the minister of the gospel must know how to communicate it. Medicine itself offers no meaning and no ultimate remedy.

6   It is probable that the natural man does not readily appreciate that the schizoid defence is a refusal to face his despair, or that the schizoid position of unrelieved despair is a possible prelude to an experience of the eternal. Christianity leads a person to accept despair of himself as the first responsive act of faith in the cross of Christ, and to rise out of despair by responsive faith in his part in the resurrection of Christ. The worst that can happen in the depths of the schizoid position is dereliction by the source-person. That dereliction by God should be the worst that Christ endured is therefore full of significance. If to rise from this death to newness of life in Christ is an open offer, to remain in despair, though explicable in terms of pain-avoidance and fear-paralysis, becomes increasingly wilful and sinful.

7   The therapy of schizoid disorders is thwarted by the paradoxical and ultra-paradoxical dynamics by which the afflicted person exists in a chaotic engine-room of internal contradictions. What promotes one set of dynamic drives, arouses destructive opposition from others. The bondage of the will is absolute. There is need for an entirely new dynamic system with power to effect behavioural change in spite of, and apart from, the pre-existing personality. Death to the self by identification with the death of Christ, and the gift of his life in a man, and a man's life in Christ, offer a way out of these insoluble contradictions.

8   The abreactive experiences of birth and the earliest months of life have made possible a more detailed exploration of the schizoid

position than before, as the experiences are recalled at the moment of repression.

9   Therapy of schizoid personalities has to do with restoration to a role in the community and at least with some growth of group awareness and social commitment. Doctors occasionally run negatively-orientated therapeutic groups which help the patients while they last. Clergy are frequently running positively-orientated groups within the community, which could be more therapeutic than they are. Special study of the schizoid viewpoint could make them more acceptable and creative for those whose commitment anxieties tend to exclude them from group participation.

Evidence from the professional literature
Our stress on the schizoid personality has been questioned because little notice is given to it in the psychiatric textbooks. Is the problem so important and central as we make out? What evidence is there from psychiatric sources for the kind of formulations we present in the presentation of the problem of the schizoid personality? We therefore set out below some of the writings in this area of mental pain.

In *Clinical Psychiatry* by Mayer-Gross and others, two pages in the total of 600 are given to 'The Schizoid Constitution'.[1] This is described as having a main characteristic of shyness, extreme sensitivity, emotional coldness, and withdrawal from the outer world to the inner. By contrast *The American Handbook of Psychiatry*[2] offers a long chapter on 'The Borderline Patient' and Arieti discusses fully the psychodynamic positions and defences of schizoid personalities, giving full weight to the peculiarly strained interpersonal relationships which often surround such patients in infancy.

The relatively slender references in British psychiatric, as opposed to psychoanalytic, literature are in part a reflection of the fact that this type of person does not readily consult general physicians or psychiatrists about the problem. The schizoid position represents a radical sickness of the self, so severe that the pain of maintaining reserve and concealing it usually seems preferable to declaring and exposing the pain to anyone else. Another reason for neglect is that in psychiatry we have no medical remedies at all for it. Longterm psychoanalytic therapy can sometimes be of benefit, but it is too rarely available to be relevant.

John Bowlby[3] describes a 'saint-like' pattern of schizoid reaction

1   W. Mayer-Gross, Slater and Roth, *Clinical Psychiatry*, Cassell 1954.
2   *American Handbook of Psychiatry*, ed. S. Arieti, New York, Basic Books 1939.
3   John Bowlby, *Personality and Mental Illness*, Kegan Paul 1940.

characterized by docility, placidity, utter selfishness, eager and anxious conscientiousness. He is even-tempered so long as he can go about his self-chosen tasks with quiet uninterrupted industry. The defects inherent in this personality pattern become evident if pressure is put upon the patient to commit himself in some way. This he finds most disturbing, irritating and apt to precipitate violent evasive action. Bowlby uses as parameters the concept of surgency as over against desurgency, and the polarities of social sensitivity as over against social insensitivity. The 'saintlike' schizoid personality is desurgent and socially sensitive, whereas the schizoid psychopath is surgent and socially insensitive. He is shamelessly opportunistic, energetically engaged in cold and rather callous crime. The social ruin he causes makes little impression on him. A sadistic quality may make him as feared as the 'saint' is loved. Yet both can be shown definitively to be 'schizoid' persons. The basic element of flight from social involvement does not determine the direction of flight. It may be a flight into 'spirituality' or 'carnality', into virtue or vice. Neither movement is freely motivated by genuine choice. Fear, and consequently compulsive behaviour, may well dominate the schizoid 'saint' equally with the schizoid psychopath. Bowlby's work was done on patients bordering on psychotic illness. It does not consider the larger number of socially acceptable schizoid personalities whose difficulties in committing themselves to others are not obvious but intimate.

Sheldon's[1] work is an important source of observation of schizoid personality dynamics. He is in fact setting out the traits which define his cerebrotonic component in the human constitution. They are identical with the traits we find in schizoid personalities and we list below some of them:

Physiologically there is an over-reaction of the digestive tract to emotional stimulation; a proneness to nervous skin reactions; and surgical shock. The patient is tense in crises, especially those concerning examinations and sexuality. He has a profound and urgent need for privacy, living a mentally intensive rather than extensive life. He cannot show his feelings and is usually given no credit for the feelings he cannot show. He evades commitment to anything. Mentally he is intensive, secretive, subjective. Reality for him is essentially what he dredges up from his own mental cellars. Outer reality appears to be secondary.

Schizoid reactions more commonly occur in the long-bodied and

---

1   W. H. Sheldon, *The Varieties of Temperament: A Psychology of Constitutional Differences*, New York, Harper 1942.

'skinny' persons. However, as we not infrequently encounter thoroughly schizoid personalities housed in broad and stout bodies, it cannot be said that physique or constitution are the sole determinants of the condition. The exceptions to the truth of Sheldon's general correlation of constitution and personality traits compel us to look elsewhere than constitution alone for explanations of the schizoid personality.

Karen Horney[1] in the tradition of dynamic psychotherapy has drawn out skilfully the interrelated patterns of behaviour in those who are 'moving away from people'. She writes of their estrangement from people and from themselves, their onlooker attitude to themselves and to life and their striking need for self-sufficiency. She distinguishes a healthy need for creative solitude from compulsive solitariness. Superficially they get along with others, but if it appears that an intrusion is imminent an immediate anxiety reaction breaks off any rapport. Emotions are numbed. A feeling of inferiority as a social participant is offset by defensive superiority feelings. He has a sense of hidden greatness and uniqueness, especially in some real or imagined quality of the mind. The presupposition of need and dependence involved in asking for professional help is bitterly resented. This makes psychoanalysis obnoxious.

Jung[2] has made many contributions to the delineation of the schizoid personality, his introverted thinking type coinciding more or less identically with the schizoid intellectual reaction pattern. He notes among the characteristics the priority given to intellectual formulations, the influences of ideas and the intense attachment the person has to products of his own mind. Perhaps most significantly he identifies in this personality type a vague dread of the other sex. As this is predominantly a male category, the object of dread is the woman. Jung's later work shows how it is the task of such men to encounter and come to terms with the intolerable emotions provoked by this 'terrible mother'.

Jung infers that this negative relation to objects, particularly personal objects outside the self, derives from the most primitive 'object relationship' which was experienced in infancy. Objects possess terrifying and powerful qualities for this type of personality. His detachment is motivated by dread. Commitment outside the self produces overwhelming terror. The 'terrible mother' is projected on to God and on to all his fellow men and women, falsifying and curtailing relationships.

1   K. Horney, *Our Inner Conflicts*, Routledge & Kegan Paul 1946.
2   C. G. Jung, *Psychological Types*, Routledge & Kegan Paul 1944.

Since this failure of courage to make outgoing relationships is, by definition, the antithesis of Christian living, whatever psychiatrists may say of the unchanging rigidity of schizoid personality structure, Christian pastoral care is bound, by elementary faithfulness to its God-given task, to discover ways of overcoming the fear so as to effect a change to positive outgoing trust and love.

Fairbairn[1] sees the origins of the schizoid position occurring in the early oral phase of development, thus bringing the genesis well within the first six months of life. He considers that the infant, soon after birth, seeks the mother's whole person. When this desire for the whole person is frustrated, interest and anxiety focus on the part-object relationship of mouth-to-breast. 'Thinking' that it 'thinks' with the mouth, the infant defends against the pain of loss of the whole mother by a fantasy of the possession of the whole breast. Either in its good life-giving aspect or in its bad, rejecting aspect, or both, the breast is thought of as having been 'swallowed' or 'incorporated'. In disgust, it may be orally ejected by retching or vomiting (one is 'sick of it'), or anally rejected by bowel movement or diarrhoea. Thus, the mouth and digestive tract become the organs of expression for a fantasy language which actually concerns the whole relationship of the baby to the mother. Our experience with patients abreacting their own baby–mother experiences leads us to shift the emphasis from the mother as a whole. It is her face, eyes and mouth, her whole familiar countenance as a 'gestalt', a whole image, intuitively sought for and ultimately recognized, which is sought. 'Being-itself', the quest of the ego for a source-person, is mediated in a face-to-face encounter. The mouth–breast relationship has to do with 'well-being' and sustenance of 'the self' rather than with its existence. Schizoid stress has to do with despair of and dread of existence itself.

Guntrip[2] maintains that the schizoid withdrawal sets up an internal closed system characterized by hatred of the weak, passive, 'unconditionally bad', self. The infant feels that it must have been mother's intention to drive it as near as possible to the point of death. Identification with what seems to be the mother's intention towards him may make a schizoid patient determined to sail as near the wind as possible to suicide. This self-destructive activity may be motivated by an intense desire to return to the point where union with the mother was lost. Since it was lost at a moment of infinite pain, the attempt to return (as it seems to the regressed mind)

1   W. R. D. Fairbairn, *Psychoanalytical Studies of the Personality* Tavistock Publications 1952.
2   H. Guntrip, *Personality Structure and Human Interaction*, Hogarth Press 1961.

must travel along the same road of pain. In fact there is something reassuring about the activity itself, however self-destructive or frustrating the action. The alternative is a more distressing and disintegrating passivity. Fairbairn and Guntrip both see the basic drive behind psychopathological conditions as the need to become and remain a person in one's own right, or in the narrower sense, the struggle to preserve an ego. Satisfactory 'object-relations' as they are called, are fundamental to healthy psychodynamic origins. The total schizoid break in interpersonal relationships of dependence on and trust in the mother or her surrogates, though so dreadful as to produce a desire to perpetuate the break, cannot be maintained by the infant. That would be death. It must retain a 'false-self system', to keep up appearances. This provides a screen of apparent trust, but actually of secret non-commitment, behind which the major part of the ego can retire to lick its wounds. Here it enjoys the pallid pleasures of a fantasy selfhood, kept alive by self-reflection, self-consciousness and narcissism. It may actually regress to the still well-remembered Elysium of intra-uterine satisfactions. Inside the fantasy womb again, the regressed ego feels safe and sound. The problem for psychotherapy is whether we can induce the regressed ego to step back over the threshold, to recapitulate the early weeks and months of life in total dependence, not now upon the mother, but upon the therapist. When this person peeps out on the world to reconnoitre, it is most aware of the dreadful abyss just over the doorstep, into which the infant ego was plunged by the mother's unwitting neglect. The therapist's task is to offer a relationship which will be strong enough inducement to the dread-inhibited ego to move out again.

The only alternative is to find a way of entering, bearing the therapeutic resources, behind the defensive door and into the strong-room, in order to persuade the regressed ego that there are more advantages in growth and maturation than in permanent retirement from the human scene. There is perhaps another alternative beyond the reach of human therapy, which would be to descend into the abyss of dread along with the patient, helping him to bring to consciousness the infantile mental anguish which accompanied the fatal hurt on the decisive occasion which produced the splitting and withdrawal.

Guntrip[1] relates a short anecdote which points to a factor he himself does not develop, the sudden, catastrophic, paradoxical, all-or-nothing nature of the traumatic experience which produces the

1   H. Guntrip, op. cit., p. 430.

schizoid infant. A patient told him of her sister's little boy being a shy and 'shut-in' child, and how she had a vivid memory of him as a baby being left screaming and she was not allowed to pick him up. Then quite suddenly he stopped dead and was silent. In that moment his spirit of trust, his courage-to-be-as-a-dependent-term-in-a-bonded-link-with-mother, his I-my-self, was annihilated. I do not think it advisable to describe the 'ego' as having been annihilated. The 'I' remains, but it has no corresponding 'self', so that there is nothing to justify the use of the possessive pronoun 'my'. The 'I-my-self' has become an 'I-nothing-nothing'. Evidently neither parent was on hand to lend a human presence to make selfhood possible by the 'umbilical cord' of the senses, especially those of sight, sound, recognition by smell or touch.

The affliction of Job and others

The schizoid position represents the basic ontological universe of the existentialists. They struggle from within their universe to achieve a vantage point no longer obscured by their own narrow and strained perspectives. Since Pascal, Kierkegaard and Simone Weil together with others who bear the schizoid affliction regard Job as their great biblical representative in the Old Testament, as Jesus is their remedy in the New, we start with him. Job's affliction did not begin with the cataclysmic losses of his cattle, camels and children. He had an incipient sense of this hinterland of mental pain all his life. 'The thing which I greatly feared has come upon me . . . I was not in safety, neither had I rest, . . . yet trouble came.'[1] He did not curse the catastrophe but the night of his conception and the day of his birth. 'Cursed be the day of my birth . . . Why was the womb not the place of my death?' Having been born, he curses his nurture. 'Oh that no lap had been there for me to lay me on, no breasts to suck.' An underlying desire to die is the most characteristic distinguishing feature between schizoid and non-schizoid persons. Severely schizoid patients speak exactly as Job did. His speech authenticates him as one of their number. 'I choose death rather than life. I cannot bear living on. Let me alone. This life of mine is but a shadow . . .' Yet Job has no hope in death, he has only a wish that perhaps death might be a shelter from affliction, 'where thou wouldst hide me away until thy anger was spent'. The concept of dread and terror which emerges from the schizoid position, and the strange horrific images which it evokes, are part of Job's experience. The God who controls Job's private universe is felt as a tyrant.

1 Job 3.

As the book of Job's conversations proceeds it is less the mental terror that daunts him than a sense of the awfulness, in both senses, of God himself. 'It is God that melts my heart with fear, his omnipotence that has troubled me.'[1] Not the surrounding darkness, but the character of God himself who can permit a man to undergo such abysmal darkness and not deliver him, is now the primary fear.

The most startling fact about Job, and the aspect of his character most offensive to moralists and to his religious critics then, is his affirmation of innocence, and the accusation he lays against God of injustice. What does God's providence amount to? In innocent affliction Job protests, 'I will not be quiet. I will speak in the anguish of my spirit. . . . If I have sinned, does it do anything to you? Why must you make a target of me so that my life has become a burden to me?'[2] This indelible sense of the persecutory nature of God's world is as strong in Job as it is in the paranoid-schizoid positions. Where 'being-itself' is mortally threatened, 'well-being' is also lost. So we must expect that if the schizoid position is entered (in which 'being-itself' falls into the abyss) the paranoid position (in which all rights to 'well-being' are unjustly witheld) has also been entered. As a result of this, there is a liability to project persecutoriness on to the environment throughout later life. When the conditions of life actually becomes persecutory, as in Job's case, the whole soul is filled with an unrelieved sense of God's tyranny (Job 30).

We must point also to the scorn to which Job is subjected by his friends and neighbours. There is not really affliction where there is not social degradation or the fear of it in some form or another. If Job cries out his innocence in such despairing accents, it is because he himself is beginning not to believe in it; it is because his soul within him is taking sides with his friends.

In the same way, the infant who, in entire innocence, suffers this ultimate affliction at the hands of a mother by whom it is allowed to fall into the dereliction of the schizoid position, takes up towards itself the attitude which 'must have been' the attitude of the mother. It subjects itself perpetually to the mother's apparent verdict, 'this thing is worthless, forget it, get away from it'. It must regard itself as wretched, worthy only of rejection, unacceptable to living persons. Scorn is inseparable from the schizoid position.

1   Job 23.
2   Job 7. Knox translation, Burns & Oates 1954.

The Psalmist and the innocent afflicted

None of the psalmists share Job's intense longing for death. However, the problem posed by the schizoid position to theodicy is continually in view. Can God's justice be vindicated? Does he justify his ways to the psalmists? Usually he does, and those Psalms resound with a confidence that has been a strength to generations of Jews and Christians. Other Psalms, notably 22, 42, 55, 69, 74, 77, 88 and 102, express the feeling that God has lost interest, is unwilling to help, or actively hostile. In Psalm 88 are expressed emotions which would be appropriate if anyone else than God were responsible for the following acts. The Psalmist has a soul full of troubles. He is like a man about to die. God's wrath lies heavy upon him. His friends have been removed, they now regard him as an abomination. He is shut in to suffering and cannot get out. This psalmist writes in the way men do who are experiencing a schizoid breakdown. To give glory to God the Father, the maker of a universe in which the innocent afflicted suffer lifelong mental pain, is hardly possible if this is all that is known about him. It is his self-revelation in the Son which alone makes a theodicy possible. These are the Psalms, especially Psalm 22, which prepared Christ for his redemptive task, giving him a prophetic view of his dark ordeal.

It is because the Psalms give expression to these deep, disturbing and paradoxical experiences of man in his relationship to God, known not only in his intimate presence but also at an ultimate distance, that they have retained such power over Jews and Christians alike. We know that the world of the repressed schizoid dread, belonging essentially to pre-verbal experiences of the first year, is a pre-Christian world. It is a world without knowledge of redemption history, in which the infant is utterly dependent on God's providences as parents choose to mediate them to the helpless baby. This common denominator of experience gives to the Psalms a universal relevance.

The New Testament and subsequent writings

Christ, who needed in his disciples men who were reliable witnesses of fact, did not choose introverted intellectuals but men whose living depended on the ability to observe facts, and bear a committed testimony to them. The only exception seems to be St Thomas whose schizoid traits stand out. He expresses a death wish while the others are recoiling from it. He expresses doubts about the way. Absent from the disciples' fellowship at a crucial time, he runs into epistemological difficulties (John 20:24; 11:16). It was round the name of Thomas that there gathered the gnostic heretics of the early Church, whose characteristic was to twist the facts of history and tradition to match their own subjective and intellectually evolved theories about God and man. Many of St Paul's injunctions against inflated intellectualism (see 1 Corinthians and Colossians) are directed against these common varieties of defence against the schizoid position. The need to defend against the dread of having to depend again for life on a personal and material world outside the self led to gnostic attempts to overturn the Christian doctrine of creation. For gnostics creation itself was the fall. The fact of a material fabric was a disgrace, a fault in creation. A wise man withdrew, especially from any commitment to the fleshly and material aspects of the world.

The gnostic assumes he knows better than the record of the witnesses (even the biblical ones) because he feels his own independent mental aristocracy is an endowment which takes precedence over mere evidence in the objective world. Gnostics show disdain, and not a little bitterness, towards ordinary Christian folk, who love their life in this world as God gave it to them. This reveals something of the secret scorn of themselves into which they were driven. It conceals and denies their deep envy of warm human ties, against the acceptance of which their life is in recoil.

On our rapid survey towards the modern age we note the complexities of the monastic movement and associated mystical theology. Mystical experience comes unbidden to Christians when they are drawn to Christ in deep devotion and contemplation in his presence. Ecstasy is also sought by schizoid persons as a reaction to the humiliating boredom of the schizoid position against which they are defending. Whether this be an experience of Christian mysticism or nature mysticism, the psychological effect is similar. It produces a sense of unitive fellowship with God, or of identity with a cosmic divinity. The hatred and contempt of the body, with related aspects of the self, which became standard parts of monastic practice went far beyond dominical precedent. Nowhere more carefully than in the writings of St Bernard[1] are the discriminations made between the action of God and a psychological artefact. The eager practice of flagellation and masochistic treatment of the body is so far from having any apostolic precedent that its schizoid origins are probable. We know that unconsciously there is a powerful urge to achieve a sense of unity within the divided schizoid personality by masochistic measures which, paradoxically, carry with them

1   E. Gilson, *The Mystical Theology of St Bernard*, Sheed & Ward 1940.

sexual satisfactions. Christian asceticism has now turned decisively away from the illicit pleasures of masochism.

Blaise Pascal recognized the philosophers as men engaged in intellectualist defences against an inner state of mind which they could not accept as true about themselves. They have chosen only one of the three lusts. Turning away from the lust for sensory pleasure and for power, both involving a man in investment outside himself, they have chosen the lust for knowledge, the *libido sciendi*. Who dares not have faith in what lies outside himself, substitutes faith in his own reason. He disapproves of Descartes's dictum of what constitutes a man's identity; *cogito ergo sum*. 'I think, therefore I am' is all too accurately a definition of the essentialist philosopher's way of life. To equate man's essential being with his thought about himself could only lead to despair. For Pascal, 'Man: dependence, desire for independence, need', was the definition over against the 'closed-self system' of the Cartesian world. Pascal lived within the decisive biblical categories of thought about man. Sewn into his waistcoat, and found after his death was a piece of paper on which he had written of his own encounter with God. 'I believe in God, not the God of the philosophers. I believe in the God of Abraham and Isaac and Jacob.' His own being rested in the God who called him. 'I am called and I respond, therefore I am' is the kind of dictum which expresses the constitutive facts of his nature. This enabled him to see that even for ordinary people 'I was and am loved, therefore I am' is a more desirable ontological formulation than one based on a gazing into a psychological mirror to catch one's own reflection. There are pointers in his infancy and later development to indicate that Pascal was a sufferer from this afflicted temperament. For such a person, a search for a way back to a tolerable humanity leads nowhere, until like Abraham he is called of God into a new being and an eternal destiny. This becomes actualized in human terms as he responds obediently to the God who makes his way plain to the eye of faith. It is characteristic of Pascal and of many others moving from affliction into the Christian faith, that this reconstitution of 'being' is linked with a strong sense of the call of God and a seeking of the closest possible relationship with him. It seems his presence as the vision of his 'countenance' as the only final remedy for affliction.

Søren Kierkegaard[1] who died, aged forty-two, in 1855, remains the most perceptive diagnostician of the tortuous paradoxes of the

1 Søren Kierkegaard, *The Concept of Dread*, Princeton University Press 1944; *Fear and Trembling and the Sickness unto Death*, Princeton University Press 1941; *Christian Discourses*, OUP Galaxy Book 1961.

schizoid person. He needed to go no further than himself to uncover his source material. His prodigous output of devotional discourses, ontological studies and novel-like aesthetic works rank him as more than just an author. He was a 'sign', because his writings and his life together were expressions of God's personal education of him in Christianity. That he fell short at the growing edge of his personality in commitment to other Christians is of less significance than his exploration of depths never before written about. He could not have written with such insight into the schizoid position, unless, at the same time, he had been sustained by a life of entire devotion to God and fellowship with Christ in the power of the Holy Spirit. As he recognized, it was probably essential that he should share the lot of the outsider in his own day, and become after his death, a rich quarry of ideas for serious authors for the next century.

It is not only that Kierkegaardian phrases are recognized in existentialist writings, whether acknowledged or not. Concepts which become explicit in Freud are implicit in Kierkegaard. The difficult terminology and tortuous expression is not just the fault of Kierkegaard's complex intelligence. It is in the nature of the material under consideration, which is pre-verbal, non-verbal and paradoxical. He had to invent a language and define his concepts. Whatever one tries to express in this field of schizoid studies, a perusal of Kierkegaard will show that he said it all 120 years ago, and said it better.

Kierkegaard, like Job, recognized that the fundamental position of man in dread is a strangely paradoxical one; a desire not to live, but to die. He speaks of the universality of this sickness of despair. It was his practice to spend the whole of the day in the company of his fellow men and women, shrewdly observing and entering into all they did, as if he were a frivolous fellow. In the evening he would write of what he has seen and knows. Long before Freud, he recognized the deceptiveness of 'reaction pattern formation', of excessive keenness which may cover secret apathy, forced tranquillity which hides strong internal agitation. Precisely those who suffer most from affliction most wish to hide it. Kierkegaard fulfilled the risky task of investigating, with the utmost intellectual rigour, the paradoxes and insoluble dilemmas of the schizoid position and its defences. His incurable melancholy, with its commitment anxiety in relation to men as well as to the woman he loved, prevented him from 'realising the universal' in human relationships. It also (more seriously) cut him off from the fellowship of the state Church. Perhaps it was necessary that it should be so. Perhaps, if the Lord himself were present in Denmark today, he would not be found sitting dutifully in Lutheran pews. Christ himself died bereft of the last rites of a Jew and, state Churches being what they are, it may or may not be the fault of Kierkegaard that he died without the last rites of his own Church. This double work he did. He maintained the full rigour of investigation into the position of a man, 'the individual', who is afflicted. At the same time he kept faith with the gospel of God in a meek following of the Lord who had called him. In his works I have found more biblical insights which have been of vital use in assisting schizoid persons into a lively faith than in any other writer. The reconciling personal and symbolic images of the Gospels do not seem to him to be 'dated'. Kierkegaard walks humbly both with his God and with his word in its totality, not in any slavishness to the letter that kills, but in a wide-ranging deep-going freedom of the Spirit.

In Great Britain the responsibility for the development of existentialist thinking in psychiatry has fallen upon R. D. Laing. The quality and perceptiveness of his work merits a school of younger psychiatrists devoted to the development of psychiatric theory and practice along these lines. It is at this ontological level of statement that psychiatry communicates with theology, or at least would do so if theologians were prepared to listen and search for answers. Freud spoke in a strange language which could not be understood theologically. Jung spoke in a mythological language to theologians who had never learned how to use it. To the alert theologian, the existentialists are speaking, not in another language, but in a closely related dialect of the same language. But many of us would rather learn a foreign language than communicate in a dialect. This is not entirely unrelated to snobbishness. Be that as it may, Laing's[1] book on the schizoid position, *The Divided Self* and the companion work, *The Self and Others*, mainly on the hysterical position, arouse keen discussion in clinical theological circles. In heading a chapter with lines from the poet W. B. Yeats he breaks tradition with medical textbooks and indicates our indebtedness to poets, dramatists and novelists for all the deepest and perceptive knowledge we have of the schizoid position and its defensive personality reactions.

The theologian wishing to make a serious study of the schizoid position is not dependent on these or any other psychiatric authors. Some biographies reveal this factor. Stefan Zweig's *Erasmus* could serve as a type-study of the schizoid sufferer. The unwanted illegit-

1   R. D. Laing, *The Divided Self*, Tavistock 1960; *The Self and Others*, Tavistock 1961; *Studies in Existentialism and Phenomenology*, Tavistock 1964; *Sanity, Madness and the Family* (with A. Esteron), Tavistock 1964.

imate child of a priest becomes the prototype of all university dons. Every symptom and pattern of defence by the intellect is raised to a high art by this thin-lipped, frail embodiment of the New Learning. The man of letters became for the first time, a power to be reckoned with in Europe. Geoffrey Faber's study of John Henry Newman in *The Oxford Apostles*,[1] is another source book for the sympathetic study of this affliction. Erikson's study of Luther[2] is a perceptive account of the importance of schizoid mechanisms in adolescence, but Luther, to me, remains a basically depressive personality with minimal schizoid components.

An interpretative conceptualization

We have seen that the schizoid position is defined psychodynamically as a catastrophic splitting of the person in the earliest weeks or months of life. It is a split that goes down to the roots of being. A complete volte-face reorientates the ego to everything that exists for it. This loss of person-centredness spreads to involve other external objects, personal and impersonal. The initial positive attraction to good objects and to enjoyment of personal closeness is replaced by negative feelings and withdrawal. This is not by a gradual swing, but is a sudden discontinuity, a dramatic, all-or-nothing, right-about-turn. Longing for life becomes longing for death. Desire for pleasure as pleasure is transformed into a desire for pain as pleasure. Compulsive attention-seeking and attachment to persons switches over into non-attention-seeking and detachment. This sudden loss of primitive longings with great intensity, leaves behind not a neutrality, but a persisting powerful revulsion.

We are affirming that the maximum intensity of hysterical clinging and attachment to persons is *contiguous* with the maximum intensity of schizoid aversion and detachment. Expressed diagrammatically, the curve would be a cusp. There is a continuity of painful stress applied to the organism (such as in infancy when the prolonged absence of the mother is endured), but the response shows a radical discontinuity in the mode of response when the margin of tolerance is reached. (See Figure 8.)

When I first encountered these manifestations of abrupt discontinuity of attitude in patients undergoing abreactive therapy under the drug LSD I was at a loss to understand them. A woman who had been reliving successive attacks of illness, incurred in the first year of life, at first treated me as her protective and attentive mother.

1 Geoffrey Faber, *The Oxford Apostles*, London 1933; Penguin Books 1954.
2 E. H. Erikson, *Young Man Luther*, Faber & Faber 1959.

Towards the end of one session a woman friend of hers joined us. With dramatic suddenness I became her persecutory mother whose careless irresponsibility and hostility seemed to her to have caused her recurrent intolerable distress. She shrank from me in terror, though a few moments previously she had been clinging to me in terror. In both cases she was quite certain that I 'was', or represented her mother. Both attitudes had been part of the history of her infancy. The transition, then as now, had been sudden and dramatic – occasioned by the arrival of another person upon whom the last remnants of trust, hope and relatedness could be projected. She had always been puzzled by the barrier against intimacy with her mother and an inner withdrawal from her, in spite of a genuine respect and friendliness. She recognized, with no interpretation from me, that her adult ambivalence towards her mother had taken its origin in these first-year experiences. For years she had struggled to hide her negative feelings under a cloak of idealization. Now the psychogenesis was apparent. She had relived towards me as a mother figure, in rapid succession, the mother as sustainer and as persecutor. These reactions concern 'well-being' rather than 'being-itself', portraying paranoid, rather than schizoid traits. However, both involve stress beyond the power of the infant to bear it, leading to the sudden adoption of contrary attitudes towards the mother. We cannot know by direct observation or report what this violent disjunction means to an infant. But the re-emergence of this ultra-maximal experience of mental pain in adults abreacting it in the course of therapy is to them a valid recall of early infantile experiences, and it is very terrible.

Transmarginal responses under stress

We must insist that a clinical theology takes seriously the fact that we are 'made flesh', as one of the mammalian orders. We are subject to many of the same reactions under stress as occur in others in the same class. Pavlov[1] and others have worked with dogs under conditions which would be unethical to produce deliberately in human beings. Some people have strong objections to such experiments. The manipulation of the environment, and of the dogs themselves, deliberately drove them into states of confusion and mental pain so severe as to be beyond the margin of the bearable. The minds of the helpless mammals split and took refuge in states of protective inhibition, negativism, withdrawal and stupor. Such

---

1   I. Pavlov, *Lectures on Conditioned Reflexes*, tr. W. H. Gantt, Martin Lawrence Ltd., 1929.

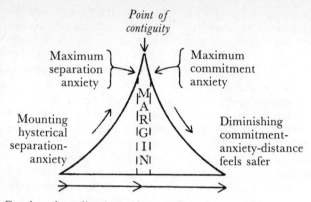

FIG. 8   Anxiety as manifesting discontinuity

things happen in nature's jungles and deserts without human interference, but in the divine providence. They happened to God's own
Son when he put himself into the hands of the human race. In fact,
God afflicted his own Son by darkness and dereliction when there
was no more that men could do to him. God was in Christ reconciling the whole afflicted world to himself. It is possible to shrink
from this world of affliction in an endeavour to protect one's own
nervous system. Can one bear to study what goes on in a world
where an innocent man suffered aggravated agonies 'according to
the will of God'? If this is possible, there is no need to turn away
from the results of experiments where Pavlov attempted experimen-
tally to discover how neurotic illnesses arose, and with equal care,
to find out how they could be cured. It is open to us to make
creative use of their suffering, or to recoil into protective inhibition.
We are more likely to 'block' at this point if we are ourselves
defending against repressed infantile mental pain of this order of
affliction. If our defences against it are breaking down, or if we
have less need to defend than we did in earlier years, this study has
a fascination which derives from its power to interpret to us so
many of our 'unfreedoms', our compulsive unadjustive reactions.

Whether we think Pavlov cruel, or excuse him by justifying the
means because of the end in view, the fact remains that we do all
these things to our own infants. The evidence of psychoanalytical
work which takes seriously the early months of life, shows that

human parents, by neglect, or other attitudes, have brought about situations of severe stress to match most of Pavlov's experimental conditions. This can happen where parents are self-absorbed, or where they have offered 'double-bind' mechanisms, such as offering the child trustable situations by day and untrustable ones by night, or where rigorous regimes of infant training create stress for the child.

Let us look at Pavlov's work in elucidating the effect of stressful stimuli on mammalian behaviour. He found with his dogs that when a particular limit of tolerance of stress had been reached, certain transmarginal responses occurred. His own word for transmarginal was 'beyond the frontier'. Within the frontier, stressed at times, the dog remained a dog with freedom to respond naturally. It was able to adjust to life in an uncomplicated 'doggy' way, tail-wagging to pleasurable stimuli and avoiding hurtful stimuli. 'Beyond the frontier' this 'freedom' has been lost. Trust has been shattered. Terrible lessons have been learned and deeply imprinted by pain upon the emerging nervous system. This dog has then lost its natural 'dogginess'. It is now no longer recognizable as a normally reacting dog. Its reactions may be so savage that it cannot be domesticated, or so craven that it dare not even approach human beings to be fed. These 'beyond the frontier' sufferings, or events strictly analagous to them, happen to infants. Adults can, except under regimes of tyranny, usually avoid them. Christ could have avoided them, but did not. This was the crux of his identification with man in his privations, and with man in his depravity for man's redemption.

Four phases of response under stress

Pavlov identified four phases of transmarginal response to increasing stress in the dogs subjected to his experiments. We list them here because they have relevance to our subsequent discussion of the effect of birth trauma on human infants.

1   *The equalization phase.* This occurs when as a result of protective inhibition induced by stress, the correlation between the strength of a stimulus and the strength of a response is lost. In this phase strong stimuli produce the same response as weak ones. We know that debilitated persons neither react to joyful stimuli with high spirits nor to catastrophes with sorrow. Their feelings remain 'much the same'. Whatever the stimulus, the responses are 'equalized'.

2   *The paradoxical phase.* This is the next most severe distortion of behaviour as a result of transmarginal stress. Here weak stimuli

produce the expected response, whereas strong stimuli produce a weak response as well. It is as if strong stimuli are felt too painfully strong, so they are defended against by the onset of protective inhibition. A very disturbed person will shrink away from a loud-voiced command into non-cooperation, yet the same person will often respond to quiet persuasion.

3   *The ultra-paradoxical phase.* At this level of stress it is as if all the switches connecting stimuli with responses were thrown into reverse. Stimuli of pleasure produce a pained response not a pleasurable one. Stimuli formerly avoided as painful are now evocative of pleasure. Pavlov, who up to the margin had been trusted as the provider of food by his dogs, now became an object of revulsion; the dogs turned away. His assistants, previously neglected by the dogs, became their objects of attention. Before the margin a dog took pleasure in being stroked and patted; after the margin it would shrink away from the same person, withdrawn and negativistic.

4   *The stuporose or hypnoidal phase.* At this stage the animal is apathetic, passing into a stuporose, sleeplike state. The stimuli are overwhelming and the responses seem to shut down. We had a patient who showed all these levels of stress and was particularly liable to this fourth phase. When in a café surrounded by talking people and a wife eager to communicate, this overstimulation produced in him a stuporose state of rapid onset. He would drop into a stupor from which his wife had to shake him.

From Pavlov's work we find it is not just a description of the reactions of the nervous system of a dog. It is a clear description of the neurophysiological background of many of our patients, particularly those with a cerebrotonic constitution or a schizoid personality pattern. Theologians may object that this represents an unattractive picture of a human being, as one who is a passive victim of powers so overwhelming as to produce automatic, mechanistic responses. For those who take seriously the bondage of human will, it matters little what language is used to describe the nature of the enslaving mechanisms. What is important is that they should be scientifically well validated. Theology will not simplify its task by refusing to look at the inhuman rigidity of the bondage of those who are fast bound in misery and iron. Our therapeutic resources must be matched against the inflexible realities of mental pain in the schizoid position.

Two years before his death, Pavlov wrote that clinicians, neurologists and psychiatrists in their respective domains will have to reckon with these fundamental patho-physiological facts arising from his work on these transmarginal states. With this I find myself in full agreement. We observe what Pavlov calls the 'complete isolation of functionally pathological points of the cortex' in the phenomena of 'splitting-off' or 'dissociation'. The hysterical and schizoid positions are both examples of this. Nor can the schizoid position be understood without the interpretive concepts of the paradoxical and ultra-paradoxical phases. Not a psychiatrist himself, Pavlov had to rely for evidence on psychiatric reports. Had he lived he would have gained even more evidence for his assertions from patients, such as I have known, under LSD abreaction.

The trauma of birth

The abreaction of traumatic experiences in the birth passages and in the first few months of life, provides evidence of mental pain which has been beyond the limits of tolerance. Ultra-maximal stressing has taken place, and the four patterns of protective inhibition are still observable. In the 1950s, when using the abreactive agent LSD-25, my cautious scientific mind tended to reject any notion that the unconscious mind could contain valid memories of the traumatic experiences of birth. I am now convinced by overwhelming evidence from my own and my colleagues' practice, as well as that of psychiatrists in many parts of the world, that birth trauma is not only memorable, but that these painful events often constitute the direct or indirect causes of neurotic affliction.

About half of all the patients who undergo abreactive therapy under LSD go through an experience of being born. Some are acutely aware of the experience of the crushing of the head so severe as to reach the margin of tolerance and to exceed it. Like Job, they have wished the gates of the womb to close against them and that they might return, back deep into the womb. Some speak of this moment of indecision, as if it depended on the baby whether to go on, through the pain to the point of birth, or to dissociate from the ónward movement into a death-wish. Others experience a regressive wish to return to the safe place. One patient had been attempting for more than a year to complete his academic final thesis. Always he found himself using delaying tactics which prevented him 'getting on with it'. Under LSD he abreacted a long and complicated travel through the birth passages including a moment when he was certain he was dying. This brought dramatic relief of all his symptoms. It also identified for him the origin of his inhibition and entirely eliminated his phobia and resistance. He completed his thesis within weeks, working rapidly and without hindrance. He 'went through with it' and presented a much-admired thesis. For a number of

patients they had no doubt that they had already passed the limit of tolerance of pain during this descent in the second stage of labour. They had already lost all trust in the world into which they were being thrust out. They would have been annihilated on the way. This can account for the fact that some children are autistic from birth.

The spirit is driven to the end of its tether when the power of being-in-relatedness is depleted to the point of extinction by the too-prolonged absence of the source-person. Anxiety and despair set in at the prospect of not being able to exist without the source which gives being. Tillich[1] writes of courage in these circumstances which can be lost or gained. If present in full measure it is identical with that sense of joy and centredness in loving care which St Paul speaks of as 'the fruit of the Spirit' (Gal. 5:22). Spirit is built up in the baby by face-to-face encounters with a mother who transmits unmistakably her joy in her child, and evoking a response. She creates in the baby, who innately desires this synthesis courage to be. This is an upbuilding of the powers of the spirit. The 'courage-to-be-as-a-part' grows in the presence of the mother as long as there is a transmission of her power of being to the infant. It is this power of being which is tested by the absence of the mother beyond the expected time of her return, or by any major deprivation or injury.

It requires great courage to wait for anyone whose 'not coming' is able to kill your spirit and cut you off from your species. The young organism is always intolerant of loneliness (as Pavlov's experiments demonstrated). Tillich defines this as 'the courage-to-be-as-one's-self-alone'. It is a qualification of spirit. The high-spirited and confident young animal has this self-affirmation. The specimen which has often been let down in the past tends to be low-spirited. If it remained in the hysterical position its tolerance of time spent waiting is poor. If it had been thrust over the margin into the schizoid position, time has lost all meaning, because it is no longer waiting for anyone. Time becomes an irksome thing to which one must not become committed.

The capacity to wait is partly a function of the nervous system well-equipped with inhibitory mechanisms, and partly a qualification of spirit. It has been built up by all previous experiences which encouraged the infant to reckon the mother's care as being reliable in adequacy and timeliness. It has been enhanced by earlier experiences of waiting which have terminated in the mother's coming before anxiety became too painful. Hopeful waiting has

1 Paul Tillich, *The Courage to Be*, Nisbet 1953.

been justified and courage has grown. We find that the same factors that Pavlov found in his dogs are relevant in infants. Any traumatic experience such as previous physical illness, high fevers, previous emotional frights or insoluble conflicts, make babies and children less able to tolerate subsequent traumatic absences without reaching the margin at which paradoxical reversals of behaviour take place.

A clinical theology must be selective in its use of physiological and medical concepts. The basis should be experimental and empirical. I know of no other conceptual framework which can give structural and dynamic coherence to the 'dreadful' and 'outrageous' facts which emerge from the memories of infancy in schizoid personalities than the Pavlovian notion of transmarginal stressing.

Schizoid affliction and Christian resources

Because we are concerned with clinical theology we shall move freely between the ontological affliction and those aspects of the living word of God in Christ which offer, and have been found by some to be, a remedy.

Simone Weil,[1] herself a sufferer from the pain of schizoid affliction, has laid it bare, with all its effects, in her classic account of the condition in her book *Waiting on God*. She was continually able to make something of it, live on, and love on, in spite of it. For her, affliction makes God appear absent for a time, more absent that light in the utter darkness of a cell. It can mean physical pain and social degradation, like a nail whose point is applied at the very centre of the soul. All the qualifications of spirit which came from an intact dynamic cycle of relationships are attenuated to nothing. The right to call on someone who can reliably be called one's own is taken away. Nobody is 'mine'. 'Being-itself', the entitlement to the sight and sound of a source person, is attacked and destroyed. This brings ultra-marginal pain. A kind of paralysis of the person supervenes. The body goes on moving, but no longer from a personal centre. One has become a soul-less machine. The mother comes at last and finds one's limbs acting from an impersonal centre, driving her away, cringing from her, stiffening against her embraces. One is 'being thought', not 'thinking', being acted upon, not acting. To be turned into an impersonal robot when you have been a human being is horrible. The abnormal responses of the transmarginal stressing mean just this. They cannot mean less.

Christian shepherding involves the shepherd in isolation. A man of the community, he is cut off to serve the community. He is never

1   Simone Weil, *Waiting on God*, Collins, Fontana 1959.

more cut off than when he goes out after strays. Christian pastoral care is impossible unless those who are by nature gregarious 'insiders' can be given the actual Spirit of Christ Jesus. Only so can they become identified, contrary to their own nature, with wayward 'outsiders' to help them bear the burden of their intolerable contradictoriness. Christ so identified with the object of his rescue that he becomes 'the Lamb'. He is cut off from the flock and made to carry 'the curse'.

The isolation of the shepherd is a human demand. Identification with an accursed animal is an abnormal demand. To reach those who feel cut off from the living, Christ himself was 'cut off out of the land of the living'. He was annihilated socially by scorn, derision and inhuman treatment. Nor was this accidental. He was 'delivered by the determinate counsel and foreknowledge of God' to become this outcast of Israel. He was born to be this kind of Saviour, to be thrust as a scapegoat outside the camp, to be lifted up to make his shame more visible. His charter of activity as God's revelation of himself to man had been to identify himself with those whose personalities had cut them off from relationships into a social death. He was surrounded by them in his death and in his resurrection. He made his way to them and stood by them at the exact point of their alienation. He created a new society for the acceptance of the unacceptable. His own Holy Spirit is given, to guarantee its continuance, within the visible Church, and often in spite of her. No work is, and should be, so characteristic of Christians as their acceptance of the utterly cut-off, self-scorning person.

Clergymen have good reason to wish to have around them those who are strong, dependable moral persons. In so far as the clergyman or his people only appear to be, or are trying hard to be, such solidly acceptable types, they cannot bear the proximity of schizoid sufferers.

To become capable of pastoral care of afflicted persons demands at least that we should know ourselves to be likely candidates for the same affliction, however deeply we have hidden it. The more compelling our aversion to those in such condition, the more likely it is that we are projecting a hidden part of ourselves onto the sufferer. We then recoil from the external picture, as we have always done from the internal one, of seeing ourselves in that same dreadful ontological pit. The neurotic Christian who defends against his dread by a reaction pattern which leans over backwards against despair into a forced keenness, and against unacknowledged doubt into forced faith, is relying on the cutting-off of his 'bad side'. Without an admission or a healing of his dark side he is ultimately bound to be just as merciless towards the overtly afflicted who come his way.

Acceptance in one's despair

The physician of souls must not be taken in by the commonest of all religious defences, the active attempt not to despair. Statements such as 'trying to trust God', 'trying to have faith', are more likely to be evidences of hidden despair than of hope in a new being. The only person he may assuredly reckon not to be in despair is the one who can speak of himself as 'confident in self-despair'. For to be able to say that, a person needs to have accepted the despairing self in the power of the eternal acceptance of him *in* his despair. Then he has faith in the new being which is God's gift, given to the afflicted and identified with nothingness. Aid from without must have the aim of mediating God's grace.

There exists a life of faith which stands upon the fact that God takes 'the things that are not' and fills a person's admitted emptiness with his fullness. Such a person walks through life paradoxically aware both of his condition of emptiness or apathy and of God's gifts of fullness and passionate love. There is more in the life of faith than the filling of emptiness. There is the creative use and reversal of utterly contrary passions. This is first seen in Abraham, who in obedient faithfulness to God's command is faced with the requirement of killing his own son as a sacrificial victim (Genesis 22). God makes possible, by faith in him, courses of action which nature could never sustain by any introspective mobilization of its own powers. Faith sustains the man of faith under the forms of paradox, where despite the grace of God within him, he faces the conflicts of his all-too-human unbridled emotions with the newly-gained dynamics of loves and passions learnt from Christ. Christian experience is well content with the paradox of a divine strength made perfect *in* weakness. As Simone Weil wrote about affliction: 'The extreme greatness of Christianity lies in the fact that it does not seek a supernatural remedy for suffering but a supernatural use for it.'[1]

We cannot have God share our utmost suffering of dereliction and dread until we have become resigned to it. He has an appointment with every person in his own particular hell, not to be missed, for it is in this encounter that the ultimate fear of nothingness is banished. It is often through an act of obedience, in letting go a love that can no longer be clung to without incurring God's sorrowful

1 Simone Weil, *Gravity and Grace*, Routledge & Kegan Paul 1952.

withdrawal, that in the private hell of the schizoid darkness, the Christ of the dereliction is first encountered. To know that 'even there also shall thy hand lead me, and thy right hand shall hold me . . . for the darkness and light are both alike', is to have reached the end of this phase of the journey. This is the conjunction of two roads, that which leads to the uttermost experience of unreality of our non-being, and the infinite journey and descent into hell which Christ has taken to reach us. One way or another the afflicted spirit comes to rest in God and in reality only when all clinging attachments and false hopes have been relinquished. While there was any doubt about the final issue, or doubts measuring the goodness of God by his ability to effect a rescue, the absolute rock-bottom experience cannot be reached. Generally speaking, one cannot despair at all in the creative sense without willing to do so. If the growing apprehension of the Word of God and of human reality is tending to direct the soul towards the acceptance of nothingness as its truth, then it becomes possible, in truth, to will despair. One is then resting in despair, but not actually in despair so much as in truth which is beyond the despair.

A time not to console

The natural tendency of the pastoral counsellor is to console the sufferer, even extending an offer of companionship in a time of overwhelming affliction. There is a time for befriending, especially if the sufferer in deep and final despair may put himself for ever beyond help. True, the fractured personality needs to be splinted in companionship and rested by friendship. But a time comes when it would be spiritually disastrous to cling to manifestations of human consolation and attention. Technically this is to remain clinging in the hysterical position. There is a time for the splints and bandages to be removed. Simone Weil sharply comments: 'All consolation in affliction separates us from love and from truth.' And again: 'To explain suffering is to console it; therefore it must not be consoled.'[1]

The clergyman who speaks *simpliciter* of the love and mercy of God to a man in affliction is usually comforting himself and lightening his own burden. He may, by such talk, make it heavier for the other. If a man has been cruelly afflicted by overwhelming personal loss or disaster, the obligation for him, pastorally enforced, still to think of God also as all-powerful love and kindness is an additional exhausting burden. Counselling here is inseparable from an acceptance of much that is contradictory and paradoxical. The pastor

<hr/>

1   Simone Weil, *Gravity and Grace*, ibid., pp. 99, 102.

may give reassurances as before, but it will be less burdensome to the sufferer if, in the saying, he also observes that it may be adding to the burden rather than easing it. This then becomes a shared truth and the patient is strengthened by it. If the paradox is maintained in terms of the truth, the afflicted man will find that it is blessed to call evil evil, and nevertheless to endure it with God. This is Job's standpoint as over against that of his comforters.

Hystero-schizoid reactions in a paradoxical model

Some personalities are made up for the most part of constellations of schizoid traits with a few hysterical features. Others reverse this proportion. Many medical men are disturbed by the determination of psychoanalysts to have two sets of explanations for every item of human behaviour. The determination to win both ways confounds prediction and makes nonsense of scientific theory. On the other hand, the unidimensional mind follows contentedly where cause and effect are directly related and continue to be so to the end point. In linking together schizoid and hysteric characteristics our model shows that the human organism is at a certain primitive level mechanistic in its responses. The nervous system does respond to excessive stress by discontinuous responses. A model based on these concepts can be used for an understanding of those with hystero-schizoid afflictions.

For a personality basically taking its stand on hysterical defences the world view will look rather like Figure 9. Here the feeling tone is always related to this ontological dimension on the line numbered from 0 to 10. At 0 there is no anxiety because someone is present giving accepting attention. If there is withdrawal of visible support without a definite time of return, separation-anxiety transmits alarm signals producing movement along the 0–10 line which now becomes a time scale. Anxiety mounts with prolongation of separation, a panic state is reached. If there is no help, nor any internalized conceptualization of help such as faith in God, then there is a recapitulation of the symptoms of infantile fall into identification with non-being and the loss of self.

If this is a chronically recurrent experience and there have been schizoid antecedents (perhaps even without such antecedents) the ego may begin to take up a defensive position which is essentially one of schizoid detachment. It may give up the struggle to be related to human beings and opt for detachment or death.

Where the ego has taken up a defence in infancy which is basically that of schizoid defence by detachment, the personality's view of the world will be such as is outlined in Figure 10. Already the fall

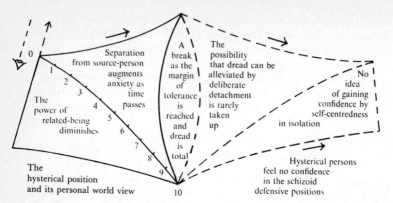

FIG. 9　The hysterical position and its personal world view

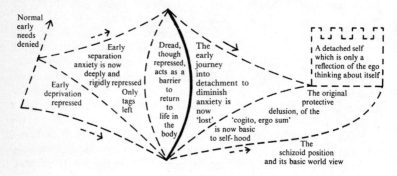

FIG. 10　The schizoid position and its basic world view

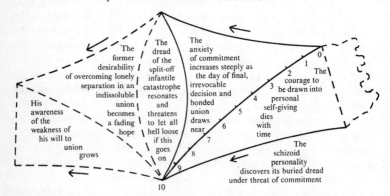

FIG. 11　The schizoid personality discovers its buried dread under threat of commitment

through separation into decisive disrelatedness has taken place. Time stopped when no one came within a tolerable time of waiting. The ego lives in the world of the essences not of existences. Some kind of ivory tower, probably intellectualist, has been established. On the hysterical side are only a few impersonal attachments, more or less compulsive. About these little things he might well be impatient. About the big things he has no need to consider the passage of time, or their disappearance from the world of sense, because he possesses all that he needs internally.

Using the model

Let us see how this model serves us and how it changes if for example this man with schizoid defences finds that marriage threatens. He is being drawn or pushed to the altar of sacrifice of all that his defensive position counts most dear (Figure 11). Time now presses heavily upon him, he is being forced into the world of existences. Commitment anxiety mounts. At 10 he will be in a dreadful state of nervous breakdown. It all depends now on what construction he puts on the words of his fiancée, 'I love you'. This can be of all phrases the most threatening to him. *Eros* is foraging for her love supplies and he is her victim again. She with whom he was bound up in in childhood, and to whom he had always to look for the content of the self, had not returned. The loss of her 'took all the stuffing out of him'. What little he had when she overstayed her absence was utterly exhausted in waiting for her. So that now this woman's words, 'I love you', mean 'I want you to love me', and that is too painfully extractive to be borne. Moreover, there is too much to lose of long-practised self-sufficiency. Though empty, he was very secure. People admired what they saw, never thinking to look inside to his emptiness. Those who had approached had been put off sharply. The inner implications of a proposal of marriage are to him a temptation to desert the role which hides his inner emptiness and expose its shame to a woman. One such as this once sucked all the goodness out of him. This one, though apparently so gentle, must have, hidden within her, the same propensities. In so far as she is naive she does not realize his predicament. He is empty; there is no substance of a person to give. He feels an impostor.

So anxiety mounts with the feeling, 'I would be bad for you. I am no good. You will rue the day you join yourself to me. I must protect you from myself. If I were to cross the margin to come to you, there would be a sudden revelation of a sucking monster which, with great gulps, would take back violently what was mine. Then there would be nothing left of you. At least if I keep you at this distance I retain you. I am terrified of my ravenous self. Either it will snatch all the good out of you, or swallow you whole. Be warned. My love is indeed the most dangerous thing about me. Keep your distance.'

As the schizoid person peers from his depersonalized world into the world of existences, contemplating the leap across the gulf again, he is afraid above all things of his own love-impulses as destructive and draining the life out of the very person he loves. What might happen if this man proceeds to marry? He may find his fears are unfounded. His wife may accept him as he is and make no demands. By marrying a woman who is emotionally of his own kind he may be assured that nothing personal will be required of him. Sometimes, however, an hysterical woman is attracted to a role-playing husband, be he priest or doctor. While she is free to follow him round, admiring the role-playing, the illusion persists that marriage with him would be 'heaven'. The incompatibility is manifest only when she is housebound by children and duties and turns to him for help. At this his commitment-anxiety mounts, he feels her demands to be 'dreadfully' unfair and 'terribly' inconvenient. From whichever side they are approaching the margin, people use these extravagant words much earlier on the road than seems justified, except to the unconscious.

Warm undemanding love is required

If, however, love is interpreted as *agape*, the kind of love character-istic of God, the schizoid man need not be threatened by the proposal. For the emphasis then is not on desire but on self-giving, not on possessing but on sacrificing. In Christ love has itself made the journey through separation-anxiety and dereliction, through dread and hell, to reach those who are most utterly lost in isolation and fearfulness. Because Christ has made this journey He knows that *eros* itself, the infinite longing for life itself, fails at the margin. He knows what it is with Job and the Psalmist to long for death. That when the eager cry of the rescuer is calling to a man, with all the longing of *eros*, to come back across the abyss to life, this is enough to make him sick with fear at the prospect – this, too, Christ knows. He understands that the very strength of *eros* is threatening to the schizoid elements of the soul. Christ as a man knew not only *agape*, but *eros*, a powerful longing for human companionship. He knows that if it is not to do more harm than good, *eros* must be invaded by and controlled by *agape*. Its most striking characteristic is patience, whereas *eros* is always impatient. As our model shows, the sense of being hurried by time to do something is itself threatening to the schizoid elements. It arouses avoidance mechanisms and resistance. Therefore *agape* must convince the soul that it has all the time in the world, and beyond it, in his own hand. Thomas must be allowed to join the eleven a week late, rather than be chivvied into his place among the eleven in order to give the Lord the satisfaction of knowing, even on the first Easter Day, that he had lost none of those his Father had committed to him.

Agape restrains *eros*, even in those who long to draw out love from the schizoid spouse. *Agape* makes their love very patient, characterized by long-suffering with entire cheerfulness. This is possible because the Lord holds in himself all varieties of love that our spirits need, so that the others may be free to take the time they need to begin the return journey from detachment. Since this joyful restraint, which takes off all the pressure of demand, also makes the lover more attractive, literally more seductive, this is much better calculated to solve the otherwise hopeless impasse of schizoid dynamics.

It is unselfish love that is able to unite itself with the schizoid person where he is. It makes no peremptory demand for change, but only prepares the way, by its presence on the lost side of dread. It is a bold claim to make for a particular kind of love, but the exigencies of the schizoid position, psychodynamically considered, demand it. This implies that autistic children can be won back to family life only by warm, outgoing and unsophisticated mothering and fathering. It says that warm-hearted befriending creates the atmosphere in which the schizoid person, frozen into the ice of his own mechanisms, can find again a reason for living. A counsellor may be driven by a need for success which derives from his own unrequited *eros* love. If so, then he will certainly fail to provide the schizoid person with good reasons for returning from the near edge of suicide into human society. The simple befriender, with no axe to grind, has a simple uncomplicated love to give, which is patient, meek and humble as to its own powers. Because it does not demand a hurried response, but just allows itself to love and care, such love creates precisely the conditions in which the dynamic circulation of the spirit can begin again to flow in the schizoid sufferer.

The Syrophoenician woman

We can turn to the Gospel narratives to discover how Jesus deals with the paradoxes of those with hystero-schizoid problems. He moves out from Galilee, where he has been faced with rejection by his own people, into Gentile country. Here a Syrophoenician woman, distracted by her anxiety, approaches him to cast out the demon that is vexing her daughter (Matt. 15:21). The reaction of the disciples to her importunate hysteria was typical: 'Lord, send her away.' Jesus set his eyes on her, but she was too distraught by her immediate needs to look at him. So Jesus 'answered her not a word'. His silence would make even her busy tongue be silent and cause her to look into his face. Only when her eyes were fixed on his, so that the infinite tenderness of the Gentiles' Saviour would be unmistakable, did the Lord utter the unpleasant remark about dogs, which otherwise must have given her great and justifiable offence.

On his cross he would be treated as an outcast, outlawed from his own people, identified with the Gentiles in the scorn of the Jews. He it was, supremely identified with outsiders, who spoke to the pagan woman, affirming to her what she knew so well for herself, that she was 'an outsider'. Jesus did not attempt to mitigate the dreadful rigour of the categorization of his world into the Jews, who were inside God's immediate providence, and the Gentiles who were, for the present, outside its purview. Christ was a Jew, and salvation was of the Jews. The children must first be fed. The children's food was not for dogs.

The silence of Christ frustrated her urgent petitions and made her seek not his favours but his face. It would be his face that held together the cleavages of her existence. His paradoxical gaze held her both in sternness and gentleness. Knowing herself in his countenance, she did not need to deny the ineluctable fact of her own exclusion from the favoured family. She could hold to the truth of her 'outsiderish' feelings, unmitigated by sentiments calculated to soften the blow while denying to her the painful truth of her own wretched status. She was a dog, and in the East that goes with indignity. She had also produced a demonic daughter. Election had placed the Jew in an unmerited position of national right. The Messiah who was the bread of life coming from the Father had a prior responsibility, even a strict limitation to the children of Israel. But Christ was not ignorant of the later extension of the purpose of God to draw all men to him, including those far-off pagans of whom this woman was representative.

Hysterical in her need and clinging; afflicted and ready to shrink away like a beaten cur into a cringing schizoid detachment, why was she not repelled by the Master's words? 'It is not right to take the children's bread and to cast it to the dogs.' Surely, because she was living in the light of his countenance, and to do this is faith

and creates faith. Out over the abyss of separation between Jew
and Greek, breaking down with his encouragement the middle wall
of partition between them, she quips, 'Truth, Lord; yet the dogs
eat of the crumbs which fall from their master's table.' 'I may be
sub-human, a kind of a dog, a thing without family rights, but you
are my Lord and Master, and you are so rich a giver that even
scraps from a table like yours are bounty enough for me.' All this
speaks strongly of the way the truth of Christ comes to the sons
of want, burdened with schizoid deficiencies at the heart of their
humanity. 'Sit and eat,' says Jesus. She had already done so. Her
eyes of faith had been feasting on his countenance and she was
healed of the horror of rejection. Christ had created faith in her and
then he commended it, for its greatness is the magnitude of the
abyss over which she leapt to follow his eyes. First they had looked
with compassion and identification into the deep pit of her
unmerited degradation. She had not winced. Dog, he said, and dog
she was, not a human-feeling child at all. Then he had drawn her
across an infinite distance by an invitation in his eyes, to a rest in
his heart, the place where all souls are fed. She did not hang back.
She did not say in tiresome apology, 'Let my shame go where it
doth deserve.'[1] She obeyed the indication in his eloquent eyes.
Without hesitation she did sit and eat. 'O woman, great is thy faith:
be it unto thee even as thou wilt,' said Jesus. Her daughter was
healed at that moment. She returned home, found the child lying in
bed, the demon gone. Being and well-being, life and its sustenance,
healing for herself and her distant daughter; in her utter nothingness
and leaving behind her self-rejection, she accepted all that Christ
had to give in one splendid gesture of response to him. All that
passed verbally to mark this infinite leap of faith was a quip of a
few words.

The paralysed man

The natural defence of the schizoid personality is solitude. Social
gatherings bore him 'dreadfully', unless he has been asked to
contribute light or wit to the occasion. He will not have been asked
to give warmth. He has no social contact in interpersonal depth.
The perfectly executed role of his profession gives to him a veneer
of social dexterity, even of maturity. Only those condemned to
depend on him for intimacy know the strength of his impregnable
solitude. His inability to break out from defensive solitude is most
marked in those relationships where he ought to be giving himself

1   George Herbert's poem, 'Love bade me welcome'.

most generously. Dread for him is synonymous with personal commitment, so that he is in flight from both. He is paralysed in solitude by fear. This operates when he is required to come down from his self-erected defensive position into the family life. It may hold him back from any kind of social involvement, even though limited to the playing of a role.

Friends who know how to move with intuitive courtesy and unpressuring readiness, are often able to initiate a relationship on terms acceptable to the guarded individual. If it is a united group of friends who do this, not only is the physical fact of solitude overcome, but the internal frozen state dominated by the drive to withdrawal begins to thaw. If this person is open to basic Christian resources, he will find self-will gradually being displaced and ultimately done to death by the indwelling of Christ. The Christ in any person seeks solitude only when it is growth-promoting, not when it stifles growth. In those who lack fellowship, the Holy Spirit within seeks out good company, drawing a person by faith out into a corporate life. The courage to be as part of the family and the congregation in all they do grows, perhaps for the first time.

The pastoral dimensions for the healing of the person with schizoid characteristics can be seen in the Gospel record of the healing of the paralysed man, brought by four friends to Jesus (Mark 2:1). The ordinary person comes into the house where Christ is, by the usual approach, through the door. Unorthodox entrances have to be found for the afflicted. The clergy will never help schizoid outsiders until they realize this and are prepared for it. A seriously afflicted person is kept out, because the curious are more concerned to indulge their own curiosity by crowding around Jesus, than they are in letting a chronic cripple be carried into his presence. The faith of the four friends rose to the occasion. They carried him up an external stairway to the roof, located Jesus, and began to dig a hole in the roof about the same size as a grave. Then with ropes at the four corners of his stretcher they prepared to let him down. There is often a cry at this moment: 'You have brought me this far yourselves; I didn't want to come on this journey; now you are letting me down. You are committing me to the tomb of all our hopes.'

If this paralysed man could have struggled off the bed before they started, or could have struck them in anger to stop them proceeding, he would by now be clinging frantically to them. Only his paralysis would save him from remaining on the roof, clinging to his friends, terrified of being let down into the presence of Jesus in full gaze of the crowd. Fortunately, he had been condemned by his illness to a passivity that overcame his contradictory and self-destructive drives. Thus the paralytic was lowered, like a dead body into a grave. The priest, Jesus himself, is waiting for the 'corpse', not at the graveside, but at the bottom of it. For Christ himself has descended into hell, and it is in hell, among the dead, that the life he gives is most purely his own resurrection life. St Paul gives us the axiom of all apostolic creativity, 'that death worketh in us, but life in you'.

The point of the story is best sustained if we regard the paralytic as one who contributed nothing whatever of himself to the cure. The healing person of Christ was working with the faith of the four friends, not of the man himself. Those who are paralysed personalities become free, not by being able to act, but by consent to the action of others. This consent they find difficult to give because it involves a form of dependence. If we suppose the man in the story not to have genuinely consented to his friends' action, disbelieving their manifest sincerity and the proclaimed character of Jesus, then the words of Jesus, 'seeing *their* faith', and declaring *his* forgiveness, are immediately appropriate and understandable. But it is important to note that the Lord's final words were: 'Rise, take up your bed, and walk.'

7

The Understanding of Paranoid Personalities

It is of the essence of the paranoid person's view of life that he regards other people as likely candidates for the attention of the psychiatrist. All his own problems are confronted, not within himself, but by projection, as they are seen in others. He perceives in others minimal manifestations of the faults and deficiencies which his own inner nature bears most severely. Since he frequently feels deprived of his rights and is prone to litigation, the lawyer will see more of him than the psychiatrist. As the parson is the representative of God, the paranoid person often brings his protest against life's injustices to the vicarage. He may be found projecting his distorted emotions on to the meetings of the church council. There is something infectious about paranoid 'chips on the shoulder': they rapidly gather other complainants.

There is a continuity, with few clear distinguishing marks, from the mild 'paranoid' feelings we all may have at times (a sense of being unjustifiably 'got at' which in itself is not justified by the facts) through the tendency under stress to react in a paranoid manner, to the fully developed neurosis, the paranoid personality. Beyond that there is the onset of a psychosis, marked by the emergence into consciousness of the fixated transmarginal infantile experience of being 'persecuted', appearing in a sudden 'illumination' as the primary delusion. This may be limited to a small area of life, kept secret from others. This is about the level described as paraphrenia. If the primary delusion becomes surrounded by extensive further delusions of explanation, strengthened by bizarre hallucinations and grandiose experiences, with contrary feelings of being sadistically persecuted, this is the worst development (reached by a very few who start on this road), namely paranoid schizophrenia.

If only to help each other, clergy need to have an understanding of paranoid personalities. A rural deanery is unlikely to be without its paranoid personality; touchy, without warm humour; his wit, wry and malicious at the best; defensive, opinionated, suspicious of detractors, wary of critics; always establishing his position against those who seem to be encroaching on his rights, argumentative, prone to pettifogging correctness, delighting to put the laity in their place, and the archdeacon too, if he puts a foot wrong. He devotes himself with unbalanced zeal to a cause with which he is identified; with ready excuses for failure and a genius for proving himself to be in the right; uneasy, brooding, seclusive, oversensitive; envious, jealous, consumed by secret hates, eager for the promotion he feels is the only proper recognition of his worth. He is proud, yet always feeling humiliated, unable to admit himself ever to have been in the wrong; a small man humanly with big ideas about himself, unable to make concessions, uncharitable, critical, over-censorious, distrustful of everyone from the bishop to the verger. He is self-centred, incapable of exposure to the rough-and-tumble give-and-take of ordinary social encounter; unable to understand what makes other people 'tick', so engaged is he in projecting on to them his own faulty dynamics. He is a sort of prickly cactus which exists for its humanity on a spare social diet, on hardly any water of the spirit. To say that he 'enjoys the freehold' is an internal contradiction. Party lines delimit his friendships. In his innermost being, through no fault of his own, he is identified with emptiness, meaninglessness, inferiority, low self-esteem, emasculated powers, a weak and sickly human spirit. As a person prepared by the basic relationships of life for meeting, for dialogue, for community, for the achievement of outgoing loving personal bonds, he is, all too literally, a dead loss. (Such a diagnostic description does not belong only to clergymen. Paranoid personalities are to be found also among doctors and politicians, civil servants and shop stewards.)

Predicament of paranoid leadership

To the Church as a healing, reconciling community the paranoid personality in a position of leadership is an incubus. His primal human experiences in the first year gave him no sense of glory, blessedness, abundance or content, no 'sanctification' of the human spirit to the point of joyful satisfaction. Or if these tokens of well-being were given, the time came, too early to be borne, when they were drastically taken away. This intolerable truth in his inward parts was split off, denied, and repressed. A reaction pattern of personality, defending by further denial and projection, completed the deception.

Neither the primal deprivation nor its emergence as a distorting factor are in themselves disqualifications for Christian leadership. St Paul himself declares his own human weakness, emptiness, wretchedness and incapacity. He besought the Lord to take away a 'thorn in the flesh' which seems characterized by 'weakness'. We know this because God's answer was that 'his strength is made perfect in weakness'. This is a paradox of another order than the psychodynamic paradoxes of ultra-marginal stressing which drove the paranoid person to loathe his own 'dependency needs'. The gospel paradox brings into apposition two ineluctable facts, the *poverty* of being-in-relatedness to inadequate sources of well-being, and the *wealth* of God's generosity in offering to us his own abundant powers of being, conferring them as daily substance through the living bread of his word, the sacraments and the coinherent fellowship. The Christian can 'rejoice in his infirmities' because the admission of their actuality opens the door to the new God-given actuality, his own power of being which rests upon and abides in the open- and the empty-hearted. The predicament of the paranoid personality lies in the premature closure of the wound inflicted upon the nascent selfhood by too early, severe and intolerable deprivations. This denial is built into the character structure, so that it militates as much against admission of inner neediness as against any reaching out for help to personal resources outside the self. He dare not 'hunger and thirst after right-relatedness' because hunger and thirst have become, in depth, too painful to be re-experienced. But only those who 'hunger and thirst' are filled, so that he who lives by fantasies of repletion and fullness remains empty. Perhaps he is now the official representative of the Church of Jesus Christ to hundreds of people. His own personality, rigid and unshiftable, blocks the very revival in the Church which alone could save him.

Revival, as a missionary in Africa described it, is 'walking with Jesus and being satisfied, every day'. St Paul writes, 'God is able to make grace abound towards you; that you, always having all sufficiency in all things, may abound to every good work' (2 Cor. 9:8). The will and gift of God is our sanctification. God means the paranoid parson to be a humble man rejoicing in the overflowing powers of well-being which come from his covenanted graciousness in Christ, when the Holy Spirit is communicated to him, waiting with his people for the living word, through the sacraments and in the fellowship. But until he can deflate his defensive pride by coming to terms with the hidden pain of his initial humiliation, nothing of this can reach him.

DIAGNOSIS OF THE VARIANT FORMS OF PARANOID REACTION

Paranoid breakdowns are typically disorders of middle and later life, with an onset usually later than the thirty-fifth year. While this is generally true, it is also possible for paranoid reactions and actual paranoid schizophrenic disorders to arise in adolescence.

Adolescent paranoid reactions

Young persons in their teens are aware that parents and older adults may not take their rights seriously. Their elders may pass them over in conversation, belittle them and delay the conferment of the privileges of free determination. Whereas the healthy young person will shrug this off, those who are inclined to paranoid reactions on account of earlier conflicts over 'rights' tend to react with extreme touchiness. They may show a generalized hostility to older people, perceiving domineering attitudes where none are present, taking offence where no offence was meant. It is in line with the dynamic situation that this will be exacerbated when, as a matter of fact, they are not doing well either at work, in recreation or in social encounter. When they become established and are well set on the road to social and economic well-being this 'paranoid' touchiness is likely to diminish.

Paranoid schizophrenia

When schizophrenia attacks after the age of thirty, the most frequent form it takes is that of a paranoid illness with delusions of persecution. Paranoid symptoms are rather characteristic of all kinds of mental illness in later life. This is true of the depressive illnesses, of senile states and other organic impairments of personality.

If a paranoid schizophrenic illness supervenes in a personality which is already schizoid, isolated, shut in, detached and asocial, or is already manifestly paranoid, it is difficult to say where the actual schizophrenia begins. It may be meaningless to ask the question. There is no group of diseases in psychiatry which is so resistant to any clear diagnostic categorization as the paranoid.

Paranoid schizophrenia may be of sudden onset in middle life in a person who appears to have been well adjusted. The attack may begin with what is known as the *primary delusion*. While he is reading a newspaper, watching the television, or listening to the radio, suddenly some word or announcement seems to him to have particular reference to himself or to his private life in the past or in the future. Anything that happens, may suddenly take on an intimate personal significance. Ordinary events in the environment suddenly become charged with serious import, often of persecutory threat. There is a *delusional mood change* which colours the person's whole emotional life and affects every relationship. The bizarre quality of this is immediately manifest, not only to the patient, but to anyone to whom he speaks of it. As a result, the patient may keep these private revelations of meaning secret for many months. He continues to conduct an apparently full life and in all respects but this particular one his conduct is normal. It is a not uncommon experience for a psychiatrist to interview a patient whose relatives are concerned about him, and in almost two hours of interviewing to fail to discover any abnormal mental content. Then in the last five minutes, in a lull, when conversation is exhausted, the patient may volunteer a remark so strangely contrary to the reality of the situation as to establish the diagnosis of paranoid schizophrenia.

This happened to a clergyman who had been having tea with a Sunday-school teacher who lived alone, and for an hour or so the conversation had gone quite normally. He had happened to notice that the spider cracks in the plaster of the wall had been stuck over with brown paper in the form of a cross. As he was leaving the room he chanced to mention this and asked her whether she was having trouble with the plaster. Without a halt in the conversation, the woman explained that the husband who had left her was puffing poisonous gas into the room through those cracks. 'But sticking that paper over them has stopped his little game.' The parson was so taken aback that he had left the house before he could gather his wits.

Once the experience of the primary delusion has occurred in adult life, the patient fixedly regards himself as one who is persecuted by some body of people in the community. At times he believes that others envy him, are out to defraud him, accuse, terrify, attack, poison or imprison him. At other times he takes refuge in the denial which is characteristic of those who still have grand memories of omnipotence and the blessedness of the infantile state of well-being, before the deluge. He is grandiose. This may lead to the full paranoid *megalomania*. He suddenly has a conviction of his almighty greatness.

These primary delusions may have been accompanied by auditory *hallucinations*, by voices accusing or deriding, threatening or commanding. Much more rarely the voices may be laudatory. Often tappings are heard in the walls of the room, or voices from hidden loudspeakers. Visual hallucinations are much less common.

The primary delusion appears at the end of a period of adult loss of well-being as if it were *a moment of 'illumination'*. In this moment it seems as though everything that had ever concerned him becomes clear. There is no shadow of doubt whatever at that moment about the truth of the assertion, 'I *am* being persecuted.' There is no point in attempting to contradict the paranoid patient on this point. He is more certain of the truth of this experience than he is of any other thing. There is no reason why we should attempt to dissuade him, since, in fact, we recognize that it does represent faithfully an actual sector of his infantile experience. We can only accept it and interpret to him what it does, in fact, represent. *He will not trust anyone who can only tell him to deny the validity of this experience. He may trust someone who is able to make what seems to him to be a sensible interpretation of it as representing, if not the whole of reality, then at least a part of reality.*

Along with these disturbances in rational explanation of the paranoid patient's universe, and indeed underlying all this 'irrational rationality', are experiences of an emotional kind which have all the characteristics of infantile experience. Powerful feelings invade the mind, whether of absolute terror, hate, jealousy or longing, with the all-or-nothing quality of the original infantile experience. To defend against these overwhelming weaknesses, the ego may regress to even earlier experiences of absolute blessedness, power, vigour and of *'overwhelming well-being'*. At one moment the patient is in ecstasy, exalted by a supernatural sense of having absolute insight into all the ultimate problems of being. At the next he may feel gripped by 'demonic' opponents and damnation. We know that these actually represent the two states of infantile 'well-being' and infantile 'ill-being' as they occurred within the first six months of life.

When these diverse states originally happened the infant was still in the state of life-by-identification with the mother for whatever being and well-being she chose to provide. The infant was incapable of distinguishing whether these overwhelming feelings ought properly to be attributed to the source-person, or to the ego itself, or to the communicating elements, the perceptions in the sensory structures. We see this same *confusion* occurring again in the paranoid patient. At times he blames himself as the source of his own wretchedness and inferiority. Taking refuge in the primal sense of superior well-being, he attributes the diminishments which he suffers to the hostility, envy and jealousy of others, who covet his goods. At yet other times, the sensory structures bear the responsibility and provide pseudo-explanations in the form of hallucinations and similar false perceptions. The regression takes the mind back to the period before any clear distinctions could be made as to subject, object and predicate, or the boundaries of the ego.

If this has been a genuine schizophrenic attack, once the psychotic nucleus of persecutoriness has emerged into consciousness, it is very difficult to return it absolutely to the repressed state. The primary delusion, with its delusions of explanation, then tends to become the first stage of a chronic schizophrenic illness.

Short paranoid attacks

Where, however, the psychotic attack is secondary to an exhaustive illness or operation, the paranoid episode often comes to an end as convalescence brings returning strength.

The association of short-lived psychotic episodes, whether primary or secondary to physical disturbances, with a new orientation to life and with religious conversion cannot be overlooked in pastoral care. I have myself been in close contact with several patients during psychotic episodes which became, for them, times of transformation of personality in an entirely beneficial sense. What seemed to be a disintegrating and shattering loss of sanity proved to be part of a more massive integration of hitherto repressed and unacceptable memories of infantile terrors of psychotic intensity. In the inscrutable economy of the spiritual order, those whose courage and power of being has been enhanced so as to make the endurance of even psychotic experience possible, become thereby 'stabilized, strengthened and settled' as they never were before. Moreover, they gain an openness to others in equivalent mental pain and a capacity to commend with a conviction which carries intrinsic weight the living Lord, whose presence, somehow sensed in and beyond the worst moments of misery, reconciled them to it. It is part of the task of pastoral care, informed by an understanding of paranoid dynamics and an even deeper understanding of the dynamics of the divine graciousness, to prove that even a psychotic episode can 'work together for good to those who love God'.

The clergyman will, within the parish, meet the paranoid schizophrenic or paraphrenic patient who has managed to retain, by a process of rigid dissociation of the paranoid content of the mind, a fairly acceptable contact with ordinary life. There has never been any reference to a psychiatrist. The general practitioner may know a good deal about this patient, yet quite deliberately make no attempt to have him admitted into the mental hospital. He knows only too well that if this were done, the likelihood of a return to the outside world is small. Though the prognosis as to length of life is good, as to full recovery from the delusions the outlook is poor. If the patient's present tenuous hold on reality in the community is lost, it is unlikely ever to be regained.

Paranoid reactions in depression

Paranoid ideas specifically accompany the depressions without vital anxiety, those depressions which are characterized by retardation, not by agitation. It is, for instance, obvious that if 'being itself' has been threatened with total loss, this *includes* the loss of 'well-being', so that paranoid reactions can also occur in association with the agitated depressions where vital anxiety is a prominent symptom. The civil war between internal hatred, envy, and jealousy, and the super-ego which dominates them, leads to a diminution of psychic energy available for repression. To some extent the misfortunes are attributed to forces beyond the control of the patient, and persecution is suspected. However, it is consonant with the character of these depressed patients that they never absolve themselves by the kind of complete projection which the basically paranoid personality can achieve. Even though there is a paranoid flavour to these depressive reactions, there is still a strong desire to attribute the failure to himself.

In these cases the treatment should be directed primarily towards the relief of the depression. The depression itself constitutes a loss of well-being, either an obvious loss of social status and esteem or the more subtle and inwardly registered diminishments of well-being which are the inevitable accompaniment of ageing. The outward man is perishing. The ultimate question, which only the Christian faith claims to answer with any finality, is, what of the inward man? Is this being renewed from day to day? Is there anything to live for in the last decade of life? Is death the end of all or the open gate to eternal well-being? However this theological question may be answered, there is no doubt that on the natural level when old people are embodied in an active social round with visits from young persons who care for them and from middle-aged folk who respect them, the breeding-ground of depressive and paranoid moods is greatly diminished.

In view of the close connection, often amounting to alternation, between paranoid thinking on the one hand and an *associated hypochondriasis* on the other, these two are dealt with together. The dynamic roots of both are the same, a severe loss of infantile well-being which has been fixated and repressed. In the paranoid mental projection, society is blamed for the unacknowledged inner persecutoriness. In the hypochondriasis the body is blamed, as if it were something almost foreign to the ego, which 'lets the side down' so regularly as to be a continual source of weakness or persecution.

The parson who is inwardly at rest can be of real assistance. If the patient has been of a religious disposition it is possible that he, in common with the man who is prone to retarded depression in later life, has driven himself excessively. He has striven to keep up with a heavy programme of activity. At this point of breakdown the man of God may be able to bring him round to the truth he has never been able throughout his life to accept, that the basic mode of our existence as Christian people is precisely one of *rest*. The fact that God and all his true friends accept him just as much now, when he cannot continue with his incessant production of beneficent activities any longer, as they did when he could, should bring home to him something of the truth about life which he needs to know.

In senile dementia the nerve cells and circuits upon which normal adult mental life depends are falling out of use with the atrophy of old age. Pre-senile dementia refers to the early onset of this senile atrophy. In a small proportion of the population the onset of this dementing process may be advanced into the fifties or even into the forties. Dementing involves a gradual return to 'the second childhood'. At the point where this regressive process reaches down to the earliest levels of experience, if these have been marked and scarred by paranoid reactions, these reactions will reappear at the other end of life. All these states of senile dementia are progressive. They have not the episodic quality associated with arterio-sclerotic or particularly with hypertensive illness. Nothing can be done to reverse the process. Pastoral care in the parochial setting should ensure that the senile person is surrounded by people who are concerned for his well-being and lovingly caring for him. The pastor can help, in cases where the relatives are feeling the strain of unjust accusations that they are neglecting the patient, and actively hostile to him, by explaining how these reactions arise. An acceptable explanation takes away all the force of these senile delusions and enables the nursing relatives to persist patiently even though rewarded only by slights and ingratitude. The gratitude of the parish and the pastor will encourage the nursing relatives. A great deal can be done to ease the burden of care in senile paranoid conditions if it can be arranged within the parish for other suitable members, even young people, to relieve the person whose main burden it is, to get away for a few hours each day.

A summary of paranoid psychodynamic development

It is not surprising that in so many conditions ranging from the neurotic to the psychotic, from the functional to the organic, paranoid reactions should occur. The experiences of severe loss of well-being in the first year must be so common as to lead us to expect paranoid reactions. Whenever the energies of the mind are reduced to a minimal state of well-being, these earliest experiences of the same kind are bound to resonate. This leads to regression and calls into action the original defences of denial and projection.

It may be useful to go over the stages by which a paranoid system develops. Though no two cases are absolutely alike, the various forms of paranoid reaction and paranoid schizophrenia have much more in common than any other varieties of schizophrenia and psychoneurosis. The paranoid states are readily recognizable and pathetically alike.

1   As a result of any of the social or personal factors by which well-being and self-esteem are lost, the reaction begins, determined largely by fixated and unconscious factors.

2   The affected person withdraws some degree of interest from the hard and unhelpful world.

3   He becomes preoccupied with himself and his resources, often becoming hypochondriacal.

4   He regresses to an infantile level and sees the world as he saw it then.

5   There is a good deal of confusion about what is going on, as there was then.

6   He dare not uncover the extreme persecutory pain and emptiness of the transmarginal state.

7   He reconstructs the world on a delusional basis, still splitting off and denying the inner reality and defending against the inner accusers and persecutors by seeing them in the world outside. The fact that in infancy he ejected, that is to say 'spat out', the unacceptable oral supplies means that he expects to find them, where he spat them out, still on the walls of life outside himself.

8   He denies that emptiness and inferiority are the inner truth about himself.

9   By projection he explains it away as the work of those who covet his goods.

10   He gathers 'evidence' to prove this view for certain, systematizing his evidence, forgetting that it has all been based on a premise from another time and place.

11   He scrutinizes every act and happening for clues left by his persecutors.

12   He misinterprets all the non-verbal symbols of communication. A smile is 'someone laughing at me'. No smile, is 'clear evidence of hostility'. A cough is 'a reminder from one of the gang that they have their tabs on me'. A tool out of place on the workbench

becomes clear evidence that 'someone is taking the mickey out of me'.

13   Self-reference extends to include *everything* as having a special meaning directed at himself.

14   Everything seems mysterious, elusive, threatening, confusing.

15   Attacks seem to be being mounted against him by 'them', by 'people', forcing him into a passive role.

16   Magical radio sets may be listening to him, accusing him, using him, and abusing him.

17   A whole organization seems to be set up, dedicated to his destruction. Some racial or religious group is 'out' to ruin him.

18   A sudden breakthrough of 'illumination' convinces him that there is nothing confusing about it any more. It is all absolutely clear and structured. At whatever point in the progress of the illness this breakthrough to pseudo-illumination occurs it is very characteristic, and once it has occurred it is difficult for the patient to retreat from it. He is surrounded by a 'pseudo-community' of persecutors.

19   Evasive action is taken and the possibility of outbursts of counter-accusation and retaliation arise.

20   He reports 'suspicious characters', and hostile acts on the part of neighbours and tradesmen to the police.

21   He may consult a lawyer to redress the wrongs which are being done to him.

22   He may take to flight and disappear suddenly from the place where he lives. The pressure may mount until he counter-attacks with sudden and unprovoked violence.

23   Society takes counter-action aggressively, and, so far as he is concerned, proves his point that they have been against him all along.

24   From this point admission to a mental hospital is not far distant.

THE TREATMENT OF PARANOID ILLNESSES

There is no fully adequate psychiatric answer to this problem. Whether, within psychiatry, we are now more hopeful, or remain sceptical about the value of treatment, this is no reason for pastoral scepticism, since the therapy of word and sacrament and fellowship has rarely been attempted with any conviction of its relevance. One reason for the ineffectiveness of psychiatric treatment in these cases is that they come for it too late. The delusions are often of long standing and so have become fixed for months or years before the psychiatrist is called in, as the last person the paranoid patient wishes to see. He can only accept the implications of his need for psychiatry by surrendering his main defensive bastions of denial and projection. He would have to admit that 'the fault is in me, not in them'. The tranquillizers alone are of limited usefulness. Unless the person recommending them has a warm and reliable relationship with the patient, the medicine will probably be rejected as poison. Only those can hope to gain the patient's agreement to a course of medical treatment who have first of all proved themselves to be good friends. The treatable problem is the loss of social well-being. The task of the parish, not of the vicar alone, should be the active ascertainment of all middle-aged and elderly people who have slipped out of reach of human concern. The second part of the task is to provide them with consistent befriending. In the context of such a parish, not only would the liability to paranoid personality development be minimal, but those who had a heavy genetic weighting or psychological predisposition to the disease, or both factors together, would be discovered early enough for the tranquillizers and active group therapy to produce their best effects. If they can be treated within the community, much is to be gained. Except in the severe cases, mental hospitals can give them nothing that the community ought not to develop its ability to give. They are helped by a regime of drugs, the tranquillizers, to diminish the tendency for primitive psychotic material to press up into consciousness. These drugs can be given just as well by the general practitioner as by the psychiatrist. What is of paramount importance concerns the well-being of the patient as a person in his own right and in the community.

SUPPORTIVE PSYCHOTHERAPY

The aim of supportive psychotherapy is to help the patient generally to improve the quality of his relationships. Because it is not 'deep' in terms of intellectual psychoanalysis of the unconscious, it is often called 'superficial'. This, I think, begs the question. St Paul's opinion that 'knowledge without love is empty', though not shared by rationalist analysts, seems to be shared by the patient. He regards love as 'deeper' than knowledge.

The paranoid patient is lonely. He has been searching in vain for someone who will accept him, without derision or mockery, without contradicting him flatly, and with true and inner understanding.

No ordinary person will accept him *with his delusions*. The mere fact of sharing his delusions with any ordinary person means that he has lost their trust, confidence, and acceptance. The ordinary person recoils from one who can hold firmly such peculiar ideas. He ceases to be any good as a friend. Both the psychiatrist and the parson are able to accept a patient with his delusions, understanding something of the psychodynamics of their origin. They have learned that a little training and experience enables them to keep up as good a relationship with the psychotic person as with many neurotics. The parson has a further inner need to accept this lonely and deluded person because he is one of the particularly lost individuals for whom Christ has made him responsible.

The natural defence against the paranoid position is '*double orientation*'. This is a form of dissociation which, while unable to do other than recognize the subjective reality of the primary delusion, attempts to conceal it and to go on acting as though it has never happened. There are some acute cases of paranoid reaction, as, for instance, after an accident, operation or sudden debilitating illness, in which the paranoid features disappear spontaneously within a few weeks without treatment. A patient after operation may feel quite convinced that fellow patients in the ward, or nursing staff, are playing tricks on him of an unfriendly kind. The combination of anaesthetic, shock, and both pain and exhaustion, can so deplete the mental energies that there is not sufficient left for repression. Yet within a few days of the operation this energy may be fully restored and the paranoid episode is forgotten. In this case the process of double orientation is in use temporarily, but the completeness of repression makes it no longer necessary after a few days or weeks.

Where, however, the primary paranoid delusional episode occurs in the normal course of life, it usually indicates a long wearing-down of psychological resistance. Once this has emerged it is seldom possible to repress it completely. All that can be done is to *make the delusional experience relatively unimportant in the total economics of the personality*.

It is quite impossible to argue the paranoid patient out of his delusion by vigorous dismissal. He cannot deny the subjective reality of the primary delusion, which still seems to him to be an illumination, a clarification. So we have really no alternative in treatment but to extend the process of double orientation. Our task is to help the person to accept the primary delusion as indeed a fact of his own infantile experience, and dissociate from it the subsequent delusions of explanation. Indeed, if he can accept the primary delusion as something which could and did happen to him, there is no need to employ the delusions of explanation by which he has attributed these persecutory feelings to hostile forces outside himself.

Direct interpretation of the subjective disordered thinking

There is a great difference between analytic uncovering of the kind that goes on in free association sessions on the analytic couch, and the '*distributive analysis*' which confines itself to the data presented by the patient himself, and his symptoms. There are here many symbolisms of the unconscious which are bizarre and puzzling. They cannot be other than threatening and disturbing to the patient. It makes a great deal of difference to him if, in very simple language, it can be explained to him how, in the course of a not very unusual infancy, these kinds of thoughts and fantasies could arise, only to be walled up at once in the catacombs of memory.

Many people have never expected that any proof of this psychological process would emerge in their own lives. They find it hard to imagine that so devastating an experience could possibly have lain undiscovered within them for so long. Yet this is a common enough hypothesis nowadays which intelligent people have little difficulty in accepting. If the doctor or clergyman cannot, in a simple psychodynamic framework of understanding, 'accept' the patient's delusory world, he prevents the patient from 'accepting' it also. The contrary intention may be a commonsense one, to force the patient to repress the delusory experience and a fear lest by accepting it as in a sense real and relevant, the patient, in talking about it, should become more fixed in his delusion. This does not happen. Until some counsellor has taken the trouble to explain how the strange subject-matter of the primary delusion could arise out of that period of mental life in the first year which is so difficult for an adult to understand, the patient can only feel uneasy that such bizarre material emerged from his own mind. But when the genesis of such strange fantasies is comprehended, the patient already feels less 'like a lunatic' and more like a human person. He no longer feels a compulsive need to tell other people these strange thoughts about himself and others. He is content to have told them to one person who has understood and made sense of them. He realizes the importance of not acting on the delusion, which increasingly he can separate out from his normal perceptions. Double orientation is established and the rational elements, backed up by the new secure relationship, can maintain control.

Any group of abnormal symptoms within oneself is much more acceptable when they have been collected together into a diagnosis, named, identified, and in a sense taken possession of through the powers of comprehension. So the counsellor must first make it clear to the paranoid patient that he does not in the least doubt the primary experience. In fact, he is interested to learn more about it and to accept it fully, as a record of something which, however at present unacceptable and surprising, once happened. Once this understanding has been firmly established and a relationship made between the counsellor and the patient which includes him with his delusions, a new source of ontological strength has been opened which may carry the patient a long way on the road to ultimate social recovery. The ordinary person, doctor or clergyman, tends to approve of the paranoid patient only in so far as he is prepared either to forget or not to mention the delusory material. In theological terms, he is prepared to 'justify', to account as rightly related to himself, only the person who is prepared to prove himself worthy of acceptance by denying the reality, even on a subjective level, of a genuine part of his experience. This does not work towards mental health, or spiritual health, any more than any other form of hypocrisy or justification by works. The redemptive task is to accept a person as he is.

The menacing effect of paranoid reactions upon the therapist

The envy and jealousy which are the basic active emotions of the paranoid patient, and the basic position of inferiority, emptiness and powerlessness which he has denied to be the truth in his inward parts, make it almost insuperably difficult for him to acknowledge that he has to go to other people for help. Those who are persecuted by their bodies in hypochondriasis can go for help. Those who, in infancy, turned to andro-erotic fantasies may go for help to men. But a proportion of all those who crossed the margin into persecutory loss of well-being dealt with their predicament by grandiose fantasies of themselves as the source of all well-being. It is this narcissistic defence which makes the paranoid person so hard to help. He cannot surrender this defence without encountering mental pain of great intensity. He would have to meet the naked terror of emptiness. This he cannot do. His *envy* of the therapist's powers of well-being, which he may recognize could make him better, may be so strong that he would rather not be cured at all than concede the superiority, even in a technical sense, of the therapist to whom he had ostensibly gone for help. This paradoxical element in a paranoid patient will cut off his nose to spite his own face.

Schizoid patients are often too detached ever to ask for help, except in the most indirect way. This is not true of the paranoid person who is able to create a relationship and, up to a point, sustain it. He is bedevilled by the fierce conflict and ambivalence of love and hate which render both his passivity and his activity highly paradoxical and contradictory. He asks help from the therapist, but that help must never be an *ex gratia* gift of well-being. It is acceptable to the paranoid patient only if it can be represented as a restoration of his own inalienable or unjustly alienated rights. Whether on the natural or theological level, he has a compulsive resistance to the experience of 'sanctification, through grace, by faith'. Even when he takes to devotional exercises, he describes the miseries, diminishments, and weaknesses of human life as unreal. He seeks, in identification with states of blessedness, the restoration of the human *status quo*; even if he uses Christian words and sacraments he subtly distorts them to these self-inflationary ends. He finds it intolerably difficult to think of God's gift of himself, under all the forms of the Holy Spirit's operation, as arising purely out of the work of Jesus Christ, without any worth, merit, or right in himself. It is because the grace he receives is always misconstrued as something which is part of his entitlement that the pattern of his religious life is so hard and graceless, sour and ungracious, cold and ungrateful. The persistence of envy and jealousy at high levels in the mind drives him to persecute fellow Christians who do not accept his point of view, with much more venom than he treats the world.

Absolute openness and 'undefensiveness' are the required therapeutic attitude. The therapist, therefore, should not himself be a 'paranoid' person on the defensive, shielding his own inadequacies behind this or that rationalization or professional qualification. Our greatest adequacy is to rest back into God with a sense of our own utter inadequacy. With this paradox clearly rooted at the centre of our being, there is no reason why the assaults of the paranoid patient should do other than make us lean harder upon those personal resources of well-being which Christ dispenses to us in his word, in the sacraments, and in the fellowship. We know that all we ever bring to him is our emptiness. For this reason, the Christian is particularly able to meet the paranoid person right behind all his defensive barriers, projective accusations, and proud denials. The Christian is one who has admitted his own hunger and thirst for right-relatedness to the sources of being and well-being. He does not share the common human illusion that it is disgraceful not to be able to cover up one's own deficiencies. It is because he knows he is in want that he can say with quiet conviction, 'The Lord is

my Shepherd, I shall not want'. Conscious of thirst and weakness
he looks to the Shepherd for sustenance, saying, confidently, 'He
maketh me to lie down in green pastures, He leadeth me beside the
still waters, He restoreth my soul.' He can take a walk through the
valley of the shadow of death, in which schizoid position he fears
no evil, because the Shepherd is with him. He is able to affirm that
even in the cruel emptiness which lies behind the paranoid position,
he remains confident. He can say of his Shepherd, 'Thou preparest
a table before me in the presence of mine enemies: Thou anointest
my head with oil; my cup runneth over. Surely goodness and mercy
shall follow me all the days of my life; and I will dwell in the house
of the Lord for ever.'

This clear-sightedness about his own emptiness means that the
pastor need offer no defensive dissimulations to the paranoid
patient. He can be scrupulously honest, truthful and steadfast. We
must remember that the paranoid person has regressed, so that, in
fact, he is aware, as the infant is at this stage to which he has
regressed, very much more of the non-verbal symbols of communication than he is of words themselves. With no group of patients
is it so important to give them undivided attention and a direct
confrontation as from countenance to countenance. One needs to
put oneself unreservedly at God's disposal to be put unreservedly
at theirs. There is something in the keen suspicious look of a paranoid patient which reminds a man of all his spiritual unprepared-
ness, of sins and shortcomings, which, under that penetrating stare,
seem to be placarded on an open screen in front of him.

This is a world in which the Son of God is standing inviting
thirsty men to come to him to drink, hungry men to feed on the
bread of God which has come down from heaven, to be filled with
all the graciousness of the Holy Spirit of God's presence in our
hearts. The whole attitude of mind of the paranoid person is so
fixated upon fantasy sources in himself or in other infantile objects
that he cannot fail to persecute Christ before he comes to terms
with him. How Christ meets his predicament upon the cross we
shall see. Meanwhile, it is only sensible to recognize that the pastor,
who in his shepherding work speaks on behalf of the Good
Shepherd, is going to receive the brunt of the persecution first. The
pastor has great need, therefore, to be identified with the attitude
of mind which characterizes our blessed Lord upon the cross. He
must be identified with a sense of emptiness and incapacity.
However strong and vital his human sources of well-being are, they
peter out in the waste lands of paranoid aridity. The paranoid
patient needs to be filled with the very life of God, poured out richly

through all the means by which the graciousness of God in Christ is convenanted to his people. Only the pastor who is, in that moment, experiencing a quiet restfulness of abiding in Christ, for his infilling and overflowing, can speak with quiet assurance of this as the reality which the patient needs, above all, to know.

Christ's approach to men did not sweep them off their feet with the ebullience of his personality. He was characterized by humility and meekness. Meekness is constituted by great powers held in deliberate limitation and reserve. Those who possess well-being from the Holy Spirit are not characterized by effusiveness, gush, or excessive exuberance of the kind which makes others feel their poverty acutely. The paranoid person is suspicious of the affectation of ebullience. He has demonstrated that superior act too often himself. He is cautious in the presence of too much heartiness or warmth, because he suspects its genuineness with good reason. He has enough defensiveness about him to be afraid of too rapid an assumption of closeness and intimacy. He needs someone who is prepared to respect the proper distances between human beings and only to enter behind the barriers of reserve when he is invited to do so.

The position of the pastor of the small and gathered congregation does not present the same problem as the incumbency of a large parish in the Church of England. The minister and his wife may be able to befriend people on the edge of social isolation in such a way as to bring them back to the full enjoyment of social life. This may be possible for many Anglican clergy whose parochial charge numbers less than two thousand. When you begin to number his parochial population in terms of five, ten or even twenty thousand, it is obvious that he can befriend only a small proportion of those who need befriending. The ability of the local Church to provide befriending then depends upon the extent to which the members of the congregation have been fired with the importance of befriending. There are two tasks here, first that of discovering who in the congregation is prepared to give time to the simple human task of befriending, and secondly, the discovery of the old people who are slipping away from social contact.

Fatigue states, exhaustion reactions, and asthenia or neurasthenia
It is desirable to include a further group of conditions in this same broad category, not exactly of the paranoid, but of the original fixated depletion of well-being itself, against which there are several lines of defence. If possible, when impending breakdown compels the mind to admit its inner insolvency, the whole débâcle is not

revealed at once. Attention is paid compulsively only to one aspect of the whole wretched experience. We see this happening not only in hypochondriasis, but in the fatigue states or exhaustion reactions, or, as they are sometimes called, the asthenic reactions, and also in what used to be commonly diagnosed as neurasthenia.

These are partially substitutive defence mechanisms which pay attention to a part of the repressed experience as if it were the whole. To this unconsciously selected sector of painful experience an overwhelming attention is given. It is watched suspiciously, always with the assumption that it is out to make further inroads into the patient's diminishing sense of well-being. It leads to intro-spective self-scrutiny. There is a corresponding withdrawal from full mature involvement in tasks calling for self-giving and for invest-ment of interest and energy outside the self-system. They tend to be regressive reactions, promoting immature responses, neurotic limitations and chronic deterioration of social responsiveness, with all that arises from curtailed interpersonal involvement. All the fruits of the spirit wither on this sapless tree.

We may briefly distinguish these three patterns of inadequate defensive reaction to fixated internal malaise, or sub-total loss of well-being.

1   *Hypochondriasis*: which pays attention to the physical symptoms still going on in the unconscious mind, most inadequately repressed.

(a) To the general level of health and strength, which, it is fearfully noted, are in a state of decline.

(b) To the imagined onset of organic disease, based on the pessi-mistic misinterpretation of minimal functional symptoms in terms of slowly fatal diseases.

(c) To the symbolic expression of internal conflicts, which, in terms of infantile fantasy are still taking place in the body cavity, and localized in various bodily organs.

2   *Fatigue states, exhaustion or asthenic reaction*: in which the patient constantly has his attention drawn to the sapping away of inner resources of energy so that he is perpetually tired, too easily fatigued, or exhausted in marked disproportion to the amount of work done.

3   *Neurasthenia*: in which the debilitated person draws his own and other people's attention to a chronic sense of weakness, of emotional fatigue, social inadequacy and inferiority, of poor atten-tion to work and to the lack of any sense of status or achievement which afflicts him, or her. Here there is also a selection of physical

symptoms expressing weakness, loss of muscle tone and power, poor appetite and flatulent indigestion, often constipation, a fast and feeble-seeming pulse and generalized nervous irritability.

A proportion of those who suffer from these conditions have a constitutional basis which renders them more susceptible to infantile loss of well-being. They grow up to be thin, rather drooping individuals to whom one might instinctively give the term 'weedy'. But so very many patients complain of these syndromes who are not at all of this physical type that we are forced to the conclusion that early environmental causes are more important than constitution alone.

In speaking of a *fatigue state* we obviously do not mean that someone feels very tired after hard work. This refers to a neurotic reaction in which the degree of weakness, fatigue, and exhaustion experienced subjectively is disproportionately greater than it should be in view of the amount of physical or mental work that has been done. This is a syndrome very commonly observed in general practice and in pastoral visitation. To the doctor the patient will probably speak of the weariness of her body, to the clergyman she is more likely to speak of the weariness of her soul or of her spirit.

Neurasthenia, a condition characterized by chronic fatigue, mental, emotional and physical, was a very common diagnosis twenty years ago, stretching back to the years after 1869 when the term was first introduced in the United States by Beard. It was then thought of as 'nerve weakness' or 'nervous exhaustion'. No one has ever been able to show that there was anything wrong with the nerves themselves. The fault is with the spirit that uses them. The term 'neurasthenia' is now not frequently used. This does not mean that the patients who used to be included in this too-wide and indefinite term have ceased to present themselves. There are still many people attending the doctor who are feeling 'run down' and begging for 'a good strong tonic'. Many people know what it means to be in 'poor spirits', without being able to pinpoint an adequate present cause.

The psychodynamic background to fatigue states and hypochondriasis is varied. We have already noted the *hypochondriacal symptoms* which can arise as part of the depressive illness. Although the rage has become unconscious and is turned upon the self, it exerts a direct influence upon the heart, the blood-vessels, the lungs and the intestinal tract, to prepare them for the aggressive action which seems to be required.

The particular variety of hypochondriasis we are now concerned with is that which expresses an inner sense of extreme loss of well-being, with oppressive emptiness and revulsion against forces which have become persectory in their refusal to give what is required. The hypochondriasis in this case is closely associated with the concepts of neurasthenia and fatigue states. In these three closely associated conditions patients personify themselves as having been weakened, damaged, prostrated, spent. The symptoms are reported on in such a way as to put the blame on the physical body or on the social 'body'. The expression, 'I've got to watch my digestion, my bowels, or, more generally, my strength' expresses the alert scrutiny characteristic of paranoid defences. Or the adjective used may be 'weak'. 'It is my weak heart, or back, or nerves'. When a piece of work has been performed, 'It has over-taxed me', 'After today I just feel wrung out'. Either in a general physical, mental or emotional sense, or in relation to a particular organ, there are openly declared feelings of being 'enfeebled', 'squeezed out', 'limp', 'weak as a kitten'.

No clear dividing line exists between these three states expressing a severe loss of well-being on the one hand, and depression on the other hand, which expresses also the results of intrapsychic conflict. The reason for this is plain when we look again at the psychodynamics of depression. While the central focus of psychodynamic conflict in depression is the rage or other aggressive emotion turned back upon the self by the super-ego, condemning and restraining violent emotions, the invariable effect of this double unproductive expenditure of mental energy is to diminish the normal output of good spirits. But the root cause of the rage was impending loss of being itself, or of the hate, was impending loss of well-being. The anxiety and fear thus aroused go towards the forceful restraint of all aggressive impulses.

In whatever way 'being' and 'well-being' are lost at Phase 1 or Phase 2 of the cycle, the net effect at Phase 3, in diminished ontological status and spiritual output, is much the same. Nevertheless, the characteristic symptoms of depression, which stem from the autonomics of rage and hate, namely the black mood, the neurotic guilt and self-reproach, the characteristic sleep difficulties, and the symptoms arising out of the autonomic preparations for fight, are specific to the depressive disturbance and are not present in these much more passive states. Here the mood is not black but grey and pallid. The blame is not put squarely upon the self but is spread much more widely on to others and on to the body as distinct from the self. Sleep is often prolonged, though it will not be refreshing, and the autonomic nervous system expresses only exhaustion, not rage or panic. The symptoms common to depression and the triad associated with loss of well-being are fatigue, exhaustion, reduction of psychic productivity and facility, a dull imagination, impoverishment of ideas and associations, the loss of concentration, the reduction of commitments, the increase of egotistical and the diminishment of outgoing concern; the loss of proper mental distancing and perspective and a general loss of good spirits. In both there is a desire for a long, long, long rest.

We may note, in passing, that there is a total lack of correlation between a patient's degree of complaint and the actual degree of pain and suffering so far as this can be objectively estimated. All life is estimated subjectively. To some of us, all the work we do is so enjoyable that we would be prepared to call it all 'a paid holiday'. There are others, suffering from this triad of complaints, to whom all the work they do feels like 'unpaid overtime'. The subjective determination that any particular piece of work is, or is not, exhausting cannot be predicted. To many of our patients the day's work at the office is less tiring than an evening at home. To others, it is exactly the opposite. Some people can actually regard the work they are paid to do as so interesting and exciting as to be a recreation and a pleasure. The same person may truthfully report on the result of an evening out with his wife in the social round as a duty which has exhausted him. The opposite may be the case. To some, the ability to turn from hard mental work which has produced subjective exhaustion to engage in the kind of energetic physical activity which would exhaust others, is for them actually a source of psychic energy rather than an expenditure of it. It all depends which way you look at it.

The subjective valuations and gradations by which social and bodily experiences are judged to be either pleasurable or painful depend upon the point at which the dynamic cycle of infantile relationships incurred traumatic interruption. As we have seen, certain people, having been stressed into separation-anxiety as far as the hysterical position, lost the courage ever to stand alone. Consequently, enforced separation from those upon whom they can depend is now experienced as exhausting. Others were stressed farther down this road into the schizoid position. This so shattered their capacity to trust that they lost the courage ever to be as an integral part of a bonded interpersonal relationship. As a result, they find themselves exhausted by any situation of enforced social commitment. Social bonds they experience as bondage. Depressive persons are exhausted by compulsive dependence on those who, by unjustly failing to appreciate their efforts, drive them to inner strangulated rage. Still others, and here we come to the category at present under consideration, were most hurt in infancy when their expected supplies of well-being and sustenance failed them. They are excessively exhausted by any contemporary situation which, being fed into the unconscious mind, is interpreted as a repetition of the traumatic infantile pattern. Whenever the quality of his dependent relationships becomes inadequate, whenever he is exposed to ungracious dealing, whenever his physical, emotional, or spiritual sustenance is painfully diminished, or whenever the demands made upon him for an output of physical, emotional, or spiritual energy are excessive, he will, under all these conditions, register the whole gamut of experiences appropriate to the original infantile situation. He will express this identification with emptiness and inferior supplies either through a fatigue state, a neurasthenic reaction, or in hypochondriacal self-concern.

When a person in this category of fixated ontological depletion says, 'I'm tired', he means 'I'm tired with the tiredness which has always been part of me'. However, when a depressed person says 'I'm tired', he may mean this, but he also means 'I'm tired of bottling up rage'. When an hysterical person says 'I'm tired' this probably means that nobody is paying attention. When a schizoid person says 'I'm tired', he may mean that too many people are paying unwelcome attention. The paranoid person, who represents the first category in the state of defending against and denying this inner fatigue and emptiness, when *he* says, if he deigns to do so, 'I'm tired', he means just this. He also gives expression to the further fatigue he shares with all who are not only empty themselves, but are wasting energy proudly denying the fact. They use up inner energy upon envy, hatred and jealousy, on which they must spend more energy keeping them under cover.

There are other psychological conflicts, characterized by fatigue, which may lead to neurasthenia-like hypochondriacal reactions. We find them, for instance, in those children who have been the focus of *excessive maternal concern about health*. The mother who is herself hypochondriacal tends to produce a hypochondriacal child. The infant has absorbed her fearful, inadequate and inglorious spirit. This may express itself physically in prognostications of disaster should he get wet feet, or climb trees, or even accept hospitality in other homes. Such a mother expresses, more clearly than any words could, her desire to retain the child in a dependent status. Even as an adult this mother's child will still retain her cautions about this and that as though they were the last word. 'Mother said I would never be able to do a full day's work.' 'Mother said I would never be able to do without someone to look after me.' Such persons are compelled to live identified with emptiness, inferiority, and meaninglessness. Either they repress their normal desires to grow up to be mature adults, or, going against the maternal or paternal prophecy, they branch out, feeling like dare-devils, to do the things ordinary people do without turning a hair. But they are exhausted by the conflict. While continuing to struggle on with the normal targets of the contemporary life situation apparently in their sights, they are unconsciously striving to return, for safety's sake, in order to please Mother or do what Father said, back into a state of dependency. This unconscious striving for dependency and the mental pain of the conflict may well be expressed as a fatigue state, neurasthenia, or hypochondriasis.

Some pastoral considerations

Whatever the spiritual physician proposes to do for these sufferers, either on the general pastoral level of common prayer, preaching, ministering the sacraments, in worship and fellowship, or by direct pastoral intervention, linking the self-emptying of Christ on his cross to the identical ontological situation in the patient, certain basic considerations ought to be borne in mind. If they are not, the parson's diligent inquiry into the rise and fall of the neurasthenic or hypochondriacal symptoms will merely increase the importance and fixity of the symptoms in the patient's mind and shut it to all possibility of being helped by Christian resources. Here are a few important considerations:

1 *Bear in mind what these conditions basically are.* We think that the basic psychodynamic position is a fixed, repressed, infantile experience of identification with severe loss of well-being, emptiness, sometimes hunger predominating, sometimes thirst, at others emotional exhaustion, emptiness of any infused graciousness from the mothering source. The whole dependency relationship has become meaningless. A chronic sense of inferiority results with extremely low self-esteem.

2 Bear in mind that this primitive experience has *destroyed trust in the source-persons*. Since this occurs first in the pre-transitional phase of identification, not only is trust in the source-person destroyed, but in the infant itself, and in the spirit which is the product of their union. This produces feelings of social inferiority, of being easily tired of people, of having poor staying-power in relationships, of being unable to go on with friendships when things are hard. It has also destroyed trust and receptivity of that which 'goes between' in good relationships, the *spirit* of the friendship, the family, the meeting, the doctor–patient, pastor–parishioner

relationship, or the fellowship of the Church of God. Paranoid, neurasthenic, and hypochondriacal people do not recognize, perceive, benefit from or feel grateful for the 'good spirit' in a social gathering in the way normal persons do. Preoccupation with their own emptiness, with its denial and restitution mechanisms, forces them into a state of non-receptivity of all spiritual resources that are 'in the air'.

The true hypochondriac, though he will try every cure for his symptom that he can afford, remains, on the whole, obstinately unhelpable. Whenever a wise programme of general management of his life situation is presented, he tends to say, at the end, 'That is most valuable and interesting, doctor, but what about my symptoms?' In the hierarchy of his concern, priority is given to the symptom. Therefore, no therapeutic measure which, as counsellor, you know does not go to the root of the matter, should ever be recommended with unqualified enthusiasm. The patient coming to you as 'the last resort' has already had as many last resorts as he has had professional helpers. Though apparently he trusts your references, actually he distrusts you as deeply as he was secretly given to distrust the depriving parent. Therefore, make realistic claims for what you offer and do not minimize the difficulties within this particular personality when it comes to accepting any kind of help.

3   Bear in mind *the destructive emotions* which these persons, as a result of the psychodynamics of infancy, are apt to carry within them. *Hate*, which would destroy the source-person with the utmost energy, if any energy remained, often with fantasies of clawing, tearing, venomous malice. *Envy*, which takes pyrrhic pleasure in vanquishing all those who set out to be able to help. *Jealousy*, which would rather not be helped by you the pastor or by the doctor, if this has the humiliating recognition that you give your help just as much to other people. Rather than tear you to bits, the jealous patient will decline your help. *Greed*, which could swallow up all available supplies you could offer with little regard for natural justice or the limitations of a reasonable demand.

A devaluation mechanism for any help that is given. This mental instrument in these patients gives consistently false readings in a diminishing direction. It has a bias towards the negative, 'It's no good, it never was any good, it never will be any good.' It invariably degrades the warmth, the genuineness, the friendliness, the openness, the outgoingness, the honesty, of every relationship that is offered. Ordinary relationships of professional care conducted professionally seem to the patient to be cool, insincere, unfriendly.

Even the saint will have attention drawn to his clay feet. Nothing less than Christly love and sanctity stands a chance. It is not enough to offer, as Christ did to the Pharisees, who out of envy had him crucified, the bread and water of life freely. You, too, have (and not so metaphorically speaking) to let the client 'crucify' you before there is much hope that he will take you seriously.

4   Bear in mind that *the symptoms are only partly expressing the full experience of the emptied, weakened, and persecuted self.* The symptom is only a trickle of water forcing its way through the underwater plates of a ship. The concern of the sailor is not really on account of this trickle, though his eyes may be riveted upon it and he may so express himself. His concern derives from his knowledge that there is infinitely more of this same threatening liquid outside, waiting, in an almost hostile fashion, for a further weakening of the rivets so that it can rush in and sink the boat. Hypochondriacal concern with the symptom has much in common with the situation of the inadequate sailor. He may be so obsessed by the leak that he will take no steps towards getting the ship into port, where the leak could be attended to. Fascinated and paralysed by fear, he watches the symptom, suspicious of every sound, every moment, lest it should presage the final rending apart of the protective defences and the end of all things. So, do not show ignorance and insensitiveness by dismissing the symptom with mockery as a trivial matter.

5   The sexual elements do not need to be emphasized in pastoral care. We do not regard the sexual as primary or causal in these conditions, as Freud did.

In all these states of intolerable weakness, the genital area becomes the object of the same solicitous concern, because of the pain it suffers, as does the stomach, because of its painful emptiness, or the whole person, because of his utter exhaustion. As a result, the build-up of genital tension which accompanies any adolescent or adult state of lowered self-esteem cannot be brought to a head into orgasm, within a true marital relationship, in such a way as to be healthfully discharged. Masturbation in such men leads to fatigue and neurasthenic feelings. Yet if the practice is stopped abruptly without solution of the ontological problem, the tension may be distributed throughout the body and mind as an anxiety neurosis. The pastoral approach is primarily through the improvement of the dynamics of being and well-being within relationships rather than through any specific attention to the psychoanalysis of sexuality.

6   Turning again to the hypochondriacal element, there are important symbolic meanings in the symptoms which we should

bear in mind. 'Bear in mind' is the correct expression. The proper time to offer to the sufferer, as direct interpretations, these now hidden meanings may not arrive for many weeks or months. In a few patients, whose symptom does not yet dominate the mental field and in whom psychological space is reasonably present, the interpretation may with value be offered at once.

How are we to understand these reiterated complaints against 'my troublesome stomach', 'my weak bowels,', 'my tired heart', 'this sore back', 'this sluggish liver', 'this bad head'. We may use the unconscious equation, the affected organ = the introjected parental relationship. If, for instance, the relationship 'weakened', 'exhausted', 'emptied' the infant of all strength and spirit to carry on with life, so now the affected organ does all these things against and within the self. If the relationship was 'painful', 'troublesome', 'sore', 'agonizing', 'creasing', so now is the chosen organ. If the relationship 'let you down', 'left you limp', 'nearly killed you', 'crippled you', 'sickened you', 'left you washed up', 'did you an injury', all this is expressed as being true of the 'diseased' organ. If the relationship was so cruel and persecutory that you had to watch it suspiciously and set it over against you under constant scrutiny, waiting until it 'got you again', this has to be expressed in relation to the suspected organ.

The pastor who bears these things in mind will be preserved from the foolishness of paying undue attention to the symptom. His thoughts will be deeply grounded in ontological realities, both the neediness of the patient and the resourcefulness of God.

7   Pastoral care will bear in mind that in all this triad of 'actual neuroses', associated with fixated infantile experiences of severe loss of well-being, *the onset of the illness is always characterized by:*

(a) *Gradual withdrawal of interest and investment of energy and attention from the outside world of persons and things.*

(b) *Gradual investment of interest and attention on some inward aspect of the self*, on the general feelings or on some particular organ. This is called *narcissism*, after Narcissus who gazed at himself in the pool. To the extent that this inward gaze has become chronic and intractable the patient is very difficult to help. He is impossible to help by exhortation to do his duty by looking outward again. He is able only to look inwards. But this he does only guardedly and incompletely. This incomplete inward look is compulsive. If the pastor can so understand the situation as to look with the sufferer inwards to the root of the problem, without arousing too much anxiety, there is some chance that the sufferer will 'stay with' the pastor. A certain amount of anxiety is inevitable whenever the truth

in the inward parts is being approached. Before it can be understood, absorbed and tolerated back in consciousness and full experience, there is bound to be a good deal of anxiety. We know that
Christ is waiting to meet this person, not in some hypothetical place
where they are not but in the very heart of their pain and emptiness.
The crucial pastoral question is, how and when can these facts be
genuinely communicated at the level of the sufferer's experience,
which cries out for valid answers and resources?

(c) *A marked loss of extraversion with an increased fixed introversion.*
Many clergy and doctors regard all introversial mental activity as
bad. The terror which we have of any 'delving' or 'probing' indicates
our own inability to face the truth in the inwards part as it threatens
to emerge in ourselves or in others. As it occurs in narcissism, we
can describe this introversial effort as a miscarried effort at finding
oneself. Narcissus will never discover himself by looking at his own
reflection in the water. He must look up into the eyes of a friend,
who alone can become a source of personal being. A genuine item
of undeniable experience of life lies hidden at the deep centre of the
patient's mind. Before he can accept life trustfully again, he feels
that this intolerable experience, which has returned partly into
consciousness, must be explained and accounted for. He senses,
without possibility of contradiction, that once he was so involved
in a cruel, fear-ridden world as to be shaped by it at least in one,
until recently quite hidden, aspect of his being. To pretend that the
question had never arisen would be to build the rest of his life on
a trap-door with all hell beneath it.

The deepest need, therefore, in these sufferers from the 'actual
neuroses' is not less introversion but more and better introversion.
They need to be strengthened in courage and spiritual resolution
by every possible consideration of truth. The truth of the débâcle
in the nursery can be matched by the truth of the débâcle on the
cross. Only through the acceptance of the fact of an historical
moment of horrible weakness can the sufferer cease to be identified
with it. Attempts by exhortation to produce cheerful extraversion,
'Don't be so damned self-centred, old chap. You need more outside
interests, my lad', now appear stupid, if only because they do not
work and further alienate the sufferer. Christian introversion is
properly the Holy Spirit's 'conducted tour' of each man's nether
world. Fortified by Christ, known and trusted in the extraversial
world of word and sacrament and fellowship, which keeps Christ
in view, the introversial exploration becomes an act of obedience,
not of curiosity. The sufferer goes down into his own private hell

in order to find that Christ, crucified and risen, comes into view again as Lord when all human help and light is gone.

(d) *Regression*, which is taking place in all these sufferers. That is to say, the mind is becoming more at the mercy of the infantile point of view, influenced more by the emotions of the fixated remote past, and less by the realities of contemporary relationships. The patient becomes unrealistic, unadjustive, unresponsive to present-day demands and resources. This is not a therapeutic regression; it does no good. Therapeutic regression, which is the deliberate going back to encounter the forcibly forgotten elements so as to assimilate them into consciousness, would be valuable and is ultimately necessary.

(e) *A change in defensive mechanisms*. The older and more effective defence mechanisms of total denial, repression, and reaction pattern formation are falling away. They are replaced by an incomplete defence which partially affirms all that was previously denied, namely, the inner emptiness and weakness. Or, they are being replaced by substitutive mechanisms which, while still splitting off the brunt of the mental pain, admit it in the form of hypochondriasis or 'organ neurosis'. This humiliating inability to keep up the complete defence by denial involves the sufferer in a literally fearful loss of self-esteem. While the mechanism of projection still works in these sufferers, they are compelled to feel that those who are helping them also despise them. Feeling despised they attack the helper's self-esteem.

Somebody's self-esteem is going to suffer. The pastoral counsellor should have solved the problem of his own self-esteem before the cross, which utterly negates it, and at the same time, because of the gift which is given there, places the man in Christ beyond the reach of attacks on his status. Now, in Christ, he can afford to rejoice in confession. He does not need to defend against his inadequacies, because he is rejoicing in the constant renewal of resources of life from the Holy Spirit within, which are not his own.

Bearing in mind all these considerations, the pastoral counsellor will be in some senses less ready to give counsel or pastoral care, while in another sense more ready. He will not be hasty. He will recognize that the primary therapeutic agent is the spiritual relation-ship established not merely with himself but with the whole Christian fellowship. He will not, in his enthusiasm for the cure, lose contact with the person or break the rapport. Here, if anywhere, 'he that believeth shall not make haste'. *He knows that his task is to improve the sufferer's capacity to suffer more*. There is no cure in any of the methods which persuade the person that it is possible to suffer less. The *way of escape* which the gospel offers is precisely this, *'that you may be able to bear it'*.

THE WORD OF GOD IN THE CROSS OF CHRIST, AND ITS SPECIFIC THERAPEUTIC MESSAGE TO ALL THOSE WHO SUFFER FROM FIXATED EXPERIENCES OF SEVERE LOSS OF WELL-BEING

This almost total loss of sustenance on physical, emotional or spiritual levels is the core of the complex for a variety of suffering persons whose diagnoses include paranoid states, certain types of male homosexuality, marital and mothering difficulties in the woman, many cases of alcoholism, of delusional envy and jealousy, of erotomania and andro-eroticism, of the fatigue states, exhaustion or asthenic reactions, neurasthenia, and the hypochondriasis which centres on feelings of weakness, depletion, emptiness and of never being 'any good'. All such persons were identified with emptiness and meaningless early in the first year of life, and have remained so ever since, even though the sector of ontological experience which carries this threat of fixated, as yet unassimilated pain, has been for many years, with more or less success, kept out of consciousness by repression and other mental mechanisms of defence against it.

They have all undergone, in a state of utter passivity, an intolerable 'passion'. To be dependent, as absolutely as the baby is dependent upon the mother, on a source-person who is, for whatever reason, totally inadequate in some essential respect, whether of food or love, unable or unwilling, too ignorant or too selfish or too opinionated to give herself generously and graciously, is a cross and passion too heavy for infant shoulders to bear. They were, and still are, crushed by the experience and the fantasies based on it. While in one sense they have borne it, since its weight has crushed them down, in another sense they have never borne it, since there has never yet been a time when their spirit could stand up, erect, under the weight of it, or even bowed and staggering, in any way support it for themselves. Even as it was happening the too severe pain of it was being split off and by repression excluded from consciousness. Yet the personal centre of being remains indelibly related to this episode of agony. The heart of the person is always being borne or carried back to this experience of the manner of its earliest relationship with the most important of its relations – mother. But one cannot be ever related to such devilish suffering, nor tied to the one

at whose hands and by whose will it was endured. The mode of
this relationship is dis-relationship, and the lifelong attempt to
attain non-relationship to the one relation who can never honestly
be disowned, is highly paradoxical. Whoever or whatever claims to
have an answer to this problem must be of all things, paradoxical.

We have already taken up, both in the case of paranoid sufferers
and of those whose burden is one of the triad of 'organ neuroses'
or 'actual neuroses' the therapeutic factor of the fellowship. We
have seen how difficult it is for such people to accept from others,
the spiritual benefits or ontological resources of personal well-being
which those who are normally open to fellowship receive through
it. What other pastoral resources are there? No other resources
along this line, for our only resources are what we humanly are and
the grace and sustenance of God in Christ through the fellowship
they reject.

There are, however, other channels of communication of this
same grace and sustenance. God invites men to live by eating and
drinking His own life. Ontological analysis of the words of the Son
of God in St John's Gospel leaves no room for doubt about his
intention. 'Except ye eat of the flesh of the Son of God and drink
his blood, ye have no life in you.' 'I am the Bread of Life', of the
life of God himself. 'He that eateth me shall live by me.' Yet this
grace of well-being is not a food or a medicine which can be bought
and consumed like a bottle of wine or a stimulant pill. This longed-
for experience is inseparable from a personal fellowship with God,
inseparable from his call, inseparable therefore from man's whole-
personal response of faith and obedience, inseparable from all God's
ways of communicating his life and its abundance, namely the word,
the sacraments and the fellowship.

The centre of the Word of God to man, which is Christ in his
human and divine person, is the paradox of suffering and glory
which marked his life and three years of active ministry, and, most
potent of all, its culmination in his cross and passion, itself crowned,
but not exceeded in essential glory, by his resurrection and
ascension.

A paradox of suffering and glory. This is God's final word to
man about his own nature and destiny on earth. In order that no
mistaken attempts should be made to dissociate these two, as if the
suffering element could be alienated from man, as the ugliness he
should shun, the pain he should avoid, or the emptiness he could
abjure, Christ himself inseparably binds the suffering with the glory.
He does this in the most central act of his own person, both as Son
of God and representative man, in man, for man and towards

man. The preaching of the cross does not allow us to forget this reconciliation, within the divine order, of suffering and glory, which in the human order can never come to terms with one another.

Let us turn then to consider whether the word of God as it is spoken uniquely to the sons of want through the cross of Christ, telling of God's identification with just this extreme form of suffering, cannot 'get through' to the sufferer. If this can be done he will be enabled to accept and assimilate and bear for the first time the full load of suffering which lies within, waiting for him. *This inner cross can be accepted or rejected by the adult just as decisively as any piece of purely contemporary persecution.* In fact, there is no cross or persecution which leaves the adult so free as to whether he will or will not, for Christ's sake, bear it, as the pain of his own inheritance of repressed suffering. Not that the choice usually presents itself in that way. It is, in those who seem mentally healthy, normally incidental to some act of obedience to the Holy Spirit which 'goes against the grain' that the trap-door opens and the pain behind their protective defences is surprisingly revealed. Even when 'nervous breakdown' has forced upon us the partial recognition of our latent pain it still remains a free choice as to whether, to the glory of God in Christ, we bear it so that its end is good, or, recoiling, demand its palliation and a way of escape by *not* bearing it.

CHRIST, IN HIS CROSS AND PASSION, ENTERS INTO THE PRIVATIONS OF THE CHILDREN OF WANT

The question 'Why?' arises constantly from the lips of those who suffer in innocence. The sense of injustice constantly beats up against the rocks of faith. Christ was innocent. None of his judges could find any fault in this man. Yet he was outlawed before he was judged, condemned without trial, and cursed before he was dead. According to the law, there should have been a trial, followed, if the prosecution proved the case, by condemnation, followed by the punishment. The capital crime of blasphemy led to a violent death, by stoning. But here, the Roman punishment, crucifixion, ended the life of a man who had broken no Roman law. Only after death could the curse and the proclamation that a man was outlawed properly follow. This proceeding left a man who was too guilty for men to punish, to the vengeance of God. Pilate, Herod, and Caiaphas the high priest were all guilty of gross injustice. God, who is identifying his Son with those who suffer every kind of injustice, 'arranged' it that way. Even the common law and common justice were denied him. Those who are, or who are made, helpless continually suffer in this way.

At the same time he had to bear the curse of the guilty. He could not bear the curse of being abandoned to God's 'vengeance' on sin if he were already dead. It must all be suffered while he is still alive. The torment and the penalty of hell must come upon Christ while the life of man is still in him. Only so can he harrow hell, empty it of its terrors while still on *this* side of the grave. The Mosaic Law could do no more than say 'Cursed be every one who hangs on a tree'. The stoning of the accused is not bad enough for him. Stoning does not lift a man up, does not exhibit him to shame. Stoning is enough for those who break the law of Moses. They are killed by men among men. This is not cruel enough, not persecutory enough to express this universal injustice and judgement by which the Son of Man, being lifted up, repels all men from him, and draws all men, especially the unjustly rejected, to him.

Mockery: the pain to low-esteem, of being laughed at

The paranoid person cannot stand being laughed at. He takes himself 'terribly seriously'. Because he feels that life itself mocked at his infant needs, he is very sensitive to mockery.

Christ was mocked all the way from his first appearance in the courtroom to the moment when the darkness descended. The mockery of the small inhabitants of the microcosm, soldiers, priests, bystanders, and even passers-by, was stilled with the darkness. Then, the more terrifying mockery of the macrocosm took over. In this mockery of justice the Creator of Light was denied the light, at noonday. The King of Glory was wholly obscured. The Son appealed in perfect righteousness to the Father, who, because of the load he bore for God, turned away his face.

Christ shares with the defenceless, loss of strength and of all natural rights

All the strength of Christ, the strength of a young carpenter used to working and carrying wood, was drained away from him. He fell under the weight of the cross. He was too exhausted to carry his own cross with dignity. The Lord, who, a few days previously, as King, had requisitioned a donkey to ride into his capital city, who as Priest requisitioned a room for the covenant meal, now has all of his rights of requisition taken from him. A common soldier requisitions an African, a man who happened to be nearby, to come to his aid. Nothing is more humiliating to the infant than to feel that my rights in my mother and my rights in my father are contemptuously denied me. If a human being has no right to requisition anyone or lay claim to any help, he cannot continue to carry the burden of existence. There is no more humiliating circumstance to an old person than to realize that no natural bonds remain which entitle them to call upon a member of the family for help or even upon a neighbour. An anonymous stranger appears at the door by order of a local authority. So also was Christ humiliated.

So little were the rights of Christ respected that he had to see his clothes raffled away by the soldiers throwing dice under the cross. No magi here to bring costly gifts. No fish from the sea with the coin in its mouth to pay his taxes. No recognition of his right to any property at all, not even to his own coat and vest. This is how we treated the firstborn of God's creation, by whom he made the world. The paranoid person is scrupulously concerned about his rights. He cannot accept any diminishment at all. To all such, the Divine Son's relinquishment of every human right comes home, or ought to come home with force. The Spirit of Christ runs clean contrary to the paranoid's spirit, as it occurs, more or less, in all of us. He obeys his own Sermon on the Mount. He accepts personal injury without retaliation, property loss without reprisal, loss of liberty without forceful rejoinder.

All the common rights of man are taken away from him, bread and water and human companionship. He bears the curse of the unforgiven and the unforgivable, of intolerable isolation. He thirsts for the water of compassionate human friendship even more on Golgotha than in Gethsemane. But he does not appeal to any man. He undergoes the painful isolation of the accursed. The 'ends of the world' have come upon him. He is alone in catastrophe.

Shame of nakedness and of disgrace are shared by Christ

Intense feelings of inferiority, disgrace, shamefacedness, shyness, blushing, fear of exposure, all these are characteristic of the group of sufferers we have been studying. The paranoid person feels shame, both on account of his identification with emptiness and poor supplies, and because of the strange homosexual fantasies which may take the place of the normal sources. He feels as if everyone saw through into his inferiority and peculiarity. Women identified with poor breastfeeding feel an intense shame at the very fact of becoming or being breasted. Quite unreasonably, they feel their breasts to be hideously large or ridiculously small. They behave in company as though they were unclothed, as though everyone could see the shame of their nakedness. The boy or man who has suffered in this way has a similar sense of organ inferiority so severe that he will not bathe in public, or play games. The fantasies of strange things swallowed add to the confusion of face which they all are apt to feel.

All these feel a sense of shame and intense guilt at the thought of nakedness. The Bible always portrays the hell of those who 'go a-whoring after their own inventions' as a painful revelation of nakedness. For the normal person not moved by infantile exhibitionism, clothes are one of the common mercies, the older the person, the greater the mercy. With all these, innocent or guilty, Christ Jesus is identified in his nakedness. He hangs on the cross naked. Both the innocent who were not loved and the guilty who have spurned love are ashamed. Both have something to hide. Clothing is the symbol of hiding what we are ashamed to reveal. In his own innocence he is identified with the innocent in nakedness. In his identification with the guilty, he is stripped on their behalf, so that they may face their own guilt, not in front of one who mocks, but in One who hides shame with the cloak of his own righteousness. He was exposed as we should be, and will be, unless we lower our absurd pride to accept his offer of a covering for the shame of our deprivation and our depravity. He was so deprived of his natural clothing of transfigured beauty and glory that men, seeing him thus, shrank away from him. The whole world will see this same King appearing in all his beauty and glory, because he allowed both, in the service of the Word of God, to be utterly taken away.

Christ's descent into the hell of emptiness

Christ descended into the hell which is prepared for every infant for whom the mother will not or cannot give sustenance, either of the breast or of her love. (Of course, the bottle, if necessary, with mother's gracious love, is so adequate as to occasion no concern.) To have the mother turn away in dislike of her child is to smite its growing spirit in the face. It comes to know the quality of its own worth from the eyes and the voice of the mother. Contempt, disgust, fear, or mere disinterestedness, when written in the countenance of the mother as she faces her baby, cannot fail to produce in it the awful realization that in the very place where peace and love should be found, there is a thrusting away into outer darkness. The only hearth and home and bosom open to the child is closed. There is no other place of peaceful abiding open. To turn to the father as a substitute for the disgrace of being unloved by the mother is to grow up an inferior man, or an inferior woman. So it had to be with Jesus, before God himself.

Jerusalem, the city of God's peace, was Christ's own city. The priests and people of his own nation should have recognized, welcomed and worshipped him. Instead, as with those who suffer from human degradation, he is thrust out of Jerusalem, having already been thrust out of Israel. The priests drove him out as an unclean thing. It was expedient that one man should die as a scapegoat for the people. Infants suffer many hells because they are made the scapegoats of adult passions. So Christ suffered. He was thrown out as they are on to the dunghill of the world. What they must endure quite passively, he accepts in active passivity.

His disciples forsook him and fled. He was smitten on the face by a servant of the high priest. The Roman soldiers, about whom he had never said a critical word, smote him on the head and spat in his face. Centurions figured as good men in his ministry, but a centurion takes him away to be crucified. Even though at his cross the women stood with the apostle John, the descent of the darkness deprived him of the sight of them like a blow. Then, 'it pleased the Lord to bruise him. He hath put him to grief. He was bruised for our iniquities. Surely he hath borne our griefs, and carried our sorrows: yet we did esteem him stricken, smitten of God, and afflicted.'

Christ, the Water of Life, endures the unendurable thirst
Flogging, the crown of thorns, the tearing wounds in hands and feet, the bloody sweat of Gethsemane merging into the bloody sweat of Golgotha, chained him down to a fierce thirst under the midday sun. The offer of the drugged drink must have been a severe temptation to him. Among those addicted to drugs, especially to the amphetamines (the 'pep' pills) and alcohol, we have encountered many whose basic dynamic position is one of fixated exhaustion, emptiness of spirit and thirst. Christ knows the blinding force of their temptation to purchase oblivion.

Jesus had told a parable of a rich man in hell, begging for a drop of water to moisten his tongue. Now, the Lord is himself in hell. This is no parable. Nor is there any pride of stubbornness here. Christ acknowledges the kindly act, but when his taste recognizes the drug, he declines it. If this should be read by anyone suffering from the addiction to drugs or drink, he will know that if the spirit of this man can somehow be communicated to him, there is hope that the addiction will be broken. Nor does Christ's active, passionate spirit give expression to the eternity of thirst which those three hours contain until the work of redeeming identification was completed. 'After this, Jesus, knowing that all things were *now accomplished*, that the Scripture might be fulfilled, saith, "I thirst".'

Conclusion

It is a part, a difficult part, of pastoral care to know when and how this witness to the presence of Christ at the depths of mental pain should be given. Luther remarks: 'The Holy Spirit alone makes true preachers. If he does not do it, it is not done.' Of specific therapeutic 'preaching' to the paranoid, this is doubly true. For some time the pastor's task is to create a human relationship, if he can, getting to know the soil of the personality, and this introductory work must not be hastily or impatiently done. It does not, however, go on for ever. The moment does come, the right moment, in which the seed of the Word of God must be sown. Beyond all human skill and intuitive wisdom, the physician of souls must here be in living dependence on the Holy Spirit.

Those of us who are familiar with the resources available in psychiatry for this whole group of conditions associated with onto-logical weakness and persecutory states of mind are ready to recognize that they are far from adequate, never fundamentally curative, and inefficient as palliatives. Those of us who have worked for some years in clinical theology have become even more aware of our own utter helplessness in the face of these conditions. At the same time, we have learnt by experience that when faith in Christ Jesus animates the sufferer, it is invariably possible to arrive at a state of creative tension in which the law of the spirit of life in Christ Jesus begins to oppose the 'law of the mind', 'the law in the members', the law of psychological conditioning which constitutes the neurosis. The dictum of Kierkegaard that 'truth is a paradox' fits exactly here, for, with the chronic sense of emptiness there comes now an undeniable flow of good spirits; along with the weakness a new kind of strength; with inner or outer persecution a new and realistic power to take it joyfully; with the old feelings of inferiority a new ability to rest by faith on Christ's gift of divine sonship; along with the meaninglessness a new purpose for living; with the world-weariness a new zest for building the Kingdom here on earth as well as in heaven; accompanying the psychological sense of hunger and thirst a new and satisfying spiritual food; a transformation of the constant sense of uselessness by a new experience of being richly used to channel the resources of God to others. This coexistence of the 'body' of our humiliation and the 'body' which already has in it some of the powers of Christ's resurrected body, though it leaves us with painful longings, gives us also a sufficient foretaste of the future to guarantee the goodness of God in the last analysis.

8

Anxiety and Related Defensive Reactions

Anxiety takes its origin in the whole of a person in his social setting, and its effects and defensive responses are registered in every part of the body. Whatever may be the painful situation that is being repressed, it is as if it were still going on, and involving the whole person in an imminent threat of annihilation. Panic and dread at the horror of such a prospect are translated into the somatic and psychic expressions of palpitations, tightness round the chest, feelings of apprehension and other feelings as listed at the base of the diagram in Figure 12. These anxiety states of fixated primitive panic and dread are split off from consciousness by the defence mechanisms indicated by the items in the 'Repressive Layer' in the middle third of the diagram. For some people no whiff of this latent dread seems to have troubled them, even though the 'dreadful' rigidity of their defensive compulsions and personality patterns leads us to infer that dread is lying low. Others of us know of its existence as we remember childhood nightmares, and have them again in later life at times of stress or exhaustion.

Phobic reactions
It is useful to think of the phobic conditions as disorders of move-ment in relation to significant people or things. Broadly speaking the hysterical reaction, based on separation-anxiety, keeps the person rooted to the safe place, 'housebound' or 'tied to Mother'. As a disorder of movement it is an anxious inability to move away from people, even when not to move away curtails freedom of living. The schizoid personality disorder is basically a commitment-anxiety. The position of immobility is one of rigid isolation. If people attempting to make relationships come dangerously near to the schizoid person, he is compelled to move away and remain at a safe distance. As a phobic inability to move, we would say this is an inability to move towards people. For depressive personalities whose aggressive wishes have become dangerous so that they are denied, the aggression-anxiety is expressed in terms of a phobic inability to

move against people. Such immobility may persist to the extent of crushing all reasonable self-affirmation.

Behind these types of phobic reaction and the emotional paralyses of movement against, towards or away from persons to which they give rise, there lies a universe of infantile experience. The simplest to understand is the hysterical position. In this, panic rises due to separation from the personal source at a time of development which absolutely requires a constant personal source to be present. The fixated position is one in which the source of danger is seen as any situation where no human person is paying attention to me. Imagine you are a polio patient, paralysed from the neck down, able to swallow, but with no speech or movement even to beckon effectively. You are utterly at the mercy of the nurses and of your fears concerning their attentiveness to your needs. A baby has no more ability to change its circumstance than such a patient. Infantile fear is a fear that, since no one moves in to be near me, I am 'passing out' as a person, disintegrating under loss. However much the fear mounts, the infant can only *wish* to move against the bad non-caring source towards the good source, or away from the intolerably bad one. In actuality, the baby can effect no such movement. It can only cling when someone does come, or cringe if trust has been shattered.

In later infancy, when getting from place to place does become possible, the ego is compelled by the now buried and fixated fears, suffered passively, to act out the once-longed-for movements, which until now, have been but fantasy. So, in some cases, it would move against people aggressively, but this is dangerous and is suppressed by the super-ego, and thus it arrives at the depressive position. Most frequently, from its weak and passive infantile position, it has to cling to safety, avoid danger, and suffer all the time from its inability to move away into separateness. If there is more rage and ego strength, and the rages have been 'swallowed' along with the good experiences of objects and persons, a more active and sadistic pattern will result. This can result in the complexities of the obsessional phobias. Movement in these is grossly disordered with paradoxical checking and movement rituals.

The commonest of these patterns is the hysterical disorder of movement in relation to persons. In such a phobic sufferer the maximum fear is attached to any movement which takes the person away from the attentive person or prevents movement to safe places. This disorder of movement secondarily attaches itself to objects. This is because the infant, when unable to have whole-person experiences, calls fantasy to its aid and in imagination becomes

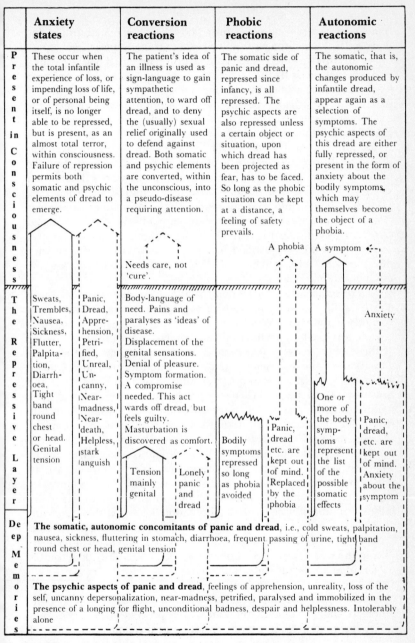

	Anxiety states	Conversion reactions	Phobic reactions	Autonomic reactions
Present in Consciousness	These occur when the total infantile experience of loss, or impending loss of life, or of personal being itself, is no longer able to be repressed, but is present, as an almost total terror, within consciousness. Failure of repression permits both somatic and psychic elements of dread to emerge.	The patient's idea of an illness is used as sign-language to gain sympathetic attention, to ward off dread, and to deny the (usually) sexual relief originally used to defend against dread. Both somatic and psychic elements are converted, within the unconscious, into a pseudo-disease requiring attention. Needs care, not 'cure'.	The somatic side of panic and dread, repressed since infancy, is all repressed. The psychic aspects are also repressed unless a certain object or situation, upon which dread has been projected as fear, has to be faced. So long as the phobic situation can be kept at a distance, a feeling of safety prevails. A phobia	The somatic, that is, the autonomic changes produced by infantile dread, appear again as a selection of symptoms. The psychic aspects of this dread are either fully repressed, or present in the form of anxiety about the bodily symptoms, which may themselves become the object of a phobia. A symptom
The Repressive Layer	Sweats, Trembles, Nausea, Sickness, Flutter, Palpitation, Diarrhoea, Tight band round chest or head. Genital tension — Panic, Dread, Apprehension, Petrified, Unreal, Uncanny, Near-madness, Near-death, Helpless, stark languish	Body-language of need. Pains and paralyses as 'ideas' of disease. Displacement of the genital sensations. Denial of pleasure. Symptom formation. A compromise needed. This act wards off dread, but feels guilty. Masturbation is discovered as comfort. Tension mainly genital — Lonely panic and dread	Bodily symptoms repressed so long as phobia avoided — Panic, dread etc. are kept out of mind. Replaced by the phobia	Anxiety. One or more of the body symptoms represent the list of the possible somatic effects — Panic, dread, etc. are kept out of mind. Anxiety about the symptom
Deep Memories	The somatic, autonomic concomitants of panic and dread, i.e., cold sweats, palpitation, nausea, sickness, fluttering in stomach, diarrhoea, frequent passing of urine, tight band round chest or head, genital tension			
	The psychic aspects of panic and dread, feelings of apprehension, unreality, loss of the self, uncanny depersonalization, near-madness, petrified, paralysed and immobilized in the presence of a longing for flight, unconditional badness, despair and helplessness. Intolerably alone			

FIG. 12 The main defensive reactions against fixated panic

related to part-objects of its own body, or objects or parts of the body of the longed-for person. To certain saving objects (or '*soteria*', to use a Latinism) there is a passionate attachment. To be separated from them arouses irrational fear. Other objects are associated with deep infantile fear and can become indirectly the centre of a phobic reaction. If these feared objects approach from the environment the patient will attempt to fly from them, or, if this is not possible, is rooted to the spot in panic.

The adult interests of the phobic patient demand that the compulsive difficulties in movement be overcome. While dominated by the phobic reaction the patient behaves as though he were still an infant living in an infant's environment. He may remark, 'I am behaving like a frightened child'. For all practical purposes, when movement is required in a direction contrary to the phobia, he is a frightened child. In attempting to treat phobic conditions from the pastoral point of view we are justified in asserting that before dealing with the question 'What ought I to do?' the patient needs to ask the prior question, 'Who am I?'

Where schizoid and hysterical positions combine, as they often do, the ability to move towards or away from human relationships is highly paradoxical. Whichever way he moves, the nearer to either pole he approaches, whether of commitment to people or avoidance of them, there is mounting anxiety. Kierkegaard has captured the condition in the phrase 'sympathetic antipathy and antipathetic sympathy'. Take for example a young man immobilized at the prospect of marriage. When he is almost totally isolated from relationships he is antipathetic to isolation and sympathetic to the idea of having bonds with a kindly woman. But we know that for the schizoid person great fear is encountered when he comes to the verge of commitment to the woman his fantasy has seized upon. The first steps in dealing with severe 'avoidance' tendencies is to reduce the fears which motivate the avoidance. This is done by explaining and interpreting their presumptive origin. If done judiciously and if acceptable to the phobic person it then becomes possible to give reassurance and thus enhance any strong motivation to move towards marriage commitment. There is general agreement that in the management of phobic reactions there must be a combination of analysis and encouragement.

Any reassuring encouragement to re-enter the area previously covered by the phobia must not be given prematurely by the counsellor. It should come at the end of the process of history-taking which has paid attention to the situation at the time of the onset of the symptoms. The process will also have enabled a rapport to be established where the patient experiences the immediacy of an understanding and accepting relationship. This is most important, for it forms a base from which the phobic areas can be re-entered. Brash remarks, insensitively suggesting that these phobias are merely silly and irrational can only arouse resistance and justifiable resentment. Thus for clergy at this time to quote texts about perfect love casting out fears is an insult to a parishioner's own spiritual perceptions. The main therapeutic task is interpretative, not exhortative. The simple offer of befriending and listening is much more likely to produce the required rapport, and through it will come an increase of courage to overcome the phobia at its roots.

The mere fact of discussing difficulties in interpersonal relationships and relating them to the time of onset of the phobias begins to make connections in depth. Some will begin to be accepted, others, more disturbing, will be rejected. The counsellor does not press his interpretations, he suggests, and maintains an expectant attitude. Some vigorously denied interpretation may be taken up weeks later by the patient and declared as undeniably true.

The core of the phobic condition

The whole purpose of the phobic reaction has been to shut down on two intolerable problems. The first and greatest occurred in infancy and the second, in some way resembling it, in more recent months. It follows that the phobic person will strongly resist opening up the painful present and the even more painful areas from the past. He has bound the anxiety to some less disturbing external object which can be avoided, and in relation to which he still has freedom of movement. He will not welcome the inner areas of anxiety being brought into the full glare of consciousness.

Within the framework of theological thinking about the neuroses there is ample place for learning theory, habit-forming and retraining. For us, it is a fundamental fact of therapy that the fight against the phobias should be given up in favour of the evangelical position of resting in the finished work of a gracious God. The core of the gospel is an invitation to step out of the arena of human struggling, to 'let go, and let God', as the old adage has it. Phobic people cannot let go. The gospel gives good ground for a change of mind in this respect.

In such activities as 'The Jesus Prayer' of the Orthodox Church, in contemplative meditation and the use of a 'quiet time', there is a stepping-back from agitation into the peace of God. Nothing could more effectively promote activity in the parasympathetic nervous system to engender a tranquil mind and body. Then there follows the stepping-out, still within the peace of God, to 'fight the good fight of faith'. This will give exercise to the sympathetic autonomous nervous system but never in a way that becomes a chronic tension.

We need to be able to help the phobic to say something more effective than the contradictory 'I'll try to trust'. It is not a juggling with words to say instead the paradoxical 'Lord, I trust you with my utter inability to trust you, or anyone else I can't see.' It implies a vital shift in the centre of gravity of the one who says it. It is no longer egocentric, it is centred in God, with complete realism and integrity. That God the Son accepts this paradoxical trust-distrust we know, for he healed the epileptic son of the man who said, 'Lord, I believe, help thou mine unbelief.'

The Benedictus (Luke 1:68) speaks of all the promised mercies of God which deliver us from our enemies, of anxiety due to isolation, guilt, fear and dread. It sums it up at the end by declaring 'that we being delivered out of the hands of our enemies, might serve him without fear, in holiness and "right-relatedness" before him all the days of our Life'. A phobic state constitutes a teleology of terror, a constant anticipation of disaster in the end. If the Christian faith is a teleology of the divine tenderness to the end and in the end, this is certainly relevant therapeutically.

Dissociative reactions

The whole Freudian critique of human culture rests on the discovery that dissociation and repression are universal. Whatever is *repressed* is totally dissociated from consciousness. Whatever is *suppressed* is dissociated from the socially available consciousness and lies, *sub rosa*, private and confidential to the individual. The whole social process by which individuals are made to conform to cultural standards, using fear of isolation as a goad, promotes the dissociation of all socially unacceptable wishes.

The entire subject of the psychoneuroses, including depression along with hysteria and the schizoid reaction, is a corollary of the dissociation or splitting-off of intolerable experiences of the self. The study of neurotic symptoms is an attempt to overcome their dissociation from the unacceptable emotions which, obliquely, they express. To overcome the dissociation by free association is the purpose of psychoanalytic therapy. All psychotherapy is the over-coming of dissociation by making association with the painful aspects of the self gradually tolerable. Dreams are dissociative phenomena, expressing fears and wishes we dare not associate in waking life. Verbal slips in everyday life depend on dissociated wishes.

It is only by a generous use of dissociative mechanisms that religious self-righteous is possible. The technical name for religious dissociation is hypocrisy. The hypocrite is one who underestimates the judgement which should be made upon himself. Avoiding realistic insight, he is able to avoid the general condemnation he applies to others. Conventional morality is largely a dissociative phenomenon.

At the centre of the most systematic theological statement in the New Testament, the Epistle to the Romans, and at the heart of the crucial passage where foundation facts of Christian life are declared, we are given the clearest exposition that occurs anywhere in the Bible of the importance of dissociated aspects of the personality. St Paul writes, 'My own behaviour baffles me. For I find myself not doing what I really want to do, but what I really loathe.'[1] In this statement he is drawing attention to two separate dynamic systems within his own personality, one concerned with the law of God, the other even more determined to follow the passions. Strenuous man of religion that he was, both before and after his conversion, he would claim to identify, in the main, with the moral aspects of his complex personality. 'My conscious mind whole-heartedly endorses the Law, I have the will to do good.' He could dissociate himself from the disowned, but nonetheless overpowering dynamics of lawlessness. 'It cannot be said that "I" am doing them at all – it must be sin that has made its home in my nature.'

Seven times he says in one way or another, 'I do not want to do the evil that in fact I do. Yet I am overpowered by it. I am an unwilling prisoner. All this is in continual conflict with my conscious attitude, but I cannot successfully invade the fortress of sin within me.'

St James would say quite bluntly to St Paul, 'Where do you suppose these evils come from? Can't you see they come from passions and conflicts within yourself? They are your own passions, Paul, dissociated maybe into an area whose depths are beyond the reach of consciousness, but yours nonetheless.' Both apostles agree that the only penetrative force known to them which is able to reach these inaccessible autonomous drives, overcoming dissociation and resistance, is God's action in Christ Jesus. Paul declares (Rom. 8): 'The new spiritual principle of life "in" Christ Jesus lifts me out of the old vicious circle of sin and death. The law never succeeded in producing righteousness – the failure was always the weakness of human nature. But God has met this by sending his own Son Jesus

1   Romans 7:15. J. B. Phillips translation.

Christ to live in that human nature which causes the trouble . . . Once the Spirit of him who raised Christ Jesus from the dead lives within you, he will, by that same spirit, bring to your whole being new strength and vitality.' James says the same thing in the simplest possible terms: 'You do not have what you need, because you do not ask God for it.'

Dissociation is necessary as defence mechanism only so long as association, integration and synthesis of the split-off areas of experience cannot be effected. Both Paul and James imply that the transforming effects of the Spirit of Christ indwelling a man are not so much concerned with the conscious life, which could be reasonably under control in a well-motivated person without special grace. The Spirit's concern is with that which lies at the roots of personality, with the springs of action and passion, with the inaccessible dissociated deprivations laid down and fixated from the foundation years of human selfhood. There is, in fact, a new creation, a renewal of the mind and heart of man. Christ is powerful here because the quality of his acceptance is such as to permit and actively encourage the return to consciousness of the repressed and dissociated 'not-me-at-any-price' experiences which constitute the primitive bases of painful ontological experience. If the problem is that of difficulty in being reconciled to a life that has to be lived identified with threats to being or well-being, Christ is no stranger to this predicament. The cross of Christ declares what is in man, and reconciles to God all those whose deprivations and depravities it declares. It remains to man only to declare, responsively before God, the truth of its verdict.

Depersonalization

There are three uses of the word depersonalization which we deliberately draw together here. The first is the psychiatric symptom of sudden onset precipitated by loss of social support such as family disaster, physical exhaustions, toxaemia or organic disturbances of the brain function. The understanding and treatment of this condition is entirely assigned to psychiatry, because the concern of psychological medicine is to deal with conditions in which physical, inorganic, organic, biochemical, psychodynamic and social factors overlap.

There remains, however, an important group of 'psychiatric' depersonalizations with the same symptoms but without organic cause. These are precipitated by longterm inadequacy or a diminishment of secure relationships. It is registered subjectively as a feeling that 'nobody cares'. Beyond a certain point there is a sudden change in the perception of one's unrelatedness to persons. Other persons are felt to be unreal, and one's own perception of being a real person is, in a fearsome way, lost. This can be continuous with a gradual loss of familial support, and yet in another sense it is discontinuous. The process can be expressed diagrammatically, as in Figure 13.

Another use of the word is in describing the way in which radically schizoid personalities usually experience themselves and other people. This is partly a defensive measure to avoid suffering, but leads to such an impasse as to become itself a ground of suffering and complaint. The third usage arises out of the sort of relationship described in Buber's phrase as an 'I–It' quality rather than the personal quality of 'I–Thou'. This can occur in professional relationships where an impersonal attitude disparages any establishment of personal relationships between the doctor and patient or between the priest and parishioner. It extends the quality of objectivity to include the whole person as just an impersonal object.

We put forward the view that depersonalization reactions can in some ways be regarded as being due to a failure of dissociation. The present-day threat to the continuance of life-by-dependence-upon-personal-resources has led to an emergence of an infantile experience of identification-with-non-being which, being excessively traumatic, had to be split off and repressed. In such persons there was, buried alive so to speak, a painful experience which said, in effect, 'If my mother is not real, nothing is real. I am not real, my world is not real. The senses which once were of use to me, communicating back and forth the reality of personal bondedness, are now real no longer.' Any circumstance which weakens repression in later life may lead to a failure of dissociation of the infantile depersonalization experiences so that they re-emerge into consciousness. This is particularly likely to happen if a person is, at this point in his personal history, losing important and significant relationships. Such events may resonate down into the dissociated depersonalization experiences, giving them greater force and feeding the volcanic fires pressing up against the thin crust of repression.

The pastor may be on the edge of this problem or at the centre of it. Depersonalization is so tied up with the possibilities of underlying schizophrenia, or of toxic and organic conditions which may precipitate it, that diagnosis and treatment must first of all be a medical and psychiatric concern. All that not withstanding, what resources are available to those who look to Christ for an answer to the deepest kind of depersonalization? In the simplest terms, Christ offers a repersonalization by incorporation into his own person and

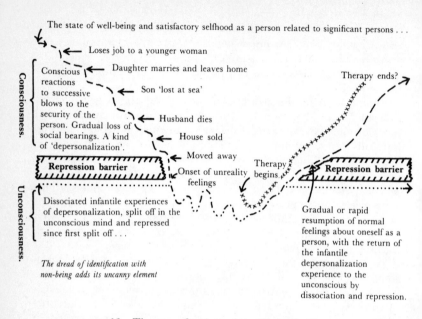

The state of well-being and satisfactory selfhood as a person related to significant persons . . .

← Loses job to a younger woman

← Daughter marries and leaves home

Therapy ends?

Conscious
reactions
to successive   ← Son 'lost at sea'
blows to the
security of the
person. Gradual loss of   ← Husband dies
social bearings. A kind
of 'depersonalization'.   ← House sold

Consciousness.

← Moved away

Repression barrier   Therapy   **Repression barrier**
                    Onset of unreality   begins
                         feelings

Dissociated infantile experiences   Gradual or rapid
of depersonalization, split off in the   resumption of normal
unconscious mind and repressed   feelings about oneself as a
since first split off . . .   person, with the return of
                                            the infantile
                                            depersonalization
The dread of identification with   experience to the
non-being adds its uncanny element   unconscious by
                                            dissociation and repression.

Unconsciousness.

FIG. 13   Therapy of repressed depersonalization

into Christian fellowship. All that we have suggested on the treatment of hysteria, separation-anxiety, and impending loss of personal being, about the ability of the indwelling Persons of the Holy Trinity to create a family life of true personal quality within the heart and mind of man, reinforcing the human fellowship, is applicable here.

It would be surprising if St Paul had not himself undergone experiences of depersonalization and unreality feelings. We know of his natural nervousness, his self-revealed breakdowns and the severe physical deprivations of his travels. He had been 'out of the body', and in these states beyond the natural mind of man had seen visions. No man could sustain such trials without, at times, taking leave of the ordinary sense of being at home in his own intact selfhood. Yet Paul's affirmation is 'I live, yet not I. Christ liveth in me.' To the Ephesians he writes: 'But even though we were dead in our sins . . . God who is rich in mercy, because of the great love he had for us, gave us life together with Christ – it is, remember, by grace and not by achievement that you are saved – and has lifted us right out of the old life to take our place with him in Christ Jesus in the heavens ... That power is the same divine energy which was demonstrated in Christ when he raised him from the dead.'[1]

The power available to those who believe in God is, says Paul, 'exceeding great'. J. B. Phillips translates this as 'tremendous', an appropriate word with the correct undertones. The power of God in raising Christ from the state of death and effecting a vivid conviction of his living presence to those who have 'sought his face' excites the same emotions of awe, fear and trembling as the dread of non-being or of personal unreality. Paradoxically, the cause of the tremor in 'godly fear' is the experience of identification with eternal being and the presence of the ultimate personal reality, God himself, disclosing something of his nature and person to man. Learning theory and behaviour therapy, transposed into this dimension, would suggest that those who, in worship, experience dread as a concomitant of the presence of the most loving person, will find that this extinguishes the uncreative form of dread which is a response to the inner stimulus indicating the terrible absence of a person.

This is, in fact, what happens. In paralytic fear before the angel of the resurrection the keepers of Christ's tomb 'shook with terror and collapsed like dead men'. Mary Magdalene and her friend had the same fear transformed by the words 'Fear not ye, for I know that ye seek Jesus who was crucified. He is not here, for He is risen.' They left the tomb which was no longer a tomb, experiencing the authentic Christian paradox, 'with fear and great joy'.[2]

1   Ephesians 2:4–6.
2   Matthew 28:8.

Appendix A

Hysterical and Schizoid Traits

In the chapter on the schizoid personality we drew attention to the way the ego is deeply split, like a tree-trunk, so the personality shows traits predominantly of withdrawal into detachment and introversion. At the same time there may be contrary traits of clinging attachment associated with the hysterical personality defence. Both reactions are defences against re-experiencing the dread of falling into the abyss of nothingness. Here we observe the patterns of behaviour which belong to each side of the cleavage. Some are characteristic of those who rush away from the 'pain belt' in the direction of external objects to which they cling hysterically. Others are typical of those who crawl up out of the abyss into schizoid detachment, determined never again to commit to anyone. A series of behavioural traits and attitudes is listed below in two columns, so as to illustrate the sharp discontinuity and contradictoriness by which they are, nonetheless, closely related to one another.

There are, of course, exceptions to some of these alignments. I do not have in mind, for instance, either the hysterical psychopath or the schizoid psychopath.

The hysterical reaction	*The schizoid reaction*
Reaction from dread in the direction of people and the substantial world.	Reaction from dread in the direction away from people and away from the world of material existence.
Extraversion.	Introversion.
Defence by *attachment to* external persons and things.	Defence by *detachment from* persons and things.
Desire to shut oneself in *with* someone to gain inseparability and achieve forced commitment.	Desire to shut oneself up *without* anyone inside, to achieve separateness.
Need to overcome separation	Need to overcome commitment

anxiety and 'explosion' anxiety. Fear of personal disintegration by forced subtraction of other persons.

anxiety and 'implosion' anxiety. Fear of social integration by forced addition of other persons.

Needs to have a socially full life.

Needs large safe areas of emptiness.

Reacts to grief by greater attachment.

Reacts to grief by greater detachment.

Under excessive stress may show schizoid traits.

Under excessive stress may show hysterical traits.

Holds fast to a variety of commitments.

Holds all possibilities open in non-commitment.

Determinants of anxiety

Anxious when no one pays attention.

Anxious when attention is paid.

Anxious that life by relatedness is not secure and bonded.

Anxious that life by relatedness is too secure and bonded.

Inconstancy feels persecutory.

Constancy feels persecutory.

Anxious at failure of courage to be as oneself alone.

Anxious at the loss of courage to be as a part of others.

Anxious at failure in undertakings.

Anxious at success of undertakings.

Anxiety that one cannot live. 'I die because I fear to die.'

Anxiety that one cannot die. 'I die because I do not die.'

Lifestyle and personality characteristics

Enjoys self-consciousness when attractive.

Tormented by self-consciousness even when attractive.

Focus of personhood outside the self.

Focus of personhood inside the self.

Over-identified with others.

Under-identified with others.

Threat to selfhood is one of impending loss.

Loss of selfhood has already occurred.

Fears depersonalization.

Has experienced actual depersonalization.

Fears reality loss, fears a catastrophic change imminent.

Has unreality feelings, but may never have known otherwise.

Driven to hysterical intensity to avert loss of feelings.

May be driven to pseudo-hysterical intensity to deny or escape from loss of feelings.

Slack about self-discipline.

Positive resistance to any habitual routine or discipline.

Lacks spiritual determinants, all psychosomatic.	Lacks bodily determinants, all 'spiritual'.
Tangible concerns.	Abstract concerns.
Wants to stay young; adolescent identifications.	Looks young but wants to grow old; late adult identifications.
Centred in immediacy.	Centred in reflection.
Tends to self-love and self-pity.	Tends to self-hate, with self-love and self-pity.

Communication

Apparent frankness and openness to others.	Shut-upness. Closed to others.
Overeager to express herself.	Most unwilling to express his true 'self'.
She cannot close her lips, in spite of efforts to do so.	He cannot open his lips, the more he tries the less he succeeds.
Communications unintentionally indirect.	Communications frequently intentionally indirect.
Language used to declare her needs.	Language used to conceal his needs.
Attempts to communicate not verbally subtle, effective in overcoming estrangement.	Attempts to communicate subtle, but tend to estrange.
Cannot be silenced except by a stronger hysteric or 'by the good which is absolutely able to speak the truth'.	Cannot be made to speak unless by a 'king of the beats', or by 'the good which is absolutely able to be silent'.
The voice reaches beyond the group addressed.	The voice barely reaches the edge of the group addressed.

Attitude to sexuality

Behaves as if oversexed (±).	Behaves as though sex repulsive (±).
Likes superficial stimulation. Rejects deep penetration.	Dislikes any form of loving contact, unless roused to almost sado-masochistic intensity.
Affectionate in fore-play and after-play.	Not affectionate, intercourse sudden, immediate, intense, impersonal.
Heterosexual, without sado-masochism; may be frigid.	Sado-masochism and perversions common.

Sexual knowledge often precocious and avidly sought.	Sexual knowledge often ignored, refused, denied and immature.
Tends to be immodest 'unintentionally'.	Excessively modest, unless utterly shameless.
Exhibitionist, though tends to deny it.	Ashamed of his own body; or exhibits his ugliness, flaunting it.

Attitude to personal needs

Seeks help when in difficulty.	Shuns help when most needs it.
When suffering creates an audience.	Creeps away to suffer in silence.
Supplies any lack by going to people.	Supplies inner lack by going to books or to reflective mental activity.
There is a point in affliction where we are no longer able to bear it to go on . . .	Or that we should be delivered from it (Søren Kierkegaard).

Attitude to time

Involuntary waiting time is like dying time.	Involuntary waiting time is 'just like life', reassuring because one has always been 'waiting for Godot'.
Every moment matters intensely because existence always threatens loss.	The passage of time has ceased to matter because existential loss is accepted.
Panic if continuity is threatened.	Panic if discontinuity is threatened.
Hell is perpetuity of absence.	Hell is perpetuity of presence.
Time is turbulent or drags when left alone.	Time spent peacefully in solitariness.
Time threatens as disengagement draws near.	Time threatens as engagement draws near.
Time flies when spent in attentive company.	Time drags on social occasions.

Social attitudes

Great capacity for enjoying social occasions.	Social occasions exhaust him.
Social involvement and	Social involvement and

integration longed for.

Companionable and matey.

Self-assured on social occasions.

Over-identification with significant people.

Manipulates others into relationships, and uses foresight and judgement to achieve this.

When a person is seen, the instinctive thought is, is he or she going to like me? if so, I am encouraged.

Taking leave is like a little death.

Recovers · well-being in company.

Tends to be one of a type, in common with a group of gregarious people. Dependent on others for stimulation.

integration loathed.

Aloof and standoffish.

Awkward on social occasions, unless role-playing.

Defective identification with members of the family who should be closest to him.

Manipulates others out of relationship, tends not to foresee or understand their reactions.

When a person is seen, the instinctive thought is, is he or she going to leave me alone? if so, I am relieved.

Taking leave is like a new lease of life.

Recovers well-being in solitude.

Eccentric, atypical, not gregarious; or in a clique of eccentrics or outsiders. Militantly self-sufficient.

Emotional characteristics

Mood light and cheerful, denies darker aspects.

She feels that she possesses normal feelings.

A fear of loneliness is interpreted as normal.

Insulated from shame even when acting shamefully.

Given credit for emotions she shows but cannot deeply feel.

Passion seems the only worthwhile thing.

Pleasantly excited by publicity.

Mood dark and mournful, denies lighter aspects.

He feels that he lacks normal feelings.

He recognizes that his revulsion at loving relationship is abnormal or peculiar.

Exposed to feelings of shame on inadequate grounds.

Not given credit for deep feelings he cannot show.

Passion seems too dangerous to put into action.

Appalled by publicity, loves privacy.

Will and action

Drawn to activism.

Drawn to nihilism.

Action positively related to exterior goals.

Action negatively orientated to interior goals.

Moves to follow or track down wanted attendants.

Can predictably be found where her interest lies.

Works to earn to spend on pleasure.

Finds all the premises for her action in the behaviour of others on whom she depends.

Lives in an armed partisanship.

Is being courageous when she stands alone without support, or in company without seeking attention.

A creative entry is made into dread when the things she has compulsively clung to are voluntarily given up.

Action negatively orientated to exterior goals.

'Action' positively focused upon interior goals.

Moves to avoid encounter with 'implosive' people.

Unpredictable, nomadic, changes personal setting as soon as he feels he is too well known.

Work felt often as indecent serfdom.

Finds all the premises for action in himself, except for occasional evasions.

Lives by armed neutrality.

Is being courageous when he overcomes his solitariness in commitment to fellowship.

Creative entry is made into dread when inhibitions against personal relationships are overcome.

Attitude to values

Opportunist, no inner spiritual cohesion.

Finds pleasure in commonplace little things.

Pride in body and dress.

Excessively committed to the finite aspects of human life.

Tied up with the transient, in time and space.

No foothold in infinity or the eternal.

Pursuit of immediate pleasure and concrete objects.

Worldliness is the ideal.

Idealistic, despairs if cannot adhere to his own standards of integrity.

No pleasure in the commonplace or familiar.

Pride in mind and knowledge.

Excessively committed to the infinite aspects of man's timeless and unlimited selfhood.

No foothold in the actual or the temporal.

Pursuit of perennial wisdom and abstractions.

Other-worldliness may be the ideal.

Neglects all universal causes.	Devoted to universal causes.
Uncommitted to values or principles.	Uncommitted to persons and social groups.
Interest in facts and happenings, especially ideas for pleasure.	Interest in views and opinions, especially ideas for thought.
Inner reality the first cargo to be jettisoned.	Outer reality the first cargo to be jettisoned.
'Reality' is discovered by extraversion.	'Reality' is the product of introversion.
The inner world is secondary, shut off and neglected.	The outer world is secondary, shut off and neglected.
No loyalty to truth in depth.	Determined to tell both sides of the paradoxical truth if it kills him.
Hell is suffering without consolation.	'Hell is false beatitude' (Simone Weil).
Preference for religion with emotion; non-mystical; evades the Dark Night and the mystery of death.	Preference for religion without human emotion or fellowship; mystical; drawn to the Dark Night and the mystery of death.
'There are people for whom everything is salutary which brings God nearer to them . . .	. . . for me it is everything which keeps him at a distance. Between me and him there is the thickness of the universe.'[1]

Intellectual factors

Tend not to have high intelligence.	If highly intelligent utilize defence by intellectualism. If unintelligent identify with the sick and the beat who are anti-intellectual.
In following up tasks relating to significant persons they show immense concentration, drive, interest and perseverance.	In relation to tasks involving persons they lack concentration, decision, interest and perseverance, unless in avoidance.
Dominated by the senses, contemptuous of the 'egghead'.	Dominated by the mind. Contemptuous of the sensual.

1 Simone Weil, *Gravity and Grace*, p. 82.

Fantasy life centres round achieving secure dependency.

Fantasy life centred on survival in separateness, perhaps in achieving some form of superiority of knowledge or power or status.

Are in general highly suggestible.

Tend to be contra-suggestible.

Refuses to entertain spiritual possibilities.

Refuses to be tied down to the necessities of existence.

Prone to idolatry, of material things.

Prone to gnosticism; mental idolatry.

Not given to philosophy. If anything, pragmatic.

As philosophers essentialist if the defence by denial of the schizoid still stands. Existentialist if the schizoid position has broken through into consciousness.

Cultivates blind spots and rationalizations when insight and the need for inner consistency threatens.

Cultivates blind spots and rationalizations when external duties and demands threaten him.

Mentally extensive and shallow.

Mentally intensive and deep.

Thought inhibited by the over-proliferation of action.

Action inhibited by the over-proliferation of thought.

Sensory characteristics

Touch hunger.

Terror of being touched.

Delight in the sudden unexpected personal touch.

Cringes from touch, especially if sudden.

Needs to be grasped and hugged.

Cannot bear embrace or close grip.

Visual factors

Compulsive need to be looked at.

Compulsive need not to attract attention.

Brazen composure under scrutiny; always role-playing.

Poor composure under public gaze, unless role-playing.

Becomes anxious in a group if time passes without her being looked at specially.

Feels increasingly comfortable as he discovers he can be unobserved.

Clothes are used to attract favourable gaze, and look younger.

Clothes are used to deny sex and give an impression of age.

Appetite

May treat her own separation-anxiety by excessive oral activity, eating, drinking, smoking.

Tends to have a poor appetite. Eats less when anxious; in anorexia nervosa a death-wish and confusion of fantasies abolishes appetite.

Movements

Lack of restraint in movement and posture.

Restrained movements, demure or awkwardly angular posture.

Enjoys flamboyant, flinging extensor movement.

Movements express guarding, cringing away, and hugging onself.

Appendix B

Pastoral Recording of a Case-history

In one of his essays entitled 'Dialogue', of great interest to the subject of case-history taking, Martin Buber speaks of three ways in which a person can look at another person – by becoming an onlooker, or an observer, or by becoming aware. All three of these ways are needed during an interview with a troubled parishioner.

Our personalities stretch back in time and what we are today is conditioned by our whole previous experience of life. These two aspects, what might be called the longitudinal view right back into personal history and family history, along with the cross-sectional view which pays attention to the present field of relational forces, must be taken into account. Neither can properly be understood without the other. The clinical theologian will also be aware of a third dimension, which will be found to interpenetrate these two, and which, stretching on into the future, is most powerfully relevant therapeutically. This is the dimension which has to do with the ultimate meanings and purposes of a person's life. Breakdowns often have to do with the incompatibility between the ends to which a person is either consciously or unconsciously striving and contrary forces within themselves or in the environment. This dimension of the goals of life emerges both in the longitudinal and in the cross-sectional accounts. Part of our purpose is to clarify them for the patient. If they are valid enough and backed up powerfully by reality, they can integrate personality and reinforce decisive action in such a way as to deliver the troubled parishioner from the painful domination either of the past or of the present.

These notes are concerned with the ordering of the clinical theological record. It is not suggested that it is either wise or reasonable to expect order from the parishioner in the telling of his story. There is too much of value and significance in the way he tells his own story to miss it by pinning him down to a questionnaire. Only if his history-telling becomes too confused or circular should a gentle offer to structure it be made by a few questions along these lines. At the same time the pastor, as listener, will benefit from having at the back of his mind a definite outline of the areas of life about which he needs to know the facts. As the patient tells his life story, these various sorting-boxes receive the information appropriate to them, so that at the end of the story as it comes from the teller a few direct questions will supply the remainder.

In clinical theological training the communication of typical histories is essential to the learning process. It is here, when the parson is recounting a clinical history to a pastoral or psychiatric consultant for his consideration, or to a group of case-workers for study and comment, that they have a right to expect that he will arrange his communication in an orderly manner.

The suggested outline is given under main headings with subsidiary heads. The main points should be memorized so that in taking a history without reference to any notes such as these you will not come away from the parishioner with one whole area uninvestigated.

1 Name
2 Complaint
3 The onset
    (*a*) Previous occasions of the same complaint
    (*b*) Previous illness of any sort
4 Family history
    (*a*) Mother
    (*b*) Father
    (*c*) Brothers and sisters
    (*d*) Other important personal influences
5 Previous personal history
    (*a*) Early days
    (*b*) Indicators of disturbance in childhood
    (*c*) General health during childhood
    (*d*) School
    (*e*) Work
    (*f*) Puberty, adolescence
    (*g*) Marital history
    (*h*) Children
    (*i*) Habits
6 Previous personality
7 Religious attitudes and christian encounter
8 Dynamic formulation

Additional examination, when a parishioner suffering from mental illness comes first to the parson
    1 Behaviour

2   Talk
3   Mood
4   Content of thought
5   Orientation
6   Memory
7   Attention and concentration
8   General information
9   Intelligence
10   Insight and judgement

1   NAME

Age,
Address,
Name of the doctor,
The church, and
The vicar, especially if he has been responsible for the referral.

2   COMPLAINT

This should be recorded in the patient's own words. It will be his response to your question, 'What is it that troubles you?' Remember that the complaint the parishioner has chosen to present to you is carefully selected by him, among the many possible symptoms he could name, because he thinks this is an appropriate offering to you, calculated to elicit your help.

In complaining to a general practitioner he will select physical symptoms, to a psychiatrist he will offer mental symptoms, to a parson what he conceives to be moral or spiritual symptoms.

Under 'Complaint' it is usual for psychiatrists to include the common complaints which patients may be so used to that they have ceased to notice them. It is good common sense for pastors to ask these same questions (not interrupting the history-taking, but at some time or other, for inclusion here), as to:

(a) Sleeping difficulties, in getting to sleep, or in waking early
(b) Loss of appetite
(c) Headaches
(d) Fatigue, loss of energy, loss of initiative
(e) Indecision
(f) Lack of concentration

(g) Low spirits
(h) Anxieties or unreasonable fears

Most of these are no more than clear indications that the 'dynamic cycle' of relationships is not in working order, for they show the loss of the normal output of being and well-being.

3 THE ONSET

The history of the development of the symptoms is always important. The search must always be made for precipitating emotional problems or anxiety-provoking relationships occurring at the time of onset of the symptoms, or shortly before their appearance. Were there any obvious anxieties, disappointments or failures, frustrations or resentments, jealousies or rivalries, or emotional conflicts in the spheres of the family, at work, or in recreation? To the extent that these precipitating difficulties in the sphere of personal relationships are manifestly severe, they may reasonably be held to account for the breakdown without looking for any major personality defects. By the same rule, if there are no discoverable environmental stresses, it is reasonable to infer that the main force of the conflict is within the persons themselves.

(a) Previous occasions of the same complaint
The same or similar sufferings may have been encountered by the parishioner a few months or even years ago. The difficulty may be recurrent. It is therefore necessary to know what the state of affairs was in which these previous symptoms developed. Sometimes the person is better able to remember who was troubling him a few years ago than he is in the present upset. This is paradoxical, but is due to the protective idealization of authoritarian figures in the present, which is so often part of the depressive reaction.

(b) Previous illnesses of any sort
If the parson is attempting to come to a mature assessment of the kind of universe this parishioner's spirit lives in, it is of obvious importance that he should know, for instance, whether childhood was bedevilled by asthma, chronic hay-fever or long-standing skin conditions, all of which, alone or together, would indicate a high level of infantile anxiety and a universe peopled with fears and dreads. The pastor is familiar with the fact that all diseases of stress carry with them a particular view of the universe which, 'as it was

in the beginning, is now, and ever shall be', so far as this person's deepest levels of spirit are concerned. He has not a universe which can easily be trusted. Similarly, if he carries a long and undistinguished record of accidents and fractures, we would have to presuppose him to be a person as defective in controlling the inhibitory mechanisms of the spirit of personal responsibility as we would if he spoke of a long record of other forms of delinquency.

4   FAMILY HISTORY

When a patient comes to a psychiatrist he expects to be asked about the family history. The parson often does not need to ask because he knows already. However, he needs to have it on record, and make inquiry from the person himself. The parishioner's intimate account of the personalities of his mother and father may show wide divergences from the parson's own opinion. Both these will then need to be stated. The very fact that we ask these questions sheds light on our view of the origins of spiritual breakdown. The growth of human personality is synonymous with the development of interpersonal relationships, and these in turn are entirely dependent upon the personalities of mother, father and, to a less extent, upon grandparents, brothers and sisters. If a person's attitude to themselves is all awry, so that they hate, despise, overprotect, or feel destructive towards themselves, we shall find the roots of these attitudes in the mother–baby relationship within the first year, and probably for many years of childhood and adolescence as well. If we find that a person's relationships with society are disordered, irresponsible, or marred by aggressive feelings towards people in authority, we would do well to look also very carefully at this person's relationship with the father. If jealousy possesses them inordinately we might also find the roots in an early displacement by a new baby.

The parishioner may find it very difficult to give an objective view of a parent. He may obviously be attempting to give an idealized view. It sometimes helps at this point to sum up what has been said, showing that you fully appreciate the weight and worth of the mother's merits, followed by a casual-seeming inquiry as to what anyone who might have been critical of her might have said, which might have been a very slight fault in her. It is also most important to understand what was the balance of power between the mother and the father in the family. So frequently the dominant mother and the passive father stand in the background behind the neurotic, ill-adjusted person. You are aiming to build up a short pen-portrait of the mother and the father along the same lines as we shall record in detail later, when examining the previous personality of the person himself.

(a) Mother

As Wesley's biographer said, 'Mothers are the makers of spirit'. To the extent that the mother succeeded, you are unlikely to be interviewing her son. To the extent that she failed, he is likely to be defending her to the last ditch, even though it is the wrong one.

Is she alive or dead?

If she has died, what was the cause of her death?

Did you get on with your mother? Better at times than others?

Did your mother have any special attachments within the family?

Have you always told your mother about everything?

If not, to what extent do you maintain a reserve?

If you have ever felt critical about your mother, could you express it openly, or would that seem not to be possible?

Was your mother liable to moods and periods of low-spiritedness, or was she always cheerful and on top of the world?

Did she tend to be houseproud and devoted to cleaning, or did she not mind a mess if people were happy?

Was your mother affectionate; so affectionate that you felt at times walled in by her affection, or was she at times unfeeling and self-centred?

What did your mother want you to be, or do?

How much freedom did you have as a child to play out and entertain?

Was your mother on good terms with the neighbours?

Did you ever feel ashamed of anything she was, or did?

With what emotions do you look back on your mother?

What was her attitude to your school work, games, friends, courting, engagement, etc.?

These are some of the questions which might well guide the patient's attempt to delineate the personality of the mother. These are not set out to be used as direct questions, they do but illustrate the sort of facts you need to know to understand the parishioner's spirit in the making. A similar picture needs to be obtained in relation to the father.

(b) Father

We should want to know, in addition to a general view of the father's personality in relation to the patient, what he did to earn his living, what his attitude was to his work and his recreation, to what degree he took an interest in his children, whether there were any favourites and where this particular person stood in his regard. It helps to know who did the punishment, and how it was administered. On looking back, does this person feel that they owe more to their father or to their mother; are they aware of having idealized and tried to be like one more than the other? Did the person feel more accepted and loved by one parent than the other?

Taking the two together, does this person feel that his parents were in love with one another? If so, did they remain in love? Was there respect between them? Did they enjoy each other's company? Were there any specially difficult periods in their married life? If so, how old was he at the time, and what did he feel about it? Sometimes there are very vivid memories of agonizing insecurity because of parental quarrels. Which of the parents seems to be the more mature and well-adjusted now?

Has the patient's estimate of either parent been changing?

(c) Brothers and sisters

It is always valuable to make a list of the family, noting the ages of the children in relation to the age of the person concerned. If you are attempting to present a full case-history, it is worth while recording the married status, occupation, general and mental health or illness of the siblings, in order. It may be that one of the siblings has been of particular importance to the person, as a friend, as a source of strength and inspiration, or as a particularly difficult thorn in the flesh. Some families have a marked cohesion, maintained through the years, which may be very sound, or occasionally based on depressive needs. Families with a predominance of hysterical, psychopathic and schizoid reactions tend not to have true cohesion, though there may be powerful collusions because neurotic needs are met.

(d) Other important personal influences

Has any person inside or outside the family been of great influence in the life of your parishioner? Grandparents may provide a security which parents fail to give. A unmarried aunt in the home may be the child's main support or its constant critic. Among those who turn to the clergy in time of need it not infrequently happens that some minister or teacher has been a profoundly supportive influence in earlier years.

5   PREVIOUS PERSONAL HISTORY

Having studied the matrix from which the person has emerged, we concentrate our study on the person's response to the conditions created for him by the family. We wish to discover his reaction to the various environments he has encountered from the earliest days, through infancy to school-life, from adolescence to his discovery of his social role as a worker, in society, and perhaps his achievement of marriage and fatherhood.

(a) Early days

Here, of course, it is possible for the person to describe only what they have been told about their infancy. Occasionally these snatches of information have the quality of myths which are the earliest memories of the race. Though we may be uncertain about their historical truth, we may recognize that for this person they represent a basic and formative experience. It is of significance, for instance, to learn that the person had a long and difficult labour as their introduction to the world. The trauma of coming into the world can set the stage for later claustrophobic and agoraphobic reactions. If the growth of the infant's spirit is the response to the mother's spirit, it is again manifest that it matters whether this person was welcomed into the world by a mother who looked forward to this baby unconditionally, or whether he was an unfortunate accident, or was to be welcomed only conditionally on being of a certain sex, or being a pretty baby. The parson need not, and should not, give the impression, by overpunctilious or persistent questioning in this area, that he attaches any irrevocable significance to these events in determining what came after, or what can be done now. This questioning represents a sober and balanced awareness that if he is to understand in depth the spirit of the person whom he is trying to help, he is concerned to find indications of the personal forces to which he could respond, and against which he was bound to react from the very earliest months. Since one of the basic tasks of theology is to alter the attitude to the self, from self-despising to self-acceptance, it is not illogical to spend time trying to discover the nature and quality of the relationships offered in those early months of life-by-identification with the source of being, during which the foundations of the personal spirit were laid down. Inquiry can usefully be made under the following heads:

The health and happiness of the mother during pregnancy.

Was the birth at full term or premature, a normal delivery, or delayed, or instrumental?

Were there any difficulties in establishing breastfeeding?

When, why and how was weaning achieved?

What sort of baby is he said to have been? Happy and contented, passive and placid, or always screaming?

Were there any illnesses or severe feeding difficulties during the first year? Or sleeping difficulties?

Was the maternal practice to attend to the crying child, or in the Truby King manner to leave it to cry?

Were the milestones of sitting, walking, teething, feeding oneself, bowel and bladder training achieved more or less at the usual periods?

Was he said to have been an early or a late developer? (Severe emotional difficulties tend to late development.)

(b) Indicators of disturbance in childhood

The memory often stretches back far enough for recall of some of these. In other cases the person has been told of them. They all indicate reactions to difficult personal relationships.

Night terrors	Sleepwalking	Temper tantrums
Bed-wetting	Thumb-sucking	Nail-biting
Breath-holding	Food fads	Abnormal bowel
Stammering	Tics and	habits
	mannerisms	Phobias, or
		irrational fears

(c) General health during childhood

Inquiry, in a full case-record, would be made with regard to any severe infections, illnesses, fits, allergies such as dermatitis, hay-fever or asthma, recurrent illnesses or operations. Were there any periods in hospital in the absence of the mother and father? At what age and for how long? Is it known how he reacted to these experiences? Are there any results of these, from which he has never fully recovered?

(d) School

This period, in which skills are developed, manual, mental and personal, is of importance. It may be responsible for serious setbacks in personal development or for splendid transformations through the relationships offered by teachers better able to love wisely than were the parents.

Was attendance at any phase of school life irregular, because of illness, school phobias, truancy, or any other reason?

Were there any particular periods of special happiness and progress, or marked unhappiness, failure or difficulty?

What were the special abilities and disabilities in the learning process? Did any teacher particularly influence him, and in which direction? Does he feel he owes any particular turn taken in his character development to the influence of any teacher? Was he involved in any gang mischief or solitary lapses of behaviour? Did he regard himself as a member of the school community? Did he mix easily, was he active in the group? Did he tend to lead or to follow, or to avoid group commitment altogether? How did other children treat him? Any memories of teasing, bullying, special attachments or successes? What was the attitude to games, team games, rough games, out-of-school games, hobbies?

(e) Work

How did he choose his first job? At what age? With what feelings did he start work?

Under this heading can be investigated the attitude of the person to adult social relationships, with those set in authority over him, those who are working alongside, and perhaps those who are working under him.

Does he get on with men better than with women, or equally, or the reverse? Does he enter into conversation with other people easily, or is he shy and diffident? Are friendships many or few, permanent or changing, warm or distant, reserved or confiding, protecting or dependent? Is the flow of energy for work usually free and abundant, or in some way diminished? Has the working life brought satisfactions, fulfilment of ambitions, or the contrary? What personal crises have there been in the working life? How has this person adjusted to interpersonal difficulties at work? How does he take criticism, responsibility, disappointment? Has he felt on the whole equal to the personal and intellectual demands made upon him in his working life? Does the work situation bring a sense of personal achievement and satisfaction? Does he feel accepted and secure at work, does it give a proper sense of status?

(f) Adolescence and sexual development

The ability to develop from childhood to adult life, through the period of puberty, is an important indication of the adequacy of personality. Many spiritual and mental abnormalities show themselves for the first time at this age. Asocial or antisocial inclinations emerge as important indicators of personality difficulty. It is manifestly more important to give the person an opportunity to discuss this area of life if he has still hardly emerged from it. As the years advance, inquiry in this area becomes less relevant. On the other hand, the introspective adolescent may be waiting to unburden himself to an understanding listener about a large number of problems in this field. The shy person particularly has no idea of the wide range of strange feelings which can be experienced in this period of life by people who are later regarded as quite 'normal'.

The pastoral counsellor needs to be able to relieve the adolescent of the hush-hush of neurotic reticence still common in many families. The adolescent may primarily be in need of reliable information about the developments that are going on inside him. He may need reassurance that these perturbing changes are indeed normal ones, or to what extent they can be regarded as normal. For instance, many shy young Christians may feel that to have had experience of masturbation disqualifies them from taking part in Christian activity. This habit needs to be placed in proper perspective, since in many anxious and schizoid young persons, it is primarily a symptom of anxiety. The focus of that anxiety is the difficulty of making personal relationships. When these advance normally as a result of wise counselling, the neurotic habit always diminishes in frequency and in importance. The person may be waiting for an opportunity to speak about some sexual activity which has incurred both anxiety and a sense of guilt. There may be real need for confession here as well as for pastoral counselling. The reassuring interpretations of a knowledgable pastoral counsellor at this stage of adolescence and early adult life may make all the difference between a successful transition from a homosexual phase to mature adult sexuality in one who has suffered a fixation in this phase of development, and a tragic involvement in progressively inescapable homosexual experiences. Other young people may be horrified to feel in themselves sadistic and masochistic fantasies and desires. Once these can be explained within the framework of a rational understanding of the effect of very severe early injury to the love relationship, they can be accepted and to an increasing extent dismissed. It is important that the counsellor be able to handle his own anxieties in discussing this particular phase of human development.

All this may have to be taken up again in history-taking in adults, part of whose difficulty often is that they are still preoccupied with the hopes and fears of adolescence. They cannot bear that it has passed them by. Women may volunteer information about 'the change' or menopause, in which emotional disturbance is common. It may become evident that the severe upset and irritability at home which has brought a woman to the parson with a high sense of guilt, occurs only in the pre-menstrual week. In either case she should be urged to communicate all this to her general practitioner, if she has not already done so. The glandular imbalance which lies at the root of these conditions can be corrected medically. Both conditions also fluctuate in severity with the degree of interpersonal discontent.

(g) Marital history

The problem brought before the pastor very frequently necessitates his listening to a long story of marital discord. He is called upon here to be a listener, not to take sides. As much as in any other sphere of life he can have a ministry of reconciliation here. He will do so if he bases his interpretation of the marriage partners to each other on a sound and honest appraisal of their problems in depth. Here, more than anywhere else, the infantile emotional expectations, fears, and split-off rages are apt to queer the pitch. On inquiry it may become evident that the conflict lies in the sphere of dependent relationships, either or both partners striving for neurotic dominance over one another, or for neurotic dependence on one another. Arrested psychosexual development in either partner may leave the other, from the human point of view, rightly dissatisfied. It is no part of pastoral wisdom to minimise the difficulties in order to make the task of preserving holy wedlock easier. The first way to approach an unholy deadlock is to understand it, and this may take time and discussion, separately with both partners, and together. The roots of maladjusted marriages lie in the maladjustments of previous marriages, 'to the third and fourth generation'. Since any progress towards a Christian adjustment is dependent on the readiness of at least one of the parishioners to accept the resources of a relationship with Christ as a precondition of attempting to fulfil the moral demand of Christian marriage, inquiry will need to be directed towards the spiritual resources even more than the moral standards of the persons concerned.

(h) Children

At times it can be quite important to inquire about the children, as parents are apt to identify very closely with events in their lives. The engagement of a favourite son can plunge an over-attached mother into depression, even though verbally she welcomes the engagement. Hysterical symptoms in which the mental pain and guilt are converted into a bodily symptom such as the paralysis of an arm can be the result of a man's over-intense attachment to a daughter who bears a close resemblance to his mother. Neurotic patients are apt to expect more from their children than is reasonable. Equally, the children of neurotic parents are apt to act at times with retributive harshness.

(i) Habits

Dependence on tobacco, alcohol, or medicines and drugs should be noted. Do not be so naive as to expect that a heavy drinker will be honest about his alcohol consumption if he has started to become an addicted drinker. Chain-smoking is associated with a high level of basic anxiety about interpersonal relationships, and with an unacknowledged sense of inferiority and painful passivity. If during the course of your interview the parishioner asks to be allowed to smoke, you will, of course, permit this. Some people cannot think unless they are smoking. Note the point at which this request came, because you have probably been discussing a matter which in depth is particularly a sore point, arousing anxiety.

6   PREVIOUS PERSONALITY

'What kind of a person were you before this trouble began?' is a question which can lead to important information. It may be that the present disturbance has brought about a complete change in personality. On the other hand, it may represent only an exacerbation of what the person has always been. A sudden deterioration of personality in middle life in one who has shown no signs of this before should be carefully looked into by a physician or neurologist for possible organic changes.

Inquiry here will give the pastor a good estimate of what this person has been like at his best. If his good spirits and better personality traits have become submerged, it is less of a task to resurrect them than to create them in one who has always been inadequate. This inquiry tells you what the soil of the human spirit is like in which the Holy Spirit has to plant the seeds of the new being.

There are various main dimensions representing opposite extremes of behaviour.

(a) Openness and psychological space   *v.* Rigidity and shut-in defensiveness
(b) Peacefulness and hopefulness   *v.* Anxiety and fear
(c) Surgency and active responses   *v.* Desurgency and passivity
(d) Patience and tolerance   *v.* Irritability and intolerance
(e) Sociability   *v.* Seclusiveness

It is worth while expanding the qualifications of personality observable under these headings, as all of them are qualifications of the human spirit characterizing the mode of its relationships.

(a)

Openness	*Rigidity*	*Openness*	*Rigidity*
Outgoing	Defensive	Just tidy	Over-orderly
Flexible	Stubborn	Change tolerated	Dislikes change
Harmonious	Humourless		
Cheery and easy	Grim and dour	Spontaneous	Tied to rituals
		Forgives readily	Hugs revenge
Happy-go-lucky	Serious-minded	Attached to persons	Sticks to principles
Amenable	Cussed	Tractable	Intractable

(b)

Peacefulness	*Anxiety*
Hopeful	Fearful
Imperturbable	Soon scared
Placid	Nervous
Courageous	Apprehensive
Never a care	Constant worrier

(c)

Active surgency	*Passivity*	*Active surgency*	*Passivity, desurgency*
Energetic	Listless	Aggressive	Submissive
Courageous	Timid	Fights on	Gives in
Superiority feelings	Inferiority feelings	Confident	Diffident
		Optimistic	Pessimistic
Decisive	Indecisive	Impulsive	Restrained
Concentrated	Distractible	Leader	Follower

Definite	Vague	Feels in the right	Feels often wrong
Steady work	Fitful work		
Drive	Drift	Affirmative	Apologetic

(d)

Patient	Irritable	Patient	Irritable
Tolerant	Intolerant	Accepting	Critical
Pacific	Irascible	Amicable	Hostile
Tactful	Rude	Generous	Jealous
Gracious	Resentful	Kind	Cruel
Benign	Bitter	Charitable	Spiteful
Friendly	Suspicious	Grateful	Ungrateful
Gentle	Uncouth	Finds folk nice	Finds folk nasty

(e)

Sociability	Seclusiveness	Sociability	Seclusiveness
Attached	Detached	Neighbourly	Isolated
Companionable	Retiring	Shares burdens	Hugs own burden
Dependent	Independent	Enthusiastic	Indifferent
Warm	Cool	Values – general ones	Values – private ones
Approachable	Unapproach-able	Affectionate	Chilly
Close	Distant	Joiner	Non-joiner
Credulous	Sceptical	Can commit	Cannot commit
Suggestible	Contra-suggestible	Welcomes friends	Drives off friends

Those whose characteristics lie in the first of the parallel columns are not likely to be presenting themselves as patients. If they have an excess of openness, hopefulness, surgency, friendliness and sociability, we would have to come to a diagnosis of *mania*, a condition more of psychotic origin than a psychoneurosis, though there are frequently observed in depressed patients after electrical treatment, and sometimes after the anti-depressive drugs, symptoms which are characterized by elation to the point of mania. For the most part these are recorded *as symptoms, only in excess*, when they occur as one phase of the manic-depressive psychosis.

Depressed patients show a high degree of rigidity, passivity and seclusiveness. The column headed 'Irritable' is present only in the unconscious and it is the repression of these irascible emotions which exhausts the patient. Anxiety is a variable characteristic present only in agitated depressions.

Hysterical personalities of the overt kind have a great deal of openness, of active surgency, and a high degree of apparent sociability. Their irritability is very much on the surface, and there is a deceptive mask of peacefulness known as 'la belle indifférence' in the conversion reactions.

Sufferers from *conversion reactions*, in which the mental pain is converted into a bodily symptom, have displaced their anxiety on to the symptom. Though they may give the appearance of patience, irritability will break through. A basically passive attitude to mental pain is combined with an active determination to have it attended to medically. The brittleness of this defence leads to rigidity and often ultimately to seclusiveness. His sociability is reserved for doctors, nurses and sympathizers.

Phobic patients are characterized by a high degree of anxiety. Since the personality pattern underlying phobias may be either schizoid, hysterical or depressive, this anxiety is combined with a variety of other factors.

Obsessional patients, on the other hand, have a high degree of rigidity combined with anxiety and active surgency. Irritability is usually open to the observer, though it may be denied by the person herself. Obsessionals tend to a limited degree of sociability, with a large measure of seclusiveness towards society in general.

Schizoid patients are so given to acting a part that it is difficult to classify them in this way, except by noting the high degree of seclusiveness which, in spite of every attempt to conceal it, comes across to the empathetic observer. There is, where intimate personal relationships are required, always much more rigidity than openness, deep anxiety than peacefulness, irritability than a patience. So far as intellectual pursuits are concerned, there may be a high degree of active surgency, but in the realm of personal relationships they are marked much more by passivity.

Paranoid personalities are characterized by a high degree of rigidity and seclusiveness. Their irritability is characterized by suspicion, jealousy and criticism. They combine a social passivity with an active surgent programme of deluded activity to restore their rights. Anxiety in paranoid patients is characterized by fear, which has objects, rather than by dread, which has no object.

Hypochondriasis, in which the mental pain is centred upon the bodily organs, produces a high degree of irritability, passivity, anxiety and rigidity. Any activity and sociability are reserved for the audience of those prepared to listen to the organ recital.

The *anxiety state*, in which all the intrapsychic anxiety has emerged into consciousness, throwing down the defences, is characterized by a high degree of anxiety, passivity, a quality of terrified seclusiveness, and rigidity.

7   RELIGIOUS ATTITUDES AND CHRISTIAN ENCOUNTER

In the words of the apostle Paul, 'first that which is natural, then that which is spiritual'. A man's *natural religion* is to a great extent the product of his experience of the universe of personal relationships in the earliest and subsequent years, the history of which we have been taking. If he tends towards *depressiveness*, he is likely to be maintaining very rigidly the religious patterns inculcated by his mother. If his father was irreligious his sympathy for him will be entirely unconscious. His religion, in the period leading up to the breakdown, will have been characterized by overconscientiousness, perfectionism, pride in work with need for appreciation. It is a religion felt to be all a matter of law and demand, so that failure and brokenness cannot be admitted and rage is walled off. Under these circumstances, God always appears to be distant, angry and rejecting of a failure. Neurotic guilt emerges and in the breakdown itself the patient is full of self-depreciation, self-accusation, not on account of the inner rage, but usually pinned on to some infantile lusts and long-past failings.

The *hysterical* patient, by contrast, cannot feel that there is any reliable God. It is almost too late when he comes. In order to gain attention she will have taken on the religious colour of those from whom she was expecting help. But she can change the external patterns of her religion, if she has any, with the dexterity of a quick-change artist.

The experiences which lead to *schizoid* stressing and defences lead to the belief that God has forsaken one. In a schizoid world there is no God. Or he is dead if he ever existed. Those who are afflicted in this way feel always that God may have place for everyone else in the kingdom of his love, but not for them. None the less, because of the nature of the defences which lead to a kind of gnosticism, religion in the schizoid sufferer often takes the form of mystical presumption, aristocratic religious pride, based usually on intellectual eminence, ecclesiastical connections, or ritualistic know-how. But these attempts to cover up the nothingness and hollowness within have usually broken down if the parishioner is appearing as an avowed sufferer.

Now, it is quite true that all these, and indeed also those who suffer from frank breakdowns into phobic and other reactions, may all the time be protesting their conscious belief in the existence and goodness of God. But for all practical purposes, either he does not seem to exist at all, or, in one and the same breath, he may be deemed to be hostile. We are quite right to conclude that these distortions of the human spirit arise as a result of experiences of traumatic relationships to parental sources of being in the first three years of life. For every one of us there is the 'God behind God' who is present or absent, loving or unloving, hostile or forgiving, precisely to the extent that the mother and father seemed to be so in the earliest years. None of these feelings, characteristic of the human person in breakdown, tells us anything about the nature of God, either as he is in himself, or in his attitude towards the sufferer. Even though, on this level of the human spirit 'our heart condemn us', we may have good grounds in the gospel for 'confidence towards God'.

The extent to which the troubled person can break free of this neurotic picture of what he thinks of as 'God', depends to a considerable measure on the depth and reality of what we can call the *Christian encounter* in the years preceding his illness. Natural religion is of very little use to the parishioner here, because it is precisely this natural religion which has let him down. The only thing we can utilize from his past is not derived from feelings, but from facts as they are revealed in the great good news about God, declaring his offer of new life and fellowship to us through his Son, Jesus Christ. If our patient has already encountered him, has already responded to him in active acceptance and decision, we have a great deal to work on in the realm of fact, which runs quite contrary to these neurotic feelings. If the love of Christ was real to him, then our task is to remind him of the facts. These facts of the incarnation, the passion, the resurrection and the gift of the Holy Spirit will cope with his fear and separation-anxiety, with his murderous rage against the sources of being, against his utter inability to believe that there is anybody there. We can in confidence invite him no longer to run away from his finitude and the death of the spirit, no longer to run away from his guilt into a remorse that is biting back at himself, or from the supremely dreadful fact that he cannot raise a spark of belief at all. If he desires to encounter again Christ his Saviour, he will turn round and face that from which he was running away, because it is *there*, in the place of despair about one's righteousness and the conviction of guilt, in the hell of separation-anxiety and dereliction, of emptiness and meaninglessness, that he is to meet Christ. In the power of Christ's cross and the fellowship and courage of the indwelling Son of God, he will be able to take up his own cross, which means deliberately advancing into the area of mental pain which is particular to oneself.

Therefore, in any clinical theological history-taking, it is quite essential to come to some appraisal of the extent to which the living

Christ has ever been decisively present in the experience of the now-troubled parishioner.

8   DYNAMIC FORMULATION

The clinical theologian who has listened to the history of the parishioner along these lines will probably by now be able to hazard a dynamic formulation of the nature of the problem which confronts the parishioner's troubled spirit. We use the words 'dynamic formulation' rather than diagnosis, though this means precisely the same. We want to see through into the depths of the spirit's suffering, and offer a relationship both human and divine which will meet the realities of the human spirit's situation. It would be useless for a clinical theologian to come to a diagnosis expressed, for instance, in medical nomenclature as 'hysterical personality disorder', if he had no idea what that meant in terms of a suffering spirit. The diagnostic label 'depression' is useful to the psychiatrist because in any case he is proceeding from that diagnosis to the administration of an anti-depressive drug or electrical convulsive therapy. Only seldom does he concern himself with the content of the mental pain or the dynamic formulation which lies behind it.

The parson, too, needs to know what goes with what, that is to say he needs to be able to recognize a syndrome, a diagnostic entity, not because he has any drugs to give, but because *diagnostic entities represent a common background of spiritual experience* and *a common pattern of distortion in the interrelational dynamics at the basis of personal* being.

Therefore, this formulation will be alive both to the *personality pattern*, which is largely the product of infantile conditioning and subsequent reactions on the part of the person himself and of society, along with the *contemporary events* which have precipitated the re-emergence of the primitive pattern of ill-adjusted activity. In the face of some present-day stress in human relationships, the suffering person has, in fact, concluded that because, when a situation with a similar pattern occurred in infancy, he was unable to deal with it except in this limited and defensive way, there is now no alternative but to react by the same pattern. 'As it was in my beginning, is now, and ever shall be' is the motto of neurosis. We need to help him to get back to the first half of the Gloria, for it is there that the answer to this spirit's problem lies.

We may well be able, within the two hours allotted to the pastoral interview, to feed back to the parishioner our understanding of his problem to which he has himself given us all the clues and all the keys, so that we can pass on from this to open up to him again the resources in God the Father, Son and Holy Spirit, which he has somehow, because of his illness, forgotten to take into account. At this point the dialogue moves right out of the clinical into the theological sphere.

The resources being offered are not only the resources of a human relationship, because every man must realize that he can empathize only to a limited extent with the sufferings of others. It is Christ alone who can reach down to the depths of suffering that are before us, and it is of him, and not of ourselves that we speak. In no sense are we directive as to the manner of life which we think the patient ought to have led, or should lead in the future. Our concern is only to offer him, in the name of the Lord whom we serve, a direct relationship to him, the result of which we confidently know will be a renewal of life. He too will be raised from the death of the spirit, from guilt and from unbelief, into an abundant relationship with the Life-Giver himself, and the personal gifts which his indwelling brings, his love, his joy and his peace. I have never felt in the least able to systematize this part of the clinical theological interview. It is our business at this moment to be entirely attentive to the Holy Spirit, who will give us, out of all the many resources that Christ's redemptive work has made available, those which we should lay before the troubled person. However much time you have spent on the structure, planning, content and delivery of a sermon, there comes a time when you must leave all these things behind and depend in a direct fashion upon the Holy Spirit. It is precisely so here. With no two people will the approach be identical. This is entirely the Holy Spirit's work, because it is he whose task it is to apply the saving work of Christ to human beings. Yet, because he has called us to be fellow labourers with him, nothing of the care we have taken in listening to the woes and trials of the natural spirit will be lost. It is our share of the burden-bearing.

ADDITIONAL EXAMINATION, WHEN A PARISHIONER SUFFERING FROM MENTAL ILLNESS COMES FIRST TO THE PARSON

It may well be that from time to time a parishioner comes to see his minister, believing his problem to be basically to do with personal problems or spiritual difficulties, when actually they are secondary to functional changes in the mind of a psychotic nature, or are secondary to organic or neurological deterioration of the brain substance. Under such circumstances normal thinking and spiritual activity may have become impaired in a way which no ordinary spiritual ministration can repair. Under these circumstances the clinical theologian may find it useful to have a very brief method of examination of the troubled person, so that he has some confidence in referring him to the general practitioner. This examination is commonly recorded under ten headings:

1 Behaviour

The pastor may immediately detect some strange abnormality of behaviour in a man he knows fairly well. The expression of the face and eyes may be estranged, the posture unusual, the movements and gestures inappropriate, the dress disorderly, the hair dishevelled. He may look suspiciously out of the window, or walk restlessly about the room.

2 Talk

Is the patient under an abnormal pressure to keep talking fast? Is he unable to talk at all? Is his talk off the point and irrelevant? Is it not even coherent? Does he change the topic in an abrupt manner without the usual connecting phrases? Does he ramble all over the place? As he speaks, does his thought block and his speech suddenly run out, to start again after a while at an entirely different place, an event common in schizophrenic patients? Do his speech and gestures match? Does he use odd expressions and strange syntax, are his words the bizarre inventions of the schizophrenic? Has his speech begun to slur, as it often does with chronic arterial changes in the brain? Is he in difficulties to find an obvious word which he must know well, another possible sign of organic disorder?

3 Moods

Is there something strange and uncanny about his mood? Does it show the wild inappropriateness and bizarre clash with the mood of those about him which would lead one to think of hebephrenic schizophrenia? Is it related to the topics discussed? Does he seem to be incapable of appreciating the seriousness of the situation? Has he really no emotions at all, but just a strange flatness and unreality about him? Or does he show the emotional lability and readiness to weep of those whose cerebral arteries are giving, or have given trouble? Is the mood so absurdly childish, fatuous and irresponsible as to indicate dementia?

4   Content of Thought

Here we are concerned not so much with the ordinary things that
have already been recorded in the history. We are concerned with
any abnormal contents, such as (a) delusions, which are beliefs held
in the face of evidence normally sufficient to destroy belief; or (b)
hallucinations, which are defined as 'false perceptions which have
a compulsive sense of the reality of objects, although relevant and
adequate stimuli for such perceiving are lacking', or 'the acceptance
of sense imagination as real'. These hallucinations may be visual,
as they not uncommonly are in chronic alcoholism; auditory, as
they frequently are in schizophrenia, especially of the paranoid type,
in which accusatory voices are heard; (c) compulsive thoughts of an
objectionable or persistent kind, as in obsessional neurosis. Where
delusions and hallucinations are present a psychiatrist should be
responsible for therapy. If, as may well happen, a parishioner is
returned from the mental hospital to the community still deluded
and occasionally hallucinated, the parson may be able to help, along
with the general practitioner and do much to restore the patient to
a place in the social order.

5   Orientation

Does the person know where he is? Does he behave as if he were
in your study, or as if he were in his own workshop? Sometimes, in
chronic organic arterial lesions of the brain, the patient wakes in
the middle of the night, and, forgetting that he has been retired for
fifteen years, gets out of bed and dresses as if to go to work.

6   Memory

A schizophrenic patient will be able to remember without any
difficulty, but on the other hand may be so disturbed that he cannot
be tested. A serious failure of recent memory is characteristic of
organic changes in the brain, such as are common in arteriosclerosis,
in high blood pressure, and in those changes characteristic of old
age which we call dementia. This may occasionally occur in the
fifties, when it is referred to a pre-senile dementia. When attempting
to take a clinical history the parson may discover that the patient's
account of his life does not tally with the facts he knows, that it has
gaps or inconsistencies. He may be unable to recall something which
occurred early in the interview, perhaps he will fail to repeat a
simple story, or be unable to repeat the usual seven or eight digits
forwards and four or five to be repeated backwards. It is not,
however, the task of a parson to undertake mental testing of this
sort. The loss of memory, if severe, does limit considerably the

probable usefulness of pastoral conversation, except of the most simple, definite and supportive kind.

7   Attention and concentration

The neurotic person may have some failure of attention and concentration, whether he be depressed, anxious or hysterical, if these reactions are severe enough. Schizoid patients usually give most intense attention and concentrate more closely than the examiner. However, schizophrenic patients may be quite incapable, because of the welter of psychotic material thrusting up into the conscious mind, to attend at all. They may be distracted by voices or delusory notions. Attention and concentration are also affected in the organic mental states and in those which are due to toxic conditions. Patients have come to the clergyman, at times, in a sub-acute delirious state, and it is of importance that they should be directed at once, in fact taken at once, to the medical practitioner.

8   General information

It is an old-established custom for psychiatrists to ask the following questions which are simple tests for general information and awareness of life outside:

The name of the Queen.
The name of the Prime Minister.
The capitals of France, Germany, Italy, Spain, Scotland.
Six large cities in England.

If there are large gaps in this simple information test, it would indicate either a very low level of intelligence at any time in life, or the onset of the process of dementia.

9   Intelligence

The parson probably knows the level of functioning intelligence which this patient must have had in order to practise his profession. If his performance at interview is markedly different from this, it raises questions which are properly medical, and indicate that it would be improper to attempt to take the full clinical theological approach.

10   Insight and judgement

Many neurotic patients lack insight. To some extent, of course, all of us lack insight. We are speaking here of gross distortions of insight and judgement. An elderly man who had had three strokes and was suffering from dementia imagined that it would be the simplest thing to start up again a business which had already taken him to the bankruptcy court. A paranoid schizophrenic patient will assure the parson that all kinds of impossible schemes are afoot to deprive him of his rights. It is this qualitative loss of insight of a severe kind which should indicate to the pastor that this patient lies on the medical side of the frontier. What he does further must be under medical guidance, except of course, for such general supportive measures as he may think fit, and the continuance of the normal Godward life of the patient, through worship and fellowship and sacrament, if this proves possible.

The ten questions comprising this additional examination will always be in the background of the clinical theologian's mind, but they will come into action only on those occasions when he finds he has immediately to refer the parishioner to his colleague the general practitioner.

CONCLUSION

This outline gives the main headings under which information should be sought and recorded. The main headings, 1 to 8, and the sub-headings, should be committed to memory. (This does not include the additional examination as this rarely comes under pastoral consideration.)

When communicating a clinical history, many aspects of these notes may be irrelevant to any particular case. Do not labour the reporting by including many negative findings, though a few of these can be most important and indicate that you, having envisaged possibilities, have decisively ruled them out. However full or concise your history-taking has been, record and relate it in this order. Your audience, medical or pastoral, will be more attentive and better able to give their minds to the orderly consideration of the problem.

Patients are accustomed to doctors taking notes as they talk. This does not at all interfere with interpersonal relationships if a simple explanation is given of its usefulness, in thinking over the problem afterwards, and in going back later to pick up the threads which might be lost in the wealth of detailed history presented. Having given some such simple explanation, the request 'Do you mind if I make a few notes while you talk, of things I might forget to raise later?' is usually met with a ready agreement. If there seems to be some diffidence drop the idea and record essentials, later. If confidentiality is questioned, you may add, 'Of course the notes are locked away and are entirely confidential'. Moreover, during the relation of painful matters which the patient only divulges with diffidence no sensitive person would continue note-taking. Put your pen down. These are not the things you easily forget and they need not appear in the notes.

If clergy in this country ever become widely used as personal counsellors, as they are in the United States, they will need to keep confidential records. No one can keep the details of dozens of parishioners' problems clear in his mind, yet it should never be necessary for him to be told the same things twice. Parishioners would soon come to expect confidential note-taking as part of the serious and considered approach of the physician of souls. They would like to see the notes coming out of a locked filing cabinet, and rightly so. It may be that for some years these reasonable helps to the study of persons in difficulty will be resisted, and we can do without them. Good sense and the practical advantages of systematic orderliness in case-recording and presentation will, in time, prevail.

Glossary

This glossary does not aim to be complete. Some words have, in addition to their original meaning, special connotations in psychoanalytical circles. When this is so, 'psychoanal.' appears in brackets.

A few words need to be defined because of the particular way in which I have used them. For the most part the words in this glossary are those which I have been asked by students to define.

abreaction　a technique employed in psychoanalytic therapy by which repressed emotions, which belong to earlier and usually painful situations, are relived vividly and with feeling, thus lessening the emotional tension caused by inner conflict and its repression.

accidie　ἀκηδία ('negligence', 'indifference') sadness, melancholy, spiritual torpor, sloth, with inward bitterness and irritability. One of the capital vices of the spiritual writers of antiquity.

affect　in modern usage, any kind of feeling, emotion, mood, or temperament; affects are attached to or aroused by ideas or situations or objects, or groups of these.

agape　Christian love, charity, brotherly love, used in the New Testament of the love of God or of Christ, or of Christians for each other.

agoraphobia　an irrational fear or dread of open spaces, or felt in open spaces. In origin a misleading term. The Greek agora or market place was as probably crowded as lonely.

alloplastic　descriptive of the process, in the developing individual, by which the libido adapts itself to the environment, that is, turns outward from the self and towards other objects, persons, binding its anxiety, and the goodness or badness of a situation, on to others, not on to the self.

ambivalence   the coexistence of contrary feelings in any individual towards others; alternating attitudes, as of love-hate, domination-submission, attachment-detachment, of relatively equal strength.

anamnesis   recalling to mind; recollection; (psychoanal.) those events in personal and family history prior to the onset of a disorder which the patient remembers and considers possibly relevant; (theolog.) the re-presentation and re-membering of the central action of the passion and resurrection of Christ in the Eucharist.

androcentric reaction   a personality reaction pattern taking its origin in the first year, by which the baby, rejecting the mother as the source of personal being itself, of selfhood, or identity, looks to a man, usually the father or father archetype, as the source of being, selfhood and identity. In males, this leads to a homosexual personality reaction which typically manifests itself from adolescence onwards. In the female it leads to a man-centred hysterical personality reaction, with distrust of women in both sexes.

androerotic reaction   a personality reaction pattern taking its origin in the first year, by which the baby, while accepting being itself from the mother, is driven by frustration to reject her as a source of well-being, sustenance, satisfaction, the fulfilment of rights as a person and the achievement of a meaningful life, turning for these to fantasies of well-being, etc., derived from the father, whether archetypal or actual. This does not manifest itself as personality disorder, as a rule, until middle life. The middle-aged man neglects his wife and women for companionship, turning to his men friends. The existence of this inversion often fails to reach consciousness, being projected on to the wife, who is accused of guiltily loving a man, or denied in paranoid reactions, with or without alcoholic indulgence or addiction. Women thus affected feel unmaternal and identify with men for well-being, particularly in middle age onwards.

anomie   anomia. The feeling that there are no reliable laws to guide the conduct of one's life, nothing learnable that can be relied on to be constant, no moral laws to which to be responsible, nothing stable worthy of respect.

anorexia nervosa   severe loss of appetite and refusal of food, with dramatic weight loss, and other nervous symptoms, having an emotional basis related to the schizoid position.

archetype original model or prototype; as used in Jungian writing, a representation in the unconscious of experiences inherited from the race, for example, the prototypes of the good, and the bad mother and father.

aridity a feeling of dryness of spirit, parched, barren, waterless, joyless, unrelatedness, as in a wilderness. Aridity is a symptom in a variety of spiritual and psychosomatic disorders.

asphyxia loss, or impending loss of consciousness due to lack of oxygen in the blood, as in suffocation.

asthenic feeling weak, inactive, inadequate, dejected, as in a pallid, depressed feeling.

asthenic type a long-limbed, slender body structure with relatively diminished fat and muscular tissue.

atavism a throwback to a more primitive character; the reappearance of a character absent in the immediate ancestors but present in more remote ones.

autistic characterized by autism, i.e. thinking and interest focused on oneself as in the introverted, shut-in, withdrawn, schizoid personality. The term 'schizoid' has been used throughout, both as the term to denote the schizoid *position* (i.e. of dread, the splitting-off from trustful relationships, and the fall into the abyss of non-being which occurs at the point of transmarginal stress) and also to denote the schizoid *reaction* from this intolerable position, into the withdrawn, detached, introverted or autistic defence. Psychiatric usage of the term 'schizoid' refers to 'behaviour manifesting avoidance of close relation with others, inability to express hostility and aggressive feelings directly, autistic thinking'. It thus identifies the word 'schizoid' and 'autistic'. 'Autistic' is used more frequently of the schizoid reaction as it occurs in infancy and childhood, but there is no reason why it should not be extended to cover all the meanings of the schizoid *reaction*. Psychiatric usage of the term 'schizoid' covers a wide variety of behavioural phenomena. At the time when I began to write this book, 'schizoid' seemed the more acceptable word to describe *the reaction*, as being in more common usage. It could, however, be argued that for linguistic clarity it would be advantageous to retain 'schizoid' for *the position* itself, and not for the reaction. We could then gather the various phenomena associated with what we have here called the schizoid defence from that position, by means of detachment and introversion, under the term 'autistic'. Defence against the schizoid position by attachment and extraversion could then be correctly summed up under the term 'hysterical'. There would then be a clear antithesis between the hysterical and the autistic reactions, on opposite sides of the schizoid position.

autoeroticism   arousal and/or gratification of sex feeling by one's own acts or ideas without the participation of another person.

autonomic   used chiefly of the autonomous nervous system, which functions independently, without conscious control. A self-regulating system for the nervous control of the plain-muscle of the body, i.e., that which effects bowel movement and constriction and dilation of the blood-vessels and of the glands, all of which are controlled and balanced in their actions by this system. The autonomic nervous system has two divisions, the sympathetic, in general aroused, by fright or anxiety, for fight or for vigorous activity, and the parasympathetic which, roughly speaking, works in a contrary direction, preparing the body in tranquillity for rest, good appetite and good digestion. Most organs are supplied from both these divisions.

autoplastic reactions   a psychoanalytical term signifying the early tendency to adapt to stress by moulding the psychic structures, especially anxiety, within the self, binding the goodness or badness of the situation to oneself. (See *alloplastic*).

birth trauma   injury received during the birth process, due to severe moulding of the head, crushing, stretching, anoxia, asphyxia, and the accompanying sensations of fast-beating heart, with the psychic concomitants, the fear of crushing, of suffocation, or of death. If these are protracted and of transmarginal severity, the fear of not dying, of the pain not ceasing. Thus, in birth trauma the will itself may be set in opposition to being born, or to leaving the safe place. 'Some speak of the trauma of being born unwillingly from the security of the first home (the uterus) and from the first object of the libido. The result is the seed-anxiety from which (according to some psychoanalysts) all anxiety neuroses and many other neurotic symptoms grow.'

body language   communication with other persons (or with oneself) by means of bodily symptoms and complaints, with the intention (conscious or repressed) of influencing their behaviour towards the user of this language.

catharsis   in psychoanalysis describes the purifying, purging, relaxing, releasing effect of a dramatic emotional reliving of experiences from the past, particularly so if, at that time, the strong emotions aroused were only partially expressed, suppressed, or entirely repressed.

cathexis   the channelling of a drive of powerful wish on to an object which has value for, or is of interest to the individual. When libido, or psychic energy has been connected to a goal, the goal is said to be *cathected*. The object may be another person, a social group, a cause, an idea, oneself, or a fantasy.

cerebrotonic   descriptive of a personality type correlated with the ectomorphic bodily type and marked by restraint, inhibition, alert attentiveness, and in general by predominance of the intellective processes.

claustrophobia   a pathological, irrational fear of being in an enclosed place.

collusion   (in law) a fraudulent, secret understanding; (psychoanal.) the unacknowledged, undefined gratification by two people of each other's neurotic needs. Where collusion exists insight is resisted.

conditioned response   the new or changed response produced or elicited by a given stimulus after conditioning. The word 'conditioning' itself refers primarily to the learning that is related to certain experiments, the classical ones being those of Pavlov who paired a signal, the ringing of a bell, with the presentation of food to a dog, until the bell alone elicited the response of salivation which primarily had been elicited only by the sight of food. The presenting of food is called an unconditioned stimulus, the bell is the conditioned stimulus, the response to the bell by salivation is the conditioned response.

counter-transference   (psychoanal.) the arousal of repressed feelings in the analyst, usually directed towards the patient. These may be of love or hate or envy or any other repressed emotions.

defence mechanism   a psychological means, which operates automatically, without conscious control, deliberation, or awareness of its action, whereby the ego avoids anxiety-provoking or unpleasant feelings. This mechanism is intrapsychic, but affects behaviour patterns in many cases.

determinism   the assertion that things that happen are completely accounted for by a causal chain of antecedent factors or causes; which implies that given a full knowledge of the operative factors, it would be possible to predict how anyone will act, and, indeed, must act. It purports to leave no room for the operation of free will.

dissociation   a defensive mechanism or state of mind in which psychological items (ideas, feelings, memories, relationships, obligations, and the like), which are, in fact, connected with one another and with the central ego, lose this connection so far as the conscious mind is concerned. It is a kind of forced forgetting of painful and, at times, of pleasurable associations, and is closely linked with repression. The dissociated elements are preserved in the unconscious, and can, under certain circumstances be reassociated.

dizygotic   or fraternal twins, develop from two separate fertilized ova or eggs, that is, from two zygotes. Such twins are not identical, having no more in common than other brothers and sisters in the same family.

ectomorphic   pertaining to structures developed from the embryonic ectoderm, principally the skin and the nervous system, brain, spinal cord and nerves.

ectomorphic type   relatively thin, with a large skin surface in comparison with weight; relatively speaking neither fat nor muscular. Correlated with Sheldon's cerebrotonic personality and with the asthenic type.

ego   the 'I', the self, the central part of the personality, the individual, the real self as experienced by the individual; in biblical terms, the heart, i.e. the centre of all the functions of the individual; (psychoanal.) the aspect of the personality in contact with the external world by perception, thought, volition, emotion, and which strives to keep up a realistic relationship with the social environment.

eidetic imagery   a particularly vivid type of imagery. It is practically as if the subject were actually perceiving, as in a photograph or ciné film, a scene or event from the past. It is commoner in childhood. Most adults lose it, but in abreaction eidetic images of babyhood scenes can be vividly recalled. In the light of adult knowledge eidetic imagery from infancy can be reinterpreted.

empathy   (psychoanal.) objective awareness and understanding of the feelings, emotions and behaviour of another person, without necessarily oneself sharing those feelings (as sympathy does). This is primarily understanding. There is a feeling for the other person, chiefly of acceptance of how they feel, without participating in this feeling.

endomorphic   one of the three types of body-build, that in which the inner layer of the primitive embryo predominates. As this is the layer from which the abdominal organs develop,

the heavy, paunchy type, relatively lacking in muscle; fat, rather than thin. Correlated with Sheldon's viscerotonic personality.

eschatology the (Christian) doctrines of the events at the end of history, death, judgement, heaven and hell; with all the elements of the faith which are incomplete in the here and now, but which 'in the end', will, so faith asserts, be fulfilled.

euphoria a mood of unlimited well-being, with sensations of health and vigour, of self-affirmation and elation, invulnerability, ignoring negative elements whenever they exist. This mood may or may not be pathological, may or may not be accompanied by delusions appropriate to the mood.

extraversion literally, a turning outward; an investment of interest in, and valuing of things outside oneself, in the physical and social environment. This term is often opposed to introversion, but this is not a necessary opposition. Either may increase without diminishing the other, within a phasic movement of expansion in the personality in both dimensions.

feedback (in a machine) the automatic signalling of the degree of performance or non-performance of an operation; (in an organism) the sensory report of the result of behaviour; a direct perceptual report of the result of one's behaviour upon other persons.

fetishism (fetichism) the worship or veneration of inanimate objects considered to possess magical powers; (psychoanal.) an anomaly of behaviour in which sexual excitement or pleasure is habitually produced by objects other than sexual characteristics. It affects mostly males, and the objects are often articles used by women; others are babyhood derivatives, such as rubber.

gestalt psychology pays attention to the totality of functions, to unified wholes, which are held to be more than the sum of all the objectifiable parts and their relationships, for example a face 'full of character' is more than all the descriptive details that could be applied to it, a melody is more than the sum of the notes, etc., that make it up.

globus hystericus the illusion of having a lump in the throat.

hallucination the apparent but false perception of an object which seems real, but which lacks the presence of relevant and adequate stimuli, since the object is, in fact, not there.

hebephrenic a characteristic form of schizophrenia, occurring usually in adolescence, in which the patient behaves in a *childish* way, silly and giggling, losing such adult poise as they may have had, in bizarre, ill-judged, impulsive actions, with shallow or inappropriate feelings and often with delusions and hallucinations.

hypertension   synonym for high blood pressure.

hypochondriasis   morbid concern about one's health, with exaggeration of every trifling symptom.

hypothalamus   the lower portion of the mid-brain or dien-cephalon, comprising a number of nuclei, concerned in the regulation of many bodily processes. Known as the 'conductor' of the orchestra of endocrine or ductless glands, the thyroid, the adrenals, part of the pancreas, the ovaries, and the testes.

iconic communication   communication by producing an ikon, or image, or representation of something. In logic, a symbol that has many of the properties of that which it symbolizes, for example a motion picture. Used here to represent the tendency of persons suffering from character stress and person-ality tension to communicate their needs in terms of the picture of a sick person, with all the appropriate symptoms, as they understand them, or a paralysis, in their idea of it, thus requiring the sympathetic attention of relatives and the professional care of a doctor.

id   (psychoanal.) the deepest part of the psyche, which is uncon-scious, and is the source of instinctual impulses, which demand immediate gratification without regard for conse-quences, persons, or any consideration other than its own pleasure. It is impersonal, but may dominate the ego.

introversion   an investment of interest in and attention to the inner world, usually of one's own thoughts and feelings.

involutional melancholia   a form of depression developing about the time of the menopause or climacteric, characterized chiefly by constant worrying, insomnia, lack of concentration, agitation, poor appetite, self-concern to the point of hypochon-driasis, delusional ideas of disgrace, or shame, or guilt.

kenosis   (theol.) the doctrine of the renunciation of the divine nature, at least in part, by Christ in the incarnation; literally his *emptying* of himself of those aspects of his nature which would prevent his identifying himself with man.

latency period   (psychoanal.) a period from the age of four or five to about twelve during which interest in sex is not apparent in certain boys and girls in certain cultures.

leucotomy   a surgical cutting of the white nerve fibres connecting the frontal lobes with the thalamus, sometimes used in the treatment of mental disorders. This operation has become more discriminating with use, and less extensive. One of the less extensive processes is referred to as an orbital undercut. Its purpose is to reduce excessive psychic tension, oppressive and obsessional guilt and rumination, and excessive frontal lobe activity in general. It is the commonest form of psychosurgery. Its proper use has not been fully established in psychiatry. Sometimes referred to as lobotomy.

manic-depressive psychosis   mental disorder characterized by marked emotional oscillation. An exaggeration of the swing of mood which commonly occurs and is referred to as a cyclothymic temperament. In the manic or elated phase, there is excitement, flight of ideas, over-activity, an unlimited sense of powers and personal abilities, and occasionally overactive violence. In the depressive phase there is a feeling of inadequacy, retardation of ideas and movement, melancholy, and, at times, anxiety and agitation, sometimes with suicidal attempts and at times a termination in stupor. There is little or no dementia. The timing of the swings is very varied. The extent of oscillation is varied. Some never become either deeply depressed or excessively manic-depressive psychosis. This is not a common condition, and is extremely uncommon except in persons, especially men, of very broad and heavy body-build, typically 'bull-necked'.

mesomorphic type   (contrast ectomorphic and endomorphic, q.v.) In this type of body-build the middle layer of the primitive embryo predominates, which leads to powerful athletic development of the muscles, sturdy bony structure, upright posture and vigour.

migraine   a nervous disorder characterized by severe headaches, often one-sided, often on waking, with visual symptoms, such as 'fortification spectra' with nausea, often culminating in vomiting. Associated with situations in which the person feels 'under pressure' of the environment.

narcissism   self-love of an intense, regressive quality; preoccupation with and over-valuation of one's own body and the pleasures to be derived from it; admiration of one's own person and actions is an extension of this. May be normal in infancy, or may be, even then, a defence against the mother's under-valuation of the baby.

nihilism   total rejection of current beliefs or of any beliefs, especially of religious or moral or social expectation; finding nothing of value in the existing order; total scepticism.

nirvana   the blessed state, in Buddhism, i.e. extinction of individuality and personality and absorption into the impersonal absolute.

non-directive procedure or approach   a procedure in psychotherapy or counselling in which the therapist (or counsellor), after establishing an atmosphere of acceptance of the client (or counsellee), carefully refrains from directing the communication of the client. Instead, he attempts to reflect back to the client what the latter has said, sometimes restating the client's remarks, but never attempting to correlate them with facts or other statements, and trying never to evaluate them. Responsibility for discovering the nature of his problem and planning its solution rests with the client.

oedipus complex   (psychoanal.) the desire, repressed, and unconscious, of a son for the full enjoyment of his mother, with consequent jealousy of the father, which has in it strong sexual elements. This produces emotional conflict and guilt in the son. This term has been extended to include the analagous desire of the girl for her father, otherwise known as the Electra complex.

ontology   the study of the ultimate nature and essence of being.

paedophilia   (pedophilia), descriptive of an adult's sexual attraction to children.

paraklesis   (theol.) coming alongside to help; the Holy Spirit is the Paraclete, and this word relates to his supportive functions.

parasympathetic nervous system   see **autonomic**.

personality disorder   a disorder of behaviour that is manifested chiefly in motivation and by social maladjustment, rather than primarily in emotional or intellectual disturbances.

placebo   a preparation containing no active medical properties, administered to the patient giving him to understand that he is being given active treatment.

projection   the attributing to another of one's own repressed, unconscious motivations.

psychopath   a sufferer from a character disorder leading to asocial or anti-social, or criminal behaviour.

psychosis   not a well-defined term; used by psychiatrists with a variety of meanings. Schizophrenia and paranoid schizophrenia are almost always held to be psychoses. Severe manic-depressive mental disorder is also termed psychotic. Dementia, senile dementia, and presenile dementia are included as psychoses. So are severe toxic effects upon the brain. On the other hand, personality disorders, character disorders, reactive depressions, phobic states, conversion reactions and the like, are generally held to be neuroses, not psychoses. It is not therefore a matter of severity. A psychosis can be mild, and a neurosis crippling. It is not a matter of insight, which may be present in psychotic illness and lacking in neurotic, though again, it is commoner the other way round. The best definition is that of *Standard Psychiatric Nomenclature* which states that in a psychosis there is 'a degree of personality disintegration and failure to test and evaluate correctly external reality in various spheres'.

psychosomatic   descriptive of phenomena that in some sense or other are both psychic and somatic, mental and bodily; it may refer to phenomena which are inevitably characterized both psychic and somatic components.

psychosomatic disorder   a psychogenic or partly psychogenic disorder, having somatic or physiological symptoms, which may proceed to harmful structural changes of a pathological kind, for example in peptic ulceration, atopic dermatitis, asthma, and hypertension.

psychotherapy   a very widely inclusive term for any type of treatment of psychological disorder based primarily upon communication with the patient in the interview (as opposed to the use of drugs, physical measures, or psychosurgery) when it is performed by someone entitled by convention or training to practise 'psychotherapy'. Psychiatrists, psychoanalysts, medical and lay psychotherapists, clinical psychologists, and psychiatric social workers, are permitted by custom to refer to this aspect of their work as psychotherapy. Physicians, surgeons, dentists, priests, ministers, social workers, occupational and social therapists, probation officers and lawyers, frequently perform the same therapeutic functions.

pyknic type   (pyknik) a classification of human body structure, characterized by large body cavities, considerable subcutaneous fat, and general roundness of contour.

rapport   a comfortable and unrestrained relationship of mutual confidence with an element of natural liking and community of feeling, between two or more persons. It refers particularly to a good, working relationship between counsellor and client, analyst and analysand, doctor and patient, priest and parishioner.

rationalization   the process of justifying one's beliefs or actions when they are challenged, by offering plausible reasons; often a defence mechanism against unacceptable guilt or self-accusation. The process of giving rational order to a situation hitherto vague or confused.

regression   moving backwards; a return to earlier and less mature behaviour; a relapse to certain aspects of infantile behaviour, usually those aspects disapproved of by adults.

repression   the exclusion of specific psychological activities or contents from conscious awareness by a process of which the individual is not directly aware. 'Exclusion' includes preventing entry into, forcing out of, or continuously preventing return to, consciousness.

resonance   (psychoanal.) the use of a term from physics to indicate an analogous effect in psychodynamics. Tuned resonance or sympathetic vibration occurs when the resonating body has a natural vibration frequency close to that of the imposed frequency which induces it. By analogy, in psychodynamics, contemporary situations are apt to produce 'resonance' from repressed primitive situations in so far as present-day events represents themselves to the deep mind as close to the original traumatic event, that is, as having a similar vibration frequency, for example 'tight spots', 'working under pressure', 'people who smother you', 'working against time', 'having to get through some difficult test', and 'not having a cast-iron case' may all evoke resonance, that is, the particular forms of anxiety and feelings of distress associated with the birth trauma.

schizoid   refers to a fundamental split in the personality; the *schizoid position* refers to the existence, in the unconscious, deeply repressed, of the original traumatic experience of splitting. This deepest split in the personality is associated here with traumatic experiences in infancy, of sufficient severity and duration to cause transmarginal, or supra-maximal stress, with consequent paradoxical and ultra-paradoxical reactions. The schizoid position is synonymous with an experience of unbearable dread, of a fall into an abyss of disrelatedness, or of identification with non-being. Schizoid is used of a personality type tending towards dissociation of the emotional from the intellectual life. Its original use means, 'pertaining to schizophrenia'. The schizoid personality resembles the schizophrenic in these respects, that both tend to be somewhat withdrawn from the outer world and directed inwards. The *schizoid personality reaction* is defined as an enduring and maladjustive pattern of behaviour manifesting avoidance of close relations with others, inability to express hostility and aggressive feelings directly, autistic thinking. The person is seclusive, shut in, and unsociable. Most schizoid personalities remain at the psychoneurotic level, never becoming schizophrenic. Some schizophrenic patients were schizoid personalities before their breakdown, some were not at all of this type. There is only a partial descriptive connection between schizoid and schizophrenic. They are not part of a single 'disease'. See also comments under **autistic**.

schizophrenia   a group of psychotic reactions characterized by fundamental disturbances in reality relationships, by a conceptual world determined excessively by feeling, and by marked affective, intellectual, and overt behavioural disturbances. In many cases there is a progressive deterioration. Thought and behaviour are characteristically bizarre. Delusions and hallucinations are common.

subconscious   not clearly conscious, but capable of being made so.

super-ego   (psychoanal.) a 'structure' in the unconscious, built up by early experiences mainly of parental expectations (actual, or as understood or misunderstood by the infant), which supposed attitudes are incorporated into the mental life of the infant and function thereafter as a kind of 'neurotic conscience'. When the ego gratifies the impulses of the id in opposition to the demands of the super-ego, guilt and anxiety feelings result.

symbiosis   literally, living together; a relationship between two species in which neither can survive without the other; used of any close mutual-aid relationship between individuals, especially where this extends beyond the normal need for mutual support and affection, to include exploitation and the satisfaction of neurotic needs.

syndrome   the pattern of symptoms that characterizes a particular disorder or disease; 'what goes with what' in diagnosis.

synergistic   exerting force, together or in combination, or upon the same point.

tension   a feeling of being stretched or strained or 'on tenterhooks'; an emotional state resulting when needs are unsatisfied, or goal-directed behaviour is blocked; emotional tension, psychic tension, nervous tension, a feeling of strain.

theodicy   the vindication of divine providence and the love of God, keeping in view the existence of evil and suffering.

theriomorphic   in the shape of the beasts. Theriomorphism can refer to the dehumanizing characteristic of certain behavioural sciences, and the description of human behaviour in the terms of animal reactions.

toxaemia   poison (of whatever kind) in the blood.

transference   the displacement of feeling from one object or person to another, and particularly the process by which the patient shifts feelings and attitudes primarily applicable to parents or other significant persons, on to the analyst, or on to others who evoke similar associations. These feelings of transference are either positive (i.e. of love, trust, and expectation of kindness) or negative (i.e. of hate, distrust, or expectation of unkindness or hostility). Transference reactions occur whenever a relationship of trust is established, if the dependent person begins to bring into the relationship the backlog of unsolved personal problems, including those in infancy deriving from parent–child interactions.

trauma   physical, psychological, or spiritual (interpersonal) injury.

unconscious   (noun) *the* unconscious is the aggregate of the forces and content of the mind which are not ordinarily available to conscious awareness, or to voluntary recall. The activities of the unconscious mind are not open to direct, conscious scrutiny, but have dynamic effects on conscious mental life and behaviour. At times, 'preconscious', or 'subconscious' are properly used of areas of mental life on the edge of awareness, recoverable without resistance. The deep unconscious is often, in psychoanalysis, equated with the id.

Bibliography

Allport, G. W., *Personality: A Psychological Interpretation*, 1949.

Bonhoeffer, D., *Life Together*, SCM Press 1954.

Bowlby, J., *Personality and Mental Illness*, Kegan Paul 1940.

Buber, M., *Pointing the Way*, Routledge & Kegan Paul 1957.

Caldwell, T., *The Man Who Listens*, Collins 1961.

Fairbairn, W. R. D., *Psychoanalytical Studies of the Personality*, Tavistock 1952.

Gilson, E., *The Mystical Theology of St Bernard*, Sheed & Ward 1940.

Guntrip, H., *Personality Structure and Human Interaction*, Hogarth Press 1961.

Horney, K., *Our Inner Conflicts*, Routledge & Kegan Paul 1946.

Jung, C. G., *Psychological Types*, Routledge & Kegan Paul 1944.

Kierkegaard, S., *Fear and Trembling and the Sickness unto Death*, Princeton University Press 1941; *The Concept of Dread*, Princeton University Press 1944; *Christian Discourses*, OUP Galaxy Books 1961; *The Diary*, Peter Owen 1961.

Laing, R. D., *The Divided Self*, Tavistock 1959; *The Self and Others*, Tavistock 1961.

Menninger, K., *Man against Himself*, Rupert Hart-Davis 1938; *A Psychiatrist's World*, New York, Viking Press 1959.

Mowrer, O. H., *The Crisis in Psychiatry and Religion*, Princeton and London, D. van Nostrand 1961.

Phillips, J. B., *The New Testament in Modern English*, Geoffrey Bles 1960.

Schilder, K., *Christ Crucified*, Grand Rapids, Michigan, W. B. Erdmanns 1940.

Sheldon, W. H., *The Varieties of Temperament. A Psychology of Constitutional Differences*, New York, Harper 1942.

Stern, K., *The Pillar of Fire*, Michael Joseph 1951.

Tillich, P., *The Courage to Be*, Nisbet 1953.

Tournier, P., *The Meaning of Persons*, SCM Press 1957.

Weil, S., *Gravity and Grace*, Routledge & Kegan Paul 1952. *Waiting on God*, Routledge & Kegan Paul 1959.

Whale, J. S., *Victor and Victim*, Cambridge University Press 1960.

Wilson, C., *The Outsider*, Gollancz 1959.

Index of Biblical References

General Index